'I know it's only February but I think I may have read the best crime novel of the year; certainly one of them . . . An absolute belter. It has a setting – South Africa rife with corruption, drugs and death squads – which makes most Scandi-crime look as if it's been set in Legoland . . . In the past I have flagged up Mike Nicol's 'Revenge Trilogy' of books – *Payback*, *Killer Country* and *Black Heart* – and once compared him to American crime-master Robert Crais. On the evidence of this stand-alone thriller, I'd place him higher'

SHOTS MAGAZINE on *Of Cops & Robbers*

'This is not just superb genre writing: it is superb writing, period. Read Mike Nicol now, before everyone else starts telling you how wonderful he is'

JOHN CONNOLLY

'Shady characters, twists, turns, murder, mayhem, humour, wonderful dialogue, white-knuckle pace and lots of authentic Cape Town colour . . . Everything I love about the genre in just the right amount'

DEON MEYER

'World class . . . pace, wonderful characters and brilliant dialogue'

ELLE MAGAZINE

'In the top rung of South African fiction writers . . . Nicol's clipped dialogue and sparse, high-impact prose recalls that of revered American recluse Cormac McCarthy'

THE CITIZEN

OF COPS & ROBBERS

ALSO BY MIKE NICOL

Payback
Killer Country
Black Heart

ABOUT THE AUTHOR

Mike Nicol was born in Cape Town, where he still lives and writes. He is the author of several works of fiction and non-fiction, including the 'Revenge Trilogy', *A Good-Looking Corpse* – an account of *Drum* magazine in the 1950s – and *Mandela: The Authorized Portrait*.

OF COPS & ROBBERS

MIKE NICOL

First published in 2014 by Old Street Publishing Ltd,
Yowlestone House, Devon EX16 8LN
www.oldstreetpublishing.co.uk

ISBN 978 1 908699 88 6

A CIP catalogue record for this title is available from the British Library.

Printed and bound by CPI Group (UK) Ltd, Croydon, CR0 4YY

OF COPS & ROBBERS

THE ICING UNIT, NOVEMBER 1977

They come down the street in a baby-shit yellow Ford Granada, going slowly, checking out the houses. A whisper of exhaust smoking from the tailpipe. A growl like the pipe is rusted, holed somewhere near the box.

Four men in the car, all wearing sunglasses. The driver's got on racing gloves, olive-coloured racing gloves. The thing about him, his face's huge and red, he's known as the Fisherman.

The man behind him's leaning back, his face in shadow. A cigarette hanging on his lower lip. A cigarette he keeps there like he's breathing through it. He's got mad wild surfer-blond hair.

The one in the passenger seat has his fingers steepled, but not in prayer or contemplation.

The man behind him sports a rictus grin standard on his face, his arm's out the window, big glitzy rings on every finger.

They rumble at a crawl down the street in their baby-shit yellow Ford Granada.

The men are all carrying Browning HPs modified for screw-on silencers. Special issue for the job. The one with the rictus grin also carries an Italian stiletto, his weapon of choice. This one a nine-incher with a hilt inlay of mother-of-pearl. Very snazzy to his way of thinking.

They approach the house. No car in the driveway, the gate in the low wall is open onto a short slasto path to the front door. Rictus Grin and Blondie get out, their soles slap on the crazy paving.

Rictus knocks. Sees the bell push, jabs it with a thumb: bing-bong.

They wait. Hear a woman's voice talking on the telephone, saying goodbye.

Rictus looks at Blondie, raises his eyebrows. Who's this?

Key turns in the lock. A woman opens the door: short hair, pretty face, long eyelashes, green eyes, no colour on her lips. Wears a brown dress to her knees, bare feet. Says brightly, 'Hello, menere. What can I do for you gentlemen?'

Rictus doesn't miss a beat. 'Mevrou?'

'Ja.'

'Mevrou, we're supposed to meet your husband at quarter past six.' He glances at his watch. 'Five minutes ago. Sorry, we're late.'

'You're early, he's late,' she says. 'He's not here yet.'

Rictus with his hands bunched into the pockets of his bunny jacket. He and Blondie not moving.

'Is it about constituency matters?'

Rictus nods. 'Ag, it's not that important.'

The woman smiles. 'Why don't you come in and wait? If he said quarter past six, I'm sure he won't be long.' She leads them into a dining room, the table piled with stacks of papers. 'This's his office,' she says, closing the curtains. She turns to face them, palms out towards two easy chairs. 'Make yourselves at home.' In that moment seeing the gun in Rictus's hand, the fear ritzing her face.

Rictus shoots her one time, chest shot, straight through the heart. What the newspapers will call point-blank. Then he's at her with the stiletto. Grunting with each stab and pull.

Blondie's rooted to the carpet. The speed of the other man's mania brings a sourness to his mouth. He lurches towards his partner, pulls him away from the woman's body. She's on the floor, ripped and still. Her face untouched, her eyes open, pearly teeth glinting between her lips.

Rictus wrenches himself free, bloody stiletto in his right hand, the Browning HP in his left. Blondie hadn't seen him pull either weapon.

Blondie shouting, 'Stop, stop, bugger it, stop.'

At the same time the bell's bing-bonging because the other two, the Commander and the Fisherman, are outside the front door.

'Okay, okay.' Rictus bends down to wipe the knife on the woman's dress, comes up folding the blade into the hilt, crimson stains on the mother-of-pearl.

He watches from his car at the far end of the gravel parking lot. Watches through a night scope the white Subaru stopped facing the beach.

A hard southeaster's blowing, hazing his windscreen with sea spray. So bad he switches on the wipers to clear his vision.

He's been there half an hour, on the west side of the Sunrise Beach parking area. Was there twenty minutes before the white Subaru pulled up. It's midnight, moonless.

Ten minutes later he sees a car peel off the traffic circle, dim its lights, come slowly across the gravel towards the white Subaru. It's a Jetta, black. Black windows. The waiting man gets out of his car. The Jetta stops alongside. Two men step out.

He watches through the scope. Watches the men talking. Their hand gestures. Like these men aren't here for a transaction as they should be, they're arguing. Sees them back off, the two from the Jetta separating either side of the other man. Sees muzzle flash: four shots from the Jetta men, two returns.

'Jesus Christ!' *Fish leans forward to start his car.*

'Don't,' *says the man in the passenger seat. The man holding the .45 at his head.* 'Keep watching, my friend. This is what happens when you play shit with us. You get fucked up.'

There're two bodies on the ground. The Jetta man hauls his mate into the car, spins off, showering the other body in dust.

'We know you, Mr Fish Pescado,' *says the man with the gun.* 'You are the next one. You kill one of ours, we kill one of yours. Last time, the man you shot died, Mr Pescado. Bad luck for you.' *He opens the passenger door, backs out. Leans in again, opens the glovebox, takes the gun stashed there. Looks at it.* 'What old rubbish is this?' *Pockets it.*

'Leave the gun,' *says Fish.*

The man says, 'You better call Emergency for your friend, my friend. They can fill out the, what's it? ... the declaration of death.'

Laughs: ha, ha, hey.

Surfers' Corner, Muizenberg, with a working sea. Waves: deep ocean storm outriders, metre and a half, two metres slamming in, breaking right. Got punch and power behind them, enough to give you the willies on the drop, a thrill across the face.

Fish Pescado and Daro Attilane in wetsuits paddle their longboards to the backline, feeling the sea surge going through the white water. When they get out to the swells and troughs, beyond where the peaks form, they're aching.

Three sets roll under them.

They let them come, go, not talking, taking a breather. Sit on the ocean in the late afternoon, in the mountain's shadow.

Then Daro says, 'I've got something to ask you.'

'Sure,' says Fish, 'long as it's not personal' – grinning while he says it.

He turns his longboard till the nose is pointing at Daro.

Daro Attilane, car dealer, member of the community police forum, veteran surfer. Short grey hair, tanned face, pale blue eyes, built like a rugby flanker.

'This is about my daughter, Steffie. Teenage stuff. Someone selling dagga at school.'

'A regular dealer?'

'Uh huh, Steffie bought some. I caught her with it in her bedroom, blowing the smoke out the window.'

'Nice one,' says Fish. 'I did that too. She give you a name?'

'Kid in her class.'

'You want me to talk to the kid, find out his supplier, I can do that.'

'I know who's the supplier. Seven's the supplier.' Daro gesturing at the beach. Fish follows his arms to the line-up of SUVs: every four parking bays more than two or three million bucks' worth of hardware. Daro's is a Nissan X-Trail. Fish's a rust-bucket Isuzu two-by-four he inherited, a good few notches outside the financial bracket of his surfing buddy. Fish frowns, realises it's not the beachfront Daro's referring to but the warren behind the upmarket apartments.

'Problem is,' says Daro, 'dagga's just the start. Next it's pills, methamphetamine, tik. It gets to tik, you've got a major show. That meth bites.'

Fish looks at Daro, Daro not meeting his gaze.

'Thing is, you know I'm on the forum.'

The forum wanting to clean up the resort. The scene in Muizenberg being hectic. Back in the warren behind Atlantic Road, crack houses, dagga dens, prozzies, young and old, putting out on the street, in the gang houses, anywhere for a globe of tik. And lord of it all, Seven. The bane.

'No secret I'm on the forum. Everybody knows it at Steffie's school. We've done talks to the kids, told the youngsters what's what. Steffie knows, you get onto the hard stuff, you're hooked, buggered. It's that bastard, Seven. He's targeting her to get at me.'

'Seven is?'

'I think so.'

'You give him that much credit?'

Daro serious, eyes on Fish now. 'I do. This's his style. This's how he does it. The last chairman of the forum's on tranquilisers, had to move away. What worries me, one day I'll answer the doorbell there's a kid, nine, ten years old standing there with a gun. Gang initiation. So long Mr Attilane.'

'So raid his place again.'

'Every time we raid, he's clean. He's got a source in the cops.'

'Don't they all,' says Fish.

Fish: Bartolomeu Pescado on his birth certificate. Nowadays has this discreet earring in his right lobe. His wild surfer hair, his quick eyes, his earring is how you notice Fish Pescado for the first time. Fish to his friends, for obvious reasons. Bartolomeu after the Portuguese explorer. No one but his mother called him

Bartolomeu. By way of earning a crust Fish's an investigator with not too much work on the go.

Fish stares down at his bare feet in the green water. A chilly sea about twelve degrees C. This sort of temperature he should wear booties like Daro. Except booties upset his balance. Make him trip and stumble. He's never worn booties. Booties are for older guys like Daro. Barefoot is cool, despite the cold.

He wipes blond hair off his face, looks at Daro, says, 'This happened before?'

'What? Steffie and drugs?'

Fish picks at a knob of wax on the board, flicks it away. 'No. Any kind of threat? Letter? Telephone call? Stalker?'

Daro laughs. 'Only the sort of threats that happen on a raid. That crazy "I'll-get-you" stuff.'

Their boards touch, both men backpaddle.

'Maybe Steffie's just experimenting.' Fish keeps backpaddling. 'You told your wife?'

'We've talked about it.'

'What's she say?'

'Teenage curiosity.'

'But you reckon Seven's the issue?'

Daro nods. 'I do. In the bigger picture.'

'I can have a word with Seven, if you want. I can say the sort of things you can't.'

Daro shakes his head. 'Nah. Maybe later.'

'So what's the thing you want to ask me?'

'What?'

'You said you want to ask me something.'

Daro's facing the open sea, points behind Fish. 'They're coming. Big ones.'

Fish and Daro see the first of a set roaring at them. Rising up, thinning at the top, feathering in the offshore breeze. You listen you can hear the hiss approaching.

'Yours,' shouts Fish, lying flat, paddling to get over the peak. He breaks through, goes down the back, there's a mother staring him in the face. A huge green wall, foaming to his right.

Fish swings the board round, stroking to get some speed, the water being sucked from under him into that mad crazy moment when the wave takes you, grips you. Fish letting out a long whoop all the way down the drop, getting to his feet, arms flung out, crunching off the pit onto the wall. Glued there, racing ahead of the white.

Fish's surfed all his life. Started as a five-year-old grommet at this very beach. Fish can't get enough. If he doesn't get a surf on any given day he's seriously miffed. Seriously. Fish drives by the ocean two or three times a day just to eye the swell. First thing in the a.m. he fires up his laptop to check the surf report. The steadycams at the peninsula's breaks.

Surfers' Corner his home zone. Okay, the waves don't carry the kick of Long Beach or Noordhoek or the Reserve, but, hey, they're a drive away. The nursery's right on his doorstep. He rides the other breaks from time to time, but for a quick pop and peak, the nursery's fine. Two minutes from his pad. He can walk here if he wants, which mostly he doesn't. Fish believes in having wheels ready because you never know when you're going to need them. A call-out. A chase. A getaway. Fish Pescado, investigator, always has wheels ready to rock 'n roll.

But now he's surfing. Kicks out of that first long ride well stoked. Paddles through the incoming rollers, taking the first opportunity. This late hour of the afternoon he can't pick and choose. The grommets and the hot kids are surfing the last light, like waves are never gonna happen again.

A glassy wall comes at him, picks him up, hollows, spits him over the falls. Bang into the washing machine. Fish tumbles, the board jerking at the leash like a wild thing. Fish with his hands clutching his head for protection.

He's seen plenty guys got hit in the face in this sort of situation. Broken teeth, broken nose, enough blood loss to whistle up every great white in the bay.

He breaks the surface gasping. Another roil of thunder bearing down. Fish takes a breath, dives. Listens as the churn passes overhead, his board tugging at the leash, dragging him. He waits out the set in the foam, then strokes for the backline with the lull.

Half an hour later Fish's taking a breather, three more rides notched, two wipe-outs that cleared his sinus passages. Daro, kneeling on his board, paddles over.

'Not bad.'

'Very cool,' says Fish. 'Way to end the day.' Would've been the way to pass the whole day for that matter, he thinks. There not being too much on his plate right now. Not being anything on his plate right now, truth be told.

'One more then I'm done,' says Daro. 'Can't keep the family waiting.'

Fish squints at him. 'If this drug thing's on your mind, you'll let me know?'

Daro nods. 'Course. Thanks.'

'Your call,' says Fish. Wondering what was the question Daro really wanted to ask.

The two of them sitting there, eyes on the backline, the ridges dark against the horizon. They're about to line up for the next set when a guy waving calls, 'Hey, Fish. There's a chickee on the beach after you.'

'They all are, man.'

'Says you should get yourself in chop-chop. Says you've got five minutes. Whatta stunner, hey. Nice rack.' The surfer cupping his hands at his chest. 'Wouldn't keep her waiting.'

'Vicki,' says Fish to Daro. 'Keep your mind clean,' he shouts at the surfer.

Gets as answer: 'Just delivering the message, bro.'

Then the next set of peaks are on them, Fish and Daro stroking over the first. Fish whooping, pivoting his board, 'Time to pump my soul.' And he's paddling down the drop, feeling the wave thump beneath the board with the gathering speed.

2

Vicki Kahn, Vicki with an 'i', stands next to her Alfa MiTo, scoping the ocean. The light's bad, one figure out there much like another. Sees she's being checked out by two young guys, zipping up their wetsuits. The one staring at her cleavage.

'Hey,' she calls to them. 'You know Fish?'

The boob starer shakes his head like he's trying to shake the inside bits into place, refocuses, says he does. 'The tallish blond guy with the earring?'

'Exactly. Tell him he's needed, here, now.'

'Sure, sure.' The surfer sliding his board out the back of his bakkie.

'Not in half an hour. Right away.' Vicki keeping the please out of her request. With waterheads you have to stay direct, simple.

She orders a flat white at Knead.

The Nigerian waitress with the pixie smile who always serves her, them, says, 'To go? We're closing up. I'll bring it to you.'

'Lovely,' says Vicki, pointing at her MiTo, the blazing red one. 'I'll be there.'

The waitress nods.

Vicki crosses to her car, hears her iPhone ping: couple or five emails waiting. One from the senior partner. The smooth-talking, American-twanged, highly connected Clifford Manuel. Not someone she trusts. Not someone you want as an enemy. Guy has family connections that go back into the bad old days of the struggle. Family connections now worth millions in fees, gratuities, introductions, heads-up at the trendy Bolshoi Bar.

She clicks open his email.

'Hi Vicki.'

Hi Vicki. Approachable, despite he lives in a suit. Impeccable suits. Silk shirts. Ermenegildo Zegna ties. Doesn't need to but wears braces. Who wears braces? Something he picked up in the States. And brogues. Never anything but brogues.

'Don't forget the meeting. This is important.'

Authoritative. Straight to the point. Wouldn't think that he could be lechie with the young associates. One even laid a harassment complaint. To no effect, except she left for other pastures.

He tried it on with Vicki at a cocktail party, not long after she'd joined the firm. Some time back now. The cocktail party to celebrate the firm's eighty years of legal practice. Cabinet ministers, MPs, DGs, CEOs, CFOs, ambassadors, consuls, judges, the legal sharks, glitterati all in attendance. And Fish. She got out of Clifford Manuel's smarm by introducing him to Fish.

Fish said, 'Howzit, nice place.'

'Yes, well, I suppose so,' Clifford Manuel replied, not smiling, trying to withdraw his hand from Fish's grip. Then massaging his fingers when he did.

'Impressive,' Fish said. 'All this artwork.'

Clifford Manuel smiled, smoothed his tie with his clean hand. 'Local artists. Kentridges, Goldblatts, Ractliffes. That statue's an Alexander. It's called *Serviceman*.'

'I know.'

'You like art, Mr Ah …?'

'Pescado,' Vicki said. Repeated.

'Mr Pescado.'

'Bartolomeu Pescado, otherwise known as Fish, consults for us,' she said.

Fish shrugged. 'I've got pictures by most of them.'

'Have you now?' Clifford Manuel looking hard at him.

'Ractliffe's dead donkey. An Alexander print, a Goldblatt photo of some graveyard. They're getting expensive. I've got to buy younger talent now.'

'Interesting.' Clifford Manuel backing away, holding out his right hand limply, like a rag. 'You're an interesting fish, Mr Pescado. Please. Have a drink. Enjoy yourself.'

'Thanks,' said Fish. 'I will.' Turned to Vicki, said, 'Mr Smooth.'

'He is.' Vicki grinning, loving it. 'But he's also my boss.'

And now Clifford Manuel so insistent on her being at a meeting. Nothing she's been briefed for.

'I just want you there. Want you to meet someone, that's all,' he said. 'Will be a good contact for you. Actually he asked for you, he knew your aunt.'

'My aunt?'

'That's what he said. He's a client, Vicki. An important client.'

Clifford Manuel being mysterious. Clifford Manuel being Clifford Manuel, never letting out all the information.

'Who?' she said.

'You'll see.'

'One flat white,' says the waitress, smiling her pixie smile. She points at the beach. 'He's come in, your boyfriend?'

'Yeah,' says Vicki. 'He knows what's good for him.'

The two of them watching Fish slide his board onto his Isuzu single cab. 'Great body in a wetsuit,' says Vicki.

The waitress giggles.

'Don't say anything.' Vicki waves at Fish and Daro, Fish giving her the thumbs up, Daro mouthing hello, heading off towards his car. 'Real beach Adonis, you can pick them up any beach around the city. All that lovely blond hair. The blue eyes, the hard bod.'

Fish comes up, peeling the wetsuit off his arms, makes to hug her.

Vicki steps back. 'Oh no you don't.'

'Doll,' says Fish, 'where's the romance?' He takes a swig of her coffee. 'That's weak. Needs two hits of espresso.' Rubs a towel over his chest. 'You're nice 'n early.'

'I'm not staying,' says Vicki.

'No?' Fish giving a side glance.

'I can't. Clifford wants me at a meeting in town. To meet a client. Guess who.'

'Tell me.'

'I had to drag it out of him.'

'Vicki?'

'Jacob Mkezi.'

'The big man himself?'

'The disgraced man.'

'He's a scapegoat.'

'You don't think he's corrupt?'

'Of course he is. But still a scapegoat. Take down the top cop, looks like you mean business. Everyone else in government pulling a scam can breathe easy.'

'That's cynical.'

'That's a fact of modern life.' He touches her face lightly. 'So come afterwards.'

'I don't think so. Tomorrow, okay? For the weekend.' She finishes the coffee. 'Promise.' Sees the suspicion in Fish's eyes, like he thinks something else's going on here. 'I'll call. Soon as I'm home I'll call.'

Fish watches her drive off, the lovely Vicki Kahn. Not like other women he's had in and out of his life. With Vicki he plays it loyal.

3

Daro's bête noire, Seven, is pulling a number. He and his pellie, Jouma, in the mammal gallery of the South African Museum. Rows of cabinets, rows of stuffed wild animals: bucks, cats, hippos, elephants paused on their savannahs, silent in the dim light. The gallery hushed.

'No, my bru, not this one. Nay, you's mad,' says Jouma.

'This one, my bru. I got a buyer.'

'Strues?'

'Strues, maybe.'

'Maybe?'

'Ja, definite maybe.'

The men stare at the rhinoceros in the glass cabinet.

'We can't, man, not in here.'

'Why not? I got a plan, my bru. Everything's sweet inna street.'

'What plan?'

'I tell you.'

The men shut up as tourists approach, the one edging the other to the far side of the cabinet. The tourists, a man and a woman in shorts and T-shirts, read that this specimen is a white rhinoceros, that it is one hundred and twenty years old, that it once roamed in the Cape. That it was donated to the museum by Cecil John Rhodes. The tourists smile at the two men through the glass cabinet, pass on. The two men smile back: the one has no front teeth.

Seven and Jouma are smartly dressed in jackets and clean jeans. Open-necked shirts, black takkies. They've been in the museum twenty minutes, paid their way in as good citizens do.

Jouma waits until the tourists have left the mammal gallery, says, 'Nay, my bru, we's not in this line.'

'We's branching out, my bru,' says Seven. 'Freelance onna

razor's edge.' He comes close to Jouma, whispers in his ear, 'Twenny grand, ek sê. Now we's talking bucks.'

Jouma stares at the rhino. 'How we gonna carry it?'

'No, my bru, what you thinking, my bru?' Seven laughs, smacking his thigh. 'Just the horns. No harm done. They make new ones that looks just like these, so when you's standing here yous can't tell the difference. Win-win situation. Who's the loser?' He wags his chin at Jouma. 'No one.'

Jouma says, 'Nooit, never, nay, my bru.'

Seven points at the rhino. 'This thing. This is a worthless thing. What they call priceless. Not for sale.' He comes up close to Jouma. 'So if it not for sale it doesn't matter if we take the horns. Like I say, they gonna make new ones.'

Jouma crouches to look more closely at the rhino. 'Yous don't know it's real. Maybe it's plastic.'

'Ag, no, my bru. Why's a museum gonna have a plastic rhino? This's for real. Check.' He squints at the legend. 'Donated by Cecil John Rhodes. This thing walked the earth, my bru, that's why it's here.' He jabs his finger at the legend. 'It says, mos. Roamed in the Cape. It's real, my bru. Real like you and me. This thing was alive. Now it's inna exhibition. Stuffed by Cecil.'

Jouma nods, looks round at the rows of silent animals. 'I suppose.'

'Better than killing a live one. No animals hurt in the making of this fortune.' Seven cackles, beckons Jouma out of the gallery.

They're playing dominoes in the security guard's office when the museum closes. Seven has won every time.

'How long we gonna wait?' says Jouma.

'There's still people working, moegoe,' says Seven. 'Yous a stupid or something?' He wins another game. Says to the security guard, 'Don't you play dominoes in Malawi, Paul?'

'Mozambique,' says Paul. Paul's a big man, tall, muscular, his shirtsleeves tight over his biceps.

'Ja,' says Seven. 'There.'

'We play dominoes.'

'But you don't win.'

'Sometimes I win.'

'Except, my bru, against an ace champion.' Seven laughs, slides tiles to Jouma and Paul.

Nine o'clock, Paul the security guard gives the thumbs up, fetches a two-kg club hammer from his locker, a small handsaw, gives them to Seven. The three men go down to the mammal chamber, the security guard leading by torchlight.

'Aaa, my bru, this is spooky,' says Jouma, the animals looming and vanishing in the beam of the torch. To Paul says, 'You like this job?'

'Not so much. Your money is better.'

'Fat bucks.' Seven holds out the hammer to Jouma. 'Take it. Come on Mr Demolisher.'

Jouma shrugs off his jacket, spits on his hand, lifts the hammer above his head. 'Here goes, meneer.' Whacks the hammer into the glass case. The glass cracks but doesn't break. Jouma drops the hammer, rubs his arm. 'Jusses.'

'Security glass,' says Paul. He hands the torch to Seven, takes the hammer from Jouma, brings a blow down on the wooden frame that shatters the glass.

'There's it,' says Seven.

Paul clears away shards of glass, reaches in to break off the horn. A couple of pulls, it doesn't budge.

'That's why we's got a saw', says Seven, taps it against Paul's elbow.

Paul takes the handsaw, goes at the base of the big horn, Seven encouraging him. Halfway through he rips it off. Holds the horn in both hands. 'Beautiful.'

'Aitsha! How's that?' says Seven, taking the horn. 'We got nine kilos here.' He passes it on to Jouma, adjusts the torchlight for Paul.

Paul starts on the smaller horn with the handsaw.

'Careful, my bru,' says Seven. 'Yous don' wanna damage it.

Yous damage it, who's gonna buy it then? Softly, my bru, slowly.'

Paul keeps on with the saw, cutting through the skin, through the model stuffing. When he's almost done, grips the horn with both hands, pushing, yanking. His wrestling with the horn topples the rhino against what's left of the glass cabinet.

'Agge nee, my bru! Now look what you's doing? You understand English, my bru, slow, hey, softly.' Seven flagging him down with an outspread hand. 'You must hold the horn, push back the head, saw some more. Ja, this makes sense?'

Paul grunts, does as Seven says, cuts off the small horn.

'What I say, my bru? What I tell you?' Seven takes the small horn from Paul, shines the torch on it. 'Very nice.' He weighs it in his hand. 'How much you say, maybe three or four kilos?' Seven whistles. 'Jackpot in one night. Everyone smiling.' He hands it to Jouma.

'Where's the money?' says Paul, puts down the handsaw.

Seven shines the light in Paul's face. 'Like I told you, my bru. We's got to get paid first. Doesn't happen all in a rush.'

Paul stands over Seven, reaches for the torch. 'You must not lie to me.' He twists the torch out of Seven's hand.

'Nee, my bru, never,' says Seven. 'In a few days everything's sweet.'

Paul puts the light on him. 'I come with you. To your house.'

Seven nods. 'Yes, my bru. Okay, okay.' He holds up a hand to shield his eyes. 'Time to go, hey.'

Paul leads them out of the gallery. Seven behind him, Jouma last, carrying the horns. Jouma complaining in Flats-speak about being the slave, about this Mozambican coming home with them. Not noticing Seven make his move, going round Paul. Jouma crashing into Paul as the big man stops, dropping the torch, his hands clutching at his chest.

In the darkness Seven dancing away, springing forward to put the flick knife in a third time. The Mozambican folding to his knees. Seven sticking him in the neck.

Jouma says, 'Yusses, my bru. You's fast.'

'Part of the plan, no foreigners,' says Seven, panting, picking up the torch. He turns it on Paul's jerking body. They watch until the security guard lies still.

THE ICING UNIT, NOVEMBER 1977

'He should of been here twenny minutes ago,' says Rictus Grin, moving into the room, flopping onto the couch. 'We had an appointment.'

The Fisherman stands, shifts aside the curtain to take a peek out the window. Black outside. Streetlights dull in the darkness. 'He's a politician. Politicians get held up. People wanting to shake their hands.'

'For how long?'

'For how long, what?' The man drops the curtain.

'For how long're we gonna wait?'

'All night if we have to.'

'Shit, this's up to shit.'

'Thanks to you.'

Rictus mumbling, 'Wasn't my fault.'

'Chrissakes. Leave it, okay?' He looks from one man to the next. 'Gloves,' he says. 'You put them on. You wipe down the door handles. The tap.' Pulling a pair of surgical gloves from his jacket pocket. The others dragging out their issue. Except Blondie.

'I left them in the car,' he says. 'In the boot.'

'Go 'n fetch them. Bring the spray can, too. May as well get that done. And go carefully, okay. You see a car you keep out of sight.'

Blondie comes back with the spray can. 'You do it,' he's told. 'In the kitchen, I'll show you.' They go through to the kitchen, all four men. 'Okay. Big letters right across the wall, across the fridge. Nice big red letters against the white. The first three together like it's a word, then a gap, then the next three. Okay? RAU TEM.'

'Rautem, what's that mean?'

'Just do it.'

'Fokkin nonsense.'

'RAU TEM, capital letters, only that. No poetry.'

Blondie shakes the can. 'Like this?' Makes the downstroke of the R. Stands back.

'Keep going, man, don't stop.' The man talking, the Commander, jerks a thumb at Rictus. 'Stay in the lounge. We don't want him walking in surprising us.'

'Yes, baas,' says Rictus. 'Whatever you say, baas.'

The Commander glares at him. 'Enough. Okay? Enough.'

Rictus salutes with two fingers to his forehead.

Blondie completes the letter, does the A and the U across the kitchen cupboards. Glances at his superior. 'You want it over the fridge, really?'

'I do.'

'Fokkin childish,' says the Fisherman.

'Not your problem. Not my problem either. Or any of us. It's an order. Ours not to reason.'

Blondie lets loose on the fridge, the letters dropping lower. Runnels of paint dripping down from the overspray. He stands back. The letters are manic, mad, angry.

Night comes down on the city.

Fish Pescado, home alone, no work, dwindling bank balance, listens to Shawn Colvin's sad take on life, hits up the regular doob buyers on the list he's inherited: some lawyers, couple of ad executives, clutch of asset management types, two doctors. But everyone's stocked. No big parties coming up for the weekend.

Next taps on some uni guys, no takers. Tries the doctor of classical something or other, always a buy when he calls. No answer. Leaves a message. These people all high-end, the sort who don't want to handle the street. Fish's their buffer. Fish's their man.

Brings him round to Professor Summers, professor of political science. Professor of bullshit, Fish reckons, but likes the man. The prof's got this fuck-you attitude. A short fellow, food stains on his ties, shirts, trousers. House stinks of cat piss and damp. And something mouldy, lingering, dead rats under the floorboards. But he buys without fail, weekly, since Fish took over the list.

Professor Summers opens with, 'Ah, Mr Pescado. Good to hear from you. A reminder to purchase, no doubt?'

'Part of the service.'

'That jerk, your predecessor, Mullet Mendes, never thought so. Not surprising he got killed. What a jerk. But there we are. "He that killeth with the sword must be killed with the sword." Revelation, Mr Pescado. The only book in the Bible worth reading.'

'I don't know it.'

'Not many do.'

'So how many, Prof?' says Fish.

'Two baggies. That's it. That's what it's going to be every week. With your predecessor, every week he'd ask me how many. Every week I'd tell him two baggies. For I don't know how long now. But that's over now. Two baggies every week, Mr Pescado.'

'Just checking. Case you're going large. You know, for the weekend.'

He hears the professor laugh. 'Brilliant, Mr Pescado, I must get with this street language. Going large, is it?'

'Can I deliver tomorrow?'

'Of course. Your predecessor always kept me waiting, that's the kind of jerk he was. Since you took over it's been a pleasure.'

He's gone before Fish can reply. In the contact list he inherited from Mullet Mendes, Professor Summers is listed under Arsehole.

Fish takes a Castle milk stout from the cupboard, room temperature his preference, stands at the back door gazing into his yard at the boat, the *Maryjane*, another thing he inherited from Mullet. Along with the rusty Isuzu bakkie. Next to that's his Cortina Perana V6: red with a black interior, black stripe over the bonnet, alloy wheels. A mean machine which gets the chicks hopping. Fish's retro indulgence. These toys and the house, the sum total of his assets. Still. No bond on the house. No finance on the Perana.

And then there's the inheritance. From a guy he hadn't known more than a year. They'd partnered up on some investigative jobs. Talked about opening a joint operation. Mendes & Pescado. Joked that it sounded like a Porra fish 'n chip shop. Joked that maybe Mullet & Fish would've been good. This weird alliance in their names.

Then Mullet takes a bullet. Two bullets, actually. Pops his clogs in the ambulance.

His last words, 'Titus Anders. Untouchables.'

Fish wants to tell him, yeah, we've met.

Next thing Fish knows he's the heir to a list of dagga clients Mullet used to run, a very nice sideline thank you, and a boat, a bakkie, assorted firearms. Also has to clear out the rest of the guy's life but that's another story.

Now the poor fucker's ashes are in a box under Fish's kitchen sink. He's been meaning to take out the boat, sprinkle Mullet on the waters of False Bay. Problem is the surf. It's been hot lately. And Fish would rather be surfing than blowing off ashes. The dead can wait. Mullet'd understand.

So Fish stares at the *Maryjane*, takes a gulp of stout. Thinks, Gumtree, the online sale site. He could advertise the boat there. The bucks would come in useful.

Takes another swallow from the bottle. Thinks, a shag would've been nice. Pity Vicki couldn't stay. He can feel her skin under his hands. Imagine sliding between those thighs.

Cool. Very cool.

His phone rings: his mother. Estelle. As she wants him to call her.

Vicki's at the Cullinan, hanging out where the bling set hang out, watching Jacob Mkezi approach.

He's come purposefully up the steps from the underground parking into the hotel foyer. A man who looks like he has a sadness on his mind. He pauses two steps from the top, straightens the knot of his tie. The foyer tinkles with piano music, the occasional splutter of female laughter. She reckons this isn't Jacob Mkezi's venue of choice. But that's Clifford Manuel for you. Clifford always on to the hip spots.

Jacob Mkezi steps onto the marble flooring, hears the crunch of grit beneath the soles of his shoes.

'Jacob.'

There are three men sitting on the couches, and the woman, Vicki Kahn. All rise. Clifford Manuel's first on his feet, beckoning him over. Next to him is Cake Mullins, which does not thrill Jacob Mkezi. Cake Mullins means the discussion's not about a building tender, a golf estate development, a toll road scheme. Cake Mullins means the discussion's about moving items.

The third man's tall, thin. Dressed casually: his shirt loose in the current style, a light jacket, jeans, loafers, no socks. Probably in his late forties. Has a tanned face. Tanned hands. An outdoor man. Maybe a bush man? Jacob Mkezi thinks. A game ranger? Cake Mullins is a bush man, always sourcing product in remote places. Might be another reason why Cake Mullins is warming a chair.

He shakes hands with his lawyer. Says, 'What's happening, Clifford?'

Clifford introducing Vicki Kahn. Jacob Mkezi takes her hand, cool and smooth, firm, gripping his hand tighter than he holds hers. 'What a pleasure.' Watches Vicki Kahn looking at him. Appraising is the word he thinks of. Wonders what it would take to get her away from Clifford Manuel, get her on board full-time to handle his legal business?

'I've heard a lot about you, Ms Kahn. And not only from Clifford. From other corporate lawyers as well. You are developing a reputation in the legal world,' he says, not letting go of her hand. 'Sharp as your aunt, I'm told. I knew her, your aunt, Amina Kahn. When she was in Paris. She was my lifeline until they murdered her.'

Sees Vicki Kahn frowning. 'Really. My aunt Amina? These days nobody wants to talk about her. Just the mention of her name brings death threats.'

'I can imagine.' Jacob Mkezi releases her hand. 'Remind me to tell you about her one day. Her tragic story. We were in exile together, you know. Have you read Goethe, Ms Kahn? I learnt German during my time in that country. There is a line of Goethe's: *Träume keine kleinen Träume* ... dream no small dreams. Your aunt found out about men with big dreams, and she didn't like it.' He smiles at her. 'I'm being deliberately mysterious. We need to talk.'

He turns to Cake Mullins, takes his hand next, strong, sweaty. Says, 'This's a surprise.'

'Been a while.' The men making quick eye contact, Jacob Mkezi glancing at Vicki Kahn, 'You've been introduced?'

'We know one another,' says Cake Mullins. 'Poker addicts. We sit at the same tables.'

'Sat,' says Vicki Kahn. 'I'm off the cards now.'

Cake Mullins grins. 'I'd forgotten. Gamblers remand. One day at a time.'

Jacob Mkezi catches the undertow, says to Cake Mullins, 'Maybe you should try it, Gamblers Anonymous,' looking away at the third man.

Clifford Manuel saying, 'Let me introduce you, Dr Tol Visagie.'

'Doctor?' says Jacob Mkezi. 'Medical?'

Tol Visagie laughs. He's loose-limbed, gangly, his arms moving like there's a puppet master pulling strings.

'Not for humans.'

'A vet.'

'Ja,' says Tol Visagie. 'Wild animals.'

Clifford Manuel signals a waiter, places Jacob Mkezi's whisky order.

The group settle into the couches, Clifford Manuel doing icebreakers with the wonders of his new car, the Lexus RX. 'Rides like you're gliding.'

Cars one of Jacob Mkezi's favourite topics. 'You like cars, Vicki?' he asks.

'If a red Alfa MiTo turns you on,' says Clifford Manuel.

'That's what you drive?'

'The only car I want to drive.'

'Nice,' says Jacob Mkezi. 'I'd have said you were a Cooper girl.'

'Why?' Vicki Kahn coming back at him, Jacob Mkezi unsure if she's flirting.

'Why?' He laughs. 'It's what young women drive. Fast. Going places. Wanting to be chic.' Likes the flash it brings to her smile.

'Too obvious,' she says.

'How's the Hummer?' says Cake Mullins, swirling the ice in his drink.

When Jacob Mkezi was police commissioner his Hummer became national news.

'As good as they said in the papers?' Cake Mullins chuckles, gets a frown from Jacob Mkezi, a squirm out of Clifford Manuel.

Clifford Manuel coming in fast, 'And you, Tol, what's your car?'

Tol Visagie snorts. 'A bakkie. Nissan double cab. Perfect for my work.'

Again Jacob Mkezi ignores the opening, leans forward, taps Cake Mullins on the knee. 'A favour?'

'Sure,' says Cake Mullins. 'Your word is my command.'

Jacob Mkezi doesn't crack a smile, keeps tapping at Cake Mullins' knee. 'My boy needs a car. Something fast.'

'I know a man's got a lovely little boutique showroom. Daro Attilane. He can get amazing cars.'

'Nothing amazing. Just something flashy for the kid.'

'Daro's the man.' Cake Mullins takes a sip of his drink, brushes off Jacob Mkezi's tapping finger.

'You do that.' Jacob Mkezi withdrawing his hand.

'I know Daro Attilane,' says Vicki.

'You do?'

'He's reliable. He organised my Alfa.'

'Really?' Jacob Mkezi smiling at her. 'Not only a recommended lawyer, a discerning taste in cars, but connections too.'

Clifford Manuel clears his throat, moving on to cricket, the wonders of the new team. Jacob Mkezi couldn't give a flying fig for cricket but he's sat through Clifford Manuel's cricket spiel often enough to know the lawyer's marking time.

Tol Visagie's a cricket man, it gets him going, talking overs and balls. Cake Mullins adds his two cents about how they're not going to shape against the Aussies. Probably be wiped.

Jacob Mkezi half-listens, watches through the tall windows the young and the beautiful around the pool drinking cocktails, whiskies, shooters. Soft winter night outside, imagines them getting among one another. Fantasises Vicki Kahn into that mix too.

His drink comes, they toast good health.

Clifford Manuel says, 'Jacob, as I told you on the phone, it was Tol asked me to arrange this meeting. He's got Cake on board already. What little I know of the project sounds exciting. Sounds very profitable. Any legal work you need me for, I'm a phone call away. So's Vicki. We're there whenever you need us, our professional opinion. So.' He raises his glass. 'To your venture. We'll leave you guys to it.'

They clink glasses, take a quick swallow.

Vicki Kahn stands. 'Don't get up.'

The men do anyhow.

'I'll be in touch,' says Jacob Mkezi, taking her hand again. 'To tell you about your aunt.'

'You want to feel the baize once more, you let me know,' says Cake Mullins. 'A table's not the same without Vicki the poker chick.'

'Thanks, Cake,' she says, easing her hand out of Jacob Mkezi's grasp. 'But no thanks. This time I'm through.'

'Of course,' says Cake Mullins. 'Why'm I doubting it?'

Jacob Mkezi takes in Vicki Kahn's figure in the black suit. Good hips, good boobs. He nods at Clifford Manuel slipping away with a little bow, smiling like a Buddha, his hands in prayer.

Jacob Mkezi thinking, the lawyer ducking because there's a stink on the wind. He sighs, turns to Tol Visagie wondering where this one's going. 'So, Tol. What's your story?'

Tol leans forward, his elbows resting on his knees. Goes through the polite spiel, an honour to meet you, kind of you to see me, grateful for your time, know you're a busy man, got a lot on your plate.

Jacob Mkezi holds up his hand, stop. 'Hey, my friend, enough. What's the juice?'

'A proposal,' says Cake Mullins.

Tol frowns at Cake Mullins. 'Something I wanna show you.'

'Now?'

Tol laughs, shaking his head. 'No, no-no, not now. It's a bloody long way away. I wanna offer you a break, out of the city.' He shifts to the edge of the couch. 'You're a birdwatcher, hey, that's what I read?'

'When I get a chance.'

'Here's it: this weekend I take you to the Caprivi.' Tol sitting back with a grin. 'Wonderful birds there. The feathered kind too.'

Jacob Mkezi stares at him. 'You know the sort of trouble that's in my life right now?'

'Ja.' Tol Visagie brushing it aside with a wave of his hand. 'The weekend, Mr Mkezi. That's all it's gonna take. We fly there Friday afternoon, fly back Sunday. It'll give you a break. Take you out of it in the bush.'

Jacob Mkezi keeps up the stare. 'You're a vet, you said? Wildlife?'

Tol Visagie nods. 'I work in the bush.'

'Then what's the story, my friend?'

'You have to see it. You have to come and see this.'

'You do, Jacob,' says Cake Mullins. 'Believe me, you've got to see this.'

'You're not going to tell me what it is?'

'No.'

Tol Visagie's shaking his head like a noddy dog. 'We can't.'

'It's just a weekend, Jacob.'

'All the luxuries,' says Tol Visagie. 'Five-star lodge on the river. The best meals.' He keeps the eye contact. 'It'll be worth your while, Mr Mkezi.'

'But you won't tell me what it is?'

'No, sir.' Tol, sucking on his lower lip. 'It's not the thing we should talk about here.'

You've done that lip-suck twice, Jacob Mkezi thinks, still giving Tol Visagie the full eyeball. The first time when you mentioned the birdwatching. Not exactly a poker player are you, my friend?

'Look, Jacob,' says Cake Mullins. 'It'll take you out of this situation.'

'You think I need that?'

'I would.'

'But I'm not you, Cake. I don't run.'

Cake Mullins sets down his glass. 'This's not running.'

'It's a break. Just a weekend break,' says Tol Visagie.

'You heard the man,' says Cake Mullins. 'A weekend break. With a business proposal on the side. It'd be worth your while, as he said.'

'Oh you know that? You know what'll be worth my while?'

'It's a manner of speaking, Jacob. Hell, man, what's your case?'

'Perhaps you haven't noticed my case. All over the newspapers.'

Cake Mullins throws up his hands. 'Oh for God's sake.'

The men sit silent. Jacob Mkezi thinking, mightn't be a bad

idea. A change of scenery. Time to relax completely out of it. Maybe take Mellanie along.

'This weekend?' he says to Tol Visagie.

Tol Visagie coming back, 'No strings. On the house.'

Jacob Mkezi turns to Cake Mullins. 'This car man you know?'

'Yeah.'

'Where's his place?'

'Tokai. You want me to set something up?'

'Tomorrow afternoon. Two thirty at your place. Court doesn't sit Friday afternoons.'

'And the weekend, Jacob?'

Jacob Mkezi stands. 'Bit bloody late notice.'

'Ja,' says Tol Visagie. 'Sorry.'

'What time you want to fly?'

'Five, would be good.'

'Alright.'

'Alone?'

'Maybe. Depends on Mellanie. Depends on her attitude.'

'No hassles either way,' says Tol Visagie.

Jacob Mkezi raises his left hand, goodbye. Walks off across the marble flooring, no crunch of grit under the soles of his shoes.

'Bartolomeu,' says the voice on his cellphone, 'have you got a moment.'

'Hey, Ma,' says Fish, uncapping another milk stout, 'Yeah, I reckon.' Fish still not able to call her Estelle.

His mother coming in fast before he can get into the how-are-you?-I'm-fine exchange. Saying, 'I was talking about you to some clients just now.'

'Uh huh?' says Fish, imagining his mother and the clients in the small boardroom in the London office of Invest South Africa, High Holborn, somewhere like that. His mother out there on one of her overseas jaunts selling investment opportunities. 'Someone's got to get this country on its feet. Someone's got to help black businesses.' His mother spinning stories of wonder and wealth to her clients.

'I was telling them, Barto, that you run a paralegal research firm.'

Fish laughed. 'That's fancy. I wouldn't have thought of it that way, Mom.'

'That's how I'd like to think of it, if you'd only finish your degree.'

'Don't start.' Fish taking a swallow of stout. This pet subject of his mother's: when're you going to complete your degree? You're thirty-three, you should settle down: career, family, children. You only need to write your majors. Really, Bartolomeu, is that too much to ask of you? Get the LLB. You can raise your fees. Get some real money for the work you do. And stop doing the work you do. All those boys'-own investigations. For heaven's sake, Bartolomeu, when're you going to join the adult world? Become a professional.

'I'm not starting, Barto, I'm reminding you of your obligations towards me and your father, may he rest in peace.'

'Mom ...'

'Estelle.'

'Mom...'

'Mom nothing. Now listen, this is business. Have you got a pen and paper?'

Fish rolls his eyes at the ceiling, brings the bottle to his lips but doesn't drink. His mother's saying, 'Prospect Deep, it's a gold mine, not in our portfolio, I need a full report on it. We're commissioning you, Barto.'

Fish thinking, This's close to home. Says, 'Isn't that a bit unprofessional? A bit like nepotism?'

He hears his mother sigh. Imagines her walking around the room. Smiles at the thought. His mother the businesswoman, in her lingo talking up blue-sky projects.

'For heaven's sake, Bartolomeu, it's a simple job. Don't get all coy on me. I can ask any researcher I like. You've done this sort of thing for me before. You can do it again. Besides, you need the money.'

True enough, thinks Fish. Says, 'Okay. Who're the clients?'

'Two Chinese gentlemen.'

'And?'

'And they heard about Prospect Deep, read there is some black economic empowerment deal in the wind, and want in. Simple.'

'Can't you just google it?'

'You don't think I've done that?'

'No.'

'I have.'

'So?'

'It's not enough. I need a bigger picture. Who owns what? What are the projections? Who precisely will be empowered in this deal? BEE's not simple, Barto.'

Fish lets it go, not saying anything, waiting for his mother to keep at it. But she doesn't.

She says, 'You still there?'

Fish says, 'Okay.'

Hears Estelle say, 'Thanks. Thank you, Bartolomeu. I appreciate this. What're your fees?'

'Five hundred rand an hour with expenses.'

'Make it three-fifty.'

'Jesus, Mom.'

'You said it, Bartolomeu. We don't want any hint of nepotism.'

'I thought …' Fish is going to make a point about nepotism being like pregnancy but goes with: '… nothing.' Hides behind a long mouthful of stout.

'You're drinking, Bartholomeu,' says Estelle.

'Yeah. Cheers, Mom.' Fish takes another pull.

'You sound like you're alone, Bartholomeu. Men who drink alone are sad. Sad and lonely. You should get a girlfriend.'

'I have a girlfriend.'

'That Indian girl?'

'She's thirty-five.'

'You know what I mean. You're still seeing her?'

'Uh huh.' Fish stares into the gloom of his back yard; the boat catching the light from the kitchen window like an accusation.

'It's your life, Bartholomeu. Prospect Deep. Write it down please.'

Fish does. Which is where Estelle leaves it, leaves Fish holding a dead phone, looking down at the words he's written: Prospect Deep.

Jacob Mkezi kerb-crawls his Hummer on Long Street direction the mountain, swings up Hout, back down Loop towards the harbour, goes left at Riebeek, takes a slow corner into Bree. Finds what he's looking for over Strand beyond the Castle intersection: bunch of boys in a doorway. He stops. They're huddled there under cardboard sheets, two lying down, three sitting, watching his black car with its black glass. He slides down the passenger window, holds up a pink fifty, waggles it. Knows the boys can see it. The boys don't move. Sit staring at him. He waggles it some more. Nothing. The boys dull-eyed. He disappears the note into his fist, slides the window up. Pulls slowly away, his eyes on the group, knowing they won't let it go.

Two boys jump up, run towards him. He stops the Hummer. Two would be interesting. They push their faces against the glass to see in: pretty boys both, despite their street life. The one with a swollen eye, a bruise on his cheek.

Again he slides down the window. Says to the one with the swollen eye, 'Just you, okay. Net jy.' Shoos the other one off with a dismissive hand.

The boy protests, says, 'Blowjob. Blowjob.'

'Away, away.' Jacob Mkezi shouting at the boy. The boy backing off, giving him the finger. The rest of the group in the doorway, standing up, ready to flee.

Jacob Mkezi waves his fingers at the one with the battered face. 'Net jy, with the sore eye. Open the door.'

The boy does, climbs onto the seat.

'We go for a drive, okay?' Jacob Mkezi speaking in Afrikaans.

The boy nods, staring out the windscreen at the quiet street, not looking at Jacob Mkezi.

'You like to have a drive?'

'Cheeseburger,' says the boy.

'You want a cheeseburger? Where's a cheeseburger this time of night?'

'McDonald's,' says the boy. 'There near the stadium they're building, my baas.'

'Anything else?'

'Double-thick shake. Chocolate 'n banana.'

Jacob Mkezi clucks his tongue. 'You want to eat at the Mount Nelson?'

The boy doesn't respond.

Getting to the McDonald's is through a mess of bollards, slip roads, mud, the cranes over the stadium like marabou storks on a rubbish site. The burger joint an island in the chaos. At the teller's window, Jacob Mkezi gives the order, gets a Coke for himself.

They sit in the parking lot in the dark. Jacob Mkezi watches the boy eat, the boy stuffing the food into his face. 'Somebody hit you?' he asks. Touches the skin beneath his own eye. The boy nods, his cheeks bulging.

Jacob Mkezi reaches over, caresses the boy's face with his fingers, softly, a tender touch on the bruised cheek, the swelling around the eye. His cock stirs. He can see it, the fist. A man's fist slamming into the boy's face, once, twice. The boy knocked down, scrabbling away, crab-style. Where would this be? In a room? On a pavement? In a lane behind a club? The man flicking his fingers after the impact. Swearing at the boy. Walking off. Turning as if to continue the beating. The boy fleeing, running, into the dark, into the alleys.

'Did it hurt? Does it still hurt?'

'Yes, my baas. It's very sore, my baas. Burning.'

'You need some muti, medicine.'

When the boy's eaten, Jacob Mkezi drives to a night pharmacy, leaves the boy in the Hummer. 'Wait. Okay. I'll get you medicine.'

He buys a tin of Zam-Buk salve, a tub of painkillers, a bottle

of water. Has the boy swallow two tablets. Gently rubs the oint-
ment into the boy's cheek, his fingertips tingling at the touch.
The boy reeks of smoke, his hair exuding a mushroom odour.
Jacob Mkezi breathes in the heady smell. He wants to feel the
boy's hair, knows it will be coarse with dirt. Wants to run his
hands over the boy's body, get the thrill of young skin, electric.

'Okay. That feel better?'

'Yes, my baas,' says the boy. 'That's very nice, my baas.'

Jacob Mkezi can't resist, he runs his fingers into the boy's
hair. It's short, knotted, gritty. 'Now we can go for a drive.'
He pats the boy's head, leans over to breathe in the tang of the
boy's hair.

'Yes, my baas. My baas's got a larney car.' The boy fastens
his seatbelt. 'Is there music?'

Jacob Mkezi presses buttons, brings up Brenda Fassie's 'Weekend Special'.

The boy says, 'Ma Brenda.'

Jacob Mkezi laughs, slaps the steering wheel. 'How'd you
know that?'

'I know Brenda.'

'Ah, come on, you're too young. Brenda's from a long time
ago.'

'I know Brenda. We have a tape, this one, "Weekend Special".'

'A tape?'

'And a blaster just no batteries, my baas. Sometimes we find
batteries to play it. Sometimes. Brenda's our mother.'

'Brenda's dead.'

'I know, my baas.' The boy fiddling with a hole in his jeans.

'Here.' Jacob Mkezi gives the medicines to the boy, the boy
stuffing them into his jacket pockets.

'Put more Zam-Buk on later.'

'Yes, my baas. My baas is very good.'

Brenda sings of love gone, of being a weekend special.

'We'll drive now,' says Jacob Mkezi.

He heads up Kloof Nek above the city, at the circle taking a left along Table Mountain Road past cars with people making out, past the cable station. No one about. Where there's a clearing, he fronts the Hummer onto the view. Below, the city, yellow, growling. Above, the mountain.

It's warm in the car, he keeps the engine idling, the heater on. Motions the boy into the back. Says, 'Undress.'

'All my clothes, my baas? It's cold.'

'Bah. There's a blanket.'

While the boy's undressing, Jacob Mkezi gets out, unzips, pisses a hot stream into the sand. The night's cold, his breath visible. He looks down on the city, the tower blocks of light, spits, the Coke gone stale in his mouth.

In the back of the Hummer he has the boy sit beside him, the boy clothed in the blanket like an initiate. Brenda Fassie sings 'If I Hurt You Little Boy'. Jacob Mkezi gets his hands wandering: shoulders, stomach, thighs, into the crotch, the small genitals, the little stiffie.

The boy says, 'What you want, my baas?'

'Just sit,' says Jacob Mkezi. He eases back, undoes his belt, shifts down his pants. 'You know what?'

'I can do it, my baas.' The boy leaning forward, his tongue out, licking.

Jacob Mkezi sighs. Looks out at the city bowl, this city where he's on trial, being held to account for doing his job. For fixing a broken country. Him, a comrade, a struggle fighter. In court before a prosecutor. Before a judge. Explaining himself.

He clenches his thighs, takes his eyes off the city, stares down at the head of the boy moving slowly.

Brenda sings.

He runs a hand along the boy's back over the spine bumps to the cheeks of his bum. Fastens his grip there. Pulls the boy towards him. His breath quickening, rasping in his throat.

'Suck,' he says.

8

Long way down the peninsula, in the dark dark night lurk Seven and Jouma.

'No, my bru, you's got to be out of your head. Nay, you's mad.'

Seven holding open the fence for Jouma to squeeze through, says, 'You think I'm mad. You think so, hey? You think what will happen if the forum come knocking. Like theys do. Like two nights ago. Hey, you think about that?'

Jouma hauls the black bag with the rhino horns through the fence, the plastic snagging on the wire.

'Yusses, man, watch it,' says Seven. He's got a torch in his hand, clicks it on. There's a long tear in the bag, the tip of a horn showing through. 'Grab it there,' he says, putting the beam on the hole.

Jouma bunches up his grip, follows Seven up the path. 'Where's it we going?'

'To hide them, moegoe,' says Seven.

'We can hide them in the ceiling. Safe and sound.'

'I told you,' says Seven. 'No. The forum comes, they find these, we's in big problems.'

'You leave them out here, someone'll find it.' Jouma beginning to pant with the uphill climb.

'Nay, my bru, no one's here. I been watching this place. We can hide them good.' He stops to catch his breath. Turns the torch on Jouma's thin face, Jouma's mouth open sucking in air, his chest heaving.

'You's battling, my bru? Yous need a workout with a active virgin.'

Jouma gasps, says, 'How long? How long you's going to leave them?'

'Dunno. Till tomorrow. Tomorrow we can fix it.'

THE ICING UNIT, NOVEMBER 1977

They sit in the lounge for the next hour, two hours, the four men, crushing out the butts on a plate, sliding the stompies and ash into a plastic bag. The Fisherman mostly glued to the box: the news in English, some stupid medical programme afterwards.

'Mondays are crap,' he says. 'Waste of time' – reaching over to kill his cigarette.

'Don't watch it.'

'I don't, at home. Except *The Villagers*.' He blows out smoke, gets up to switch off the set, stands there unsure.

'You watch *Derrick*? *Bonanza*? *Charlie's Angels*? *Rich Man, Poor Man*?'

'All of them.'

'Why're you complaining then?'

'That's four shows. Inna whole week.'

'You want in?'

The Fisherman scratches his armpit. 'Nee wat! Cards aren't my thing.' He sags back onto the couch. 'A drink woulda been nice.'

'No drinking,' says the Commander.

'A dop, one shot, man. Oke's got to have some Klippies somewhere?'

'No drinking.'

'Fokkit. What's the problem with a dop? A dop's not gonna hurt. Steady our hands.'

'No.'

'Where's this oke anyways?' Blondie says. 'Supposed to be here quarter past six. It's what, bloody four hours later.'

'He's got a girlfriend.'

'Ag kak,' says Rictus Grin, looking at his cards, looking at the Commander. 'True's? That's where he's? Right now?'

'I'm guessing.'

'But you know he's got a poppie?'

'Yes. And I know sometimes he visits her on his way home.'

'Sies! Does she know?' – Rictus jerking his thumb at the dining room.

'Chrissakes.'

'Ja, okay, you know what I mean. Before.'

The Commander licks his fingertips. Discards a card. 'No. We don't think so.'

'Naughty boykie. Full of secrets.'

The card players go through half a dozen hands, the matches piling up in front of their commander. The Fisherman snores on the couch.

Twenty to eleven they hear a car in the street, slowing down, turning into the driveway, the curtains blazing yellow in the glare of the headlights.

Rictus throws down his cards. 'Full house.'

The Commander leans over, holds a finger against the rictus lips. 'Sshh.' Draws his pistol. Whispers, 'No nonsense, okay.'

Rictus grins, bringing up his pistol.

The light at the curtains dies. They wait for the car door to open, the four men screwing silencers to their Brownings. Blondie with a fag in his face, suppressing the tremor in his fingers.

No sound from outside.

They're standing there, the four men, the icing unit. Listening.

'What's he doing?' Rictus tiptoes to the front door.

'You let him come right inside,' says the Commander. 'He gets away …'

'Not gonna happen.'

'Damn right it isn't.' To Blondie he says, 'Take his briefcase. Keep it, don't open it, don't give it to anyone. Even the prime minister. Take it home with you to Cape Town.' They hear the car door open, slam shut. The man clear his throat. The strike and scrape of his shoes on the slasto path. His key scratching into the lock.

9

Ambulance sirens in the distance, getting closer.

There's a man in the car, fallen sideways across the gear shift into the passenger seat.

The car's a Mercedes-Benz S600. It's rolled forward a few metres from the junction, come to rest against the kerb.

The man's wearing a jacket with the collar skew, his tie is undone. There's a bullet wound in his head. Another in his chest. There are blood sprays on the windscreen.

Traffic cones cordon off the scene. Cops stand around talking to tow-away vultures. Blue strobe lights flash on the man's face.

'Must be a rich bloke. With a car like that.'

'Someone's got an order on it.'

'Someone's gonna be pissed off it wasn't delivered.'

A man walks out of the crowd of onlookers, four, five paces into the darkness, keys on his cellphone. He turns to face the people bunched around the Benz.

'Chief,' says the Voice, 'talk to me. What's happening? Tell me things. Things I want to hear. Ticks in all the boxes. Is it done?'

'Yes,' says Mart Velaze. Mart Velaze a smart guy in jeans, a black leather jacket. Good shoulders, slim waist. Carrying no fat, no stomach swell.

'What's the talk?'

'From the cops a botched hijacking.'

'Everyone's happy with that?'

'I would say so.'

'Ah ha. Well done.' The Voice repeating the refrain, 'Ah ha, ah ha. No one saw you?'

'No one.'

'Of course not, my silly question.'

Mart Velaze has never met the woman he's phoned. The

Voice. All instructions come telephonically. He pictures the Voice as a big woman. Big stomached. Braided hair. Moving like an elephant, a matriarch, in her creased suits. Power-dressed as a man would. All he knows is the Voice is deep inside security. That's what he hears from colleagues. Not national intelligence, or military, or police, but something else, somewhere else. You get told to expect a call from her you pay attention. You do what she asks, you get a cash payment.

The Voice says, 'Go home, chief.'

'And Jacob Mkezi?' says Mart Velaze.

'You stay loyal to him, my brother. We're getting to him, chief. Patience. The English virtue. Patience. His days are short. Mr Mkezi is an embarrassment.' The Voice laughs. 'Chief, you have done very well. We appreciate you, Bra Mart. Go with the ancestors.'

10

On the backline in a mellow sea, Fish Pescado and Daro Attilane sit their boards, noses towards the shore. Their feet in the water: Fish's feet numb with the cold, Daro's snug in booties.

Yesterday's swell has gone down, the sets coming in at long intervals. There's not much action. The next front is a day out with the promise that the scene'll start cooking. Until then there's this ripple. But a ripple is better than a flat sea.

The last two sets, Fish and Daro tried for waves, the little greenies sliding beneath them. They're too far out, they need to move in. Only, they move in they lose some of the view.

Right now they're enjoying the view: watching the sun rise. This shoo-whaa spectacle that shifts Muizenberg mountain through a colour spectrum: pink, orange, tawny.

Daro breaks their daydreaming. Checks his watch, says, 'Got to go. Got an order last night on a Subaru. You ever heard of Cake Mullins?'

Fish splashes water. 'Yeah, I've heard of him. Weird name.'

Daro laughs. 'No kidding.'

'He's a card player,' says Fish. 'Vicki knows him. Played cards with him. Before.'

'He might be. The way I know him he's one of those agents, you know, arranges things for expensive people.'

'A fixer?'

'Sort of thing. But a sale's a sale. These days a rare event.'

Tell me about it, thinks Fish, work being such a rare event he'd even spring to a divorce job. Even a muscle job. Or a murder. Lots of people wanting private investigators to take on murder hunts. But Fish's not sure he wants those. He's done three. Nailed the killer before the cops. But it wasn't nice work.

'Let's go closer in,' he says. 'Jump on some of the little boogers.'

They lie down on their boards, paddle in to where there's more chance of catching a ride. Reluctant to end the session, sitting again, waiting for the ripples. Fish gazing at his feet, his toes white, bloodless. The peaceful mood on him.

Daro says, 'Can I ask a favour? Two favours?'

'Sure,' says Fish, wondering if this is yesterday's ask that never happened.

'This afternoon with this Subaru, if the guy takes it I'll need a lift back.'

'No problem,' says Fish.

'I'm buying your time,' says Daro. 'At your hourly rate.'

'Ah, man, this's a favour.'

'No, I mean it. It's a job.'

Fish picks at wax lumps on his board. 'I could use the cash.'

'There you go. I'll call you when I'm heading out.'

'And the other thing?'

'The other thing … Oh, yes, the other thing. You mentioned once about someone you know, used to be a junkie.'

'Uh huh.' Fish keeping his eyes on the sea, watching for ripples. 'Why're you asking?'

'You said she gives talks to schools.'

'She does. Has this routine of taking off her peg leg, throwing it to the kids to look at. Very bizarre. Very effective when she tells them her leg was cut off because the needle sticks went gangrene.'

'Interesting,' says Daro.

'You could say,' says Fish, 'why d'you ask?'

Daro shrugs. 'Was wondering if she'd give her talk to Steffie's class. You know, through the forum. Part of our programme.'

'No problem,' says Fish. 'What about the Seven business?'

Daro holding up his hands. 'We're working on it.'

'Offer's still open,' says Fish, getting prone, stroking to ride the first of a small set. He and Daro catching the ankle snapper, going in side-by-side, 1960s style.

11

Jacob Mkezi, in his Hummer in the traffic, says on his hands-free to Mart Velaze, 'You know, comrade, this is pissing me off.' Jacob Mkezi on his way to court for another day of the corruption showdown.

'Mr Mkezi, did you accept as a gift a pair of crocodile-skin shoes?'

'They were not a gift.'

'You went into a shoe shop with the man who bought them, correct?'

'Yes.'

'You tried on the crocodile shoes?'

No response.

The judge: 'Please answer, Mr Mkezi.'

'Yes, I did.'

'You liked them. You decided to buy them?'

'I didn't have my credit card.'

'You liked them, the shoes?'

'Yes.'

'You asked the shop assistant to keep them for you?'

'I can't remember.'

'Then your friend said he would buy them for you as a gift. And you accepted?'

'I said I would refund him.'

'Ah, you would refund him. And have you, Mr Mkezi, re-funded him?'

'Yes.'

'You can prove this? An EFT transaction? A cheque?'

'It was cash.'

'I'm sure it was.'

Mr Mkezi's advocate on his feet, the judge waves him down.

'Cash. Almost three thousand rand in cash. That's a lot of cash, Mr Mkezi. Did you make a special withdrawal for that cash?'

On and on about the crocodile shoes. The newspapers loving it: 'Jacob's sleazy shoes'; 'Top cop gets expensive shoes as gift'; 'Hood and cop on shopping spree'.

And now he's known as the man in the crocodile shoes, which Jacob Mkezi likes. Jacob Mkezi, no longer the top cop. Now Jacob Mkezi, businessman, African Enterprises (Pty).

He's wearing the offending shoes on his way to court while he talks to Mart Velaze.

'Comrade,' he says. 'Comrade, you're pissing me off, I don't read the newspapers. I don't need to know the news.' Jacob Mkezi is speaking in English because that's their common language. 'We should not be talking.'

He hears Mart Velaze sigh. He catches this despite the traffic noise, the Hummer growl, he catches this shift of exasperation. 'You know,' he says, 'you know, comrade, that this was important. You are the man I trust, comrade. Don't let me down.'

'Never, comrade,' says Mart Velaze. 'I am your man.'

'I trust you, comrade. I do not need reports.'

'No, comrade.'

Jacob Mkezi stares down at the commuters in the car alongside him: a man and a woman, husband and wife maybe, she's doing her make-up, he's on his cellphone, breaking the law. No one gives a toss for the law. Politicians, citizens, the high and mighty, the lowlife all doing their thing, no problem. Except he can't be gifted a pair of shoes it doesn't make headline news.

The man in the crocodile shoes.

Well, the man in the crocodile shoes is on it. The sorter. The saviour. The cleaner. The man who helped everyone into Armani suits, Breitling watches, Gucci handbags.

'Cheer up, comrade,' he says to Mart Velaze. 'We can live with it. You hear what I'm saying? It's what the Americans call pre-emptive. Or as the proverbs tell us, better to be the safe ones than the sorry ones. Are we on the same page?'

He hears Mart Velaze grunt 'Uh huh', thumbs him off.

The trouble with Mart Velaze, thinks Jacob Mkezi, is that sometimes he doesn't get the bigger picture. Sometimes he gets stuck on the details. Which is the trouble with intelligence agents. Their focus is too narrow. But most times you cannot have everything accounted for. The world doesn't operate like that. In this world you work with what you've got. What Jacob Mkezi calls the AK tactic. Shoot everything. It's safer that way.

His cell rings: Mellanie. Pronounced Mel-lar-nie. Never Mel or Melly. Only Mellanie. Or in Jacob Mkezi's dulcet tones: Sisi. As in, 'Hey, sisi.'

'Hey, sweets,' Mellanie says back, that edge to her tone, sarcastic. Then cuts the crap. 'Listen, sweets,' she says. 'I'm not going to make it. Client meetings all day.'

Mellanie, as in MM Coms, as in Mellanie Munnik Communications, spins for a big fishing company, a short-term insurer, the vulture tow truck industry, the building industry and any BEE company screwing up its stock exchange profile because the directors are skimming or incompetent or both. Spins for African Enterprises. Top of her preference are those companies because they don't mind her fees. Large fees. Outrageous fees.

'Mr Mkezi,' she said to him at a dinner to honour Madiba's eighty-ninth birthday, 'very snazzy shoes. Crocodile skin?' Not a glow of a smile on her face. He was police commissioner then. The top cop.

He looked at her, she gazed back at him, unwavering.

'Sisi,' he said, 'be careful. I've always worn crocodile skin.'

'Sweets,' she said, 'you're the one in the headline shoes. Here're my contact details' – snuck a business card into his top pocket. 'Give me a call.'

Which Jacob Mkezi did. Two days later was a client of MM Coms. Three dinners later found himself lying naked, except for his socks, beneath Mellanie Munnik, handcuffed to her four-poster bed.

'Sisi,' he said, 'this is not my culture.'

'Sweets,' she said, 'too bad, it's mine.'

Now she's telling him she's not going to be in court. She's been beside him through his resignation from the cops, through the bad press conferences, she's spun his story that his resigning was strategic, that it wasn't about fraud, wasn't about unaccounted-for expenses, that he wasn't fraternising with organised crime, he was working an angle.

'I want you there,' says Jacob Mkezi. 'It's what I'm paying you for. It's important.'

'Sweets,' says Melanie, 'you're paying me to make you Mister Goodfellow. Not hold your hand.'

Jacob Mkezi hears her saying off-phone: 'Put him on hold. Won't be a minute' – as if talking to him, Jacob Mkezi, is part of her morning checklist. Mellanie coming back to him: 'Sweets, you're in the grey suit, pale blue shirt, dark tie with the thin green stripes, the crocodile shoes? Tell me, yes.'

'Yes,' he says.

'Good,' she says.

She's turned the crocodile-skin shoes into his brand. Like Batman's cape. When Jacob Mkezi, even a tainted Jacob Mkezi, shows up at social events in his crocodile-skin shoes then there's a charge in the room. Women touch their hair. Men pour larger drinks. Politicians, cabinet ministers, directors-general pay attention before the man in the crocodile-skin shoes.

'Later,' Mellanie says.

Jacob Mkezi would like to tell her cancel everything, but goes with, 'We're going on safari this weekend. This afternoon.'

'We?' she says. 'This is the first I've heard of it.'

'I'm telling you now.'

'This afternoon, Jacob!' No more Sweets.

'Thank God.' Jacob Mkezi tries a laugh.

'I'm running a business, Jacob. Clients who need my time.'

'I need your time,' he says, his tone hardened. The voice of the man in the crocodile-skin shoes. 'I need your time today with me in court.'

A silence.

Mellanie says, 'I'll see what I can do, Jacob.' Pauses. 'I'm not promising anything.'

'Be there.'

He disconnects. And that's Mellanie gone and Jacob Mkezi coming down Eastern Boulevard in three lanes of solid traffic for another day at the High Court, in this city beneath the mountain. The mountain huge, looming behind the city; the city sharp and white, lying at its harbour edge the ocean, perfect. Smooth, blue, shiny. This irritating city. This city that has him on trial. Jacob Mkezi thinking, he's the man who knows what's really going on in government, yet he's in court for fraud, corruption, embezzling, associating with known criminals, the whole nine yards, the whole rooty-tooty, the complete kraal and reed dance. Except Jacob Mkezi will not be hung out to dry.

THE ICING UNIT, DECEMBER 1977

Couple of days before Christmas the Commander calls the blond agent tells him the time has come to deliver the briefcase.

The next morning the Commander arrives to collect Blondie in his Benz. The Commander wearing the same jacket and tie he wore the RAU TEM night. They drive to the winelands, not talking.

What the Commander doesn't know is that Blondie's been into the briefcase. That night, after they dropped him at the hotel, the flea-ridden Station Hotel, he tried the locks. Combination locks. Not expecting them to open. But they did, flipped up with a sharp click. Inside: election flyers, letters for signing, newspaper clippings, draft of a speech, and ...

And under that a sheaf of photocopies. Blondie flipped through them saying, Jeez, man, jeez, man. Wondering: that man, the politician, couldn't be so rich? No, man, never. This was about something else. This was why he'd been told not to open the briefcase. This was stuff the politician shouldn't have had, these copies of numbered Swiss bank accounts holding millions. You got killed for having this sort of information. Your own had you killed.

Blondie propped himself on the bed, smoked two cigarettes staring at the open briefcase. A thing he'd been told on training, always take insurance. Especially documents, photographs. Anything looks like it might have value, take it. You never know. The thing about insurance, mostly you don't need it but sometimes ...

The first opportunity he made photostats. Bank statements of all the accounts, deposit slips, correspondence. Then closed the briefcase, spun the combinations. Safe my mate.

That briefcase right now on the back seat of the Merc.

'You ever heard of Dr Gold?' says the Commander.

Blondie sucks on the cigarette, exhales. 'Of course. The minister of finance.'

'Was minister of finance. Now ambassador to Switzerland. You know why they call him Dr Gold?'

'Nah.' The cigarette dangling on his lips, trademark-style.

'Because he shifted our country's gold from London to Zurich, at a profit.'

Blondie thinking, makes sense of the millions in the bank accounts. Makes sense of blotting the RAU TEM politician, if the politician had found out what was going on. Blondie doesn't know what's going on but he thinks it has to be some get-rich scheme for Dr Gold and his mates.

'This's who we're going to see,' says the Commander. 'To give him the briefcase.' The Commander glancing at him. 'You didn't open it?'

Blondie blows out smoke. 'It's locked.'

'Not a problem for some people.'

'Ja, well. I didn't.'

Blondie reckons the Commander's not convinced. Tough tittie.

The Commander half-looking at him, one eye on the road, smiling. Says, 'There's a boykie.'

Blondie, eyes on the mountains ahead hazed in the heat, lets a trickle of smoke curl up the side of his face, disappear in his blond surfer's thatch. They drive in silence, the Commander tapping the steering wheel with his fingers. The road narrow through the winelands, past silos, sheds, the Commander going wide round a donkey cart, children in the cart waving.

On a hill he slows, turns off the tar onto a dirt road, the road ungraded, the Merc's underbelly scraping on the bumps. Takes them through a labourers' settlement of low white cottages, women staring at them, children and dogs running out.

At the end of the settlement they swerve between two cottages into a plantation of bluegum trees, the track smoother, covered in brittle eucalyptus leaves, still heading upwards. On the rise the trees clear, the vista opening into a valley, a pond below, beyond that lawns rising to the gabled house.

Blondie whistles.

'Built 1730,' says the Commander. 'Says so on the gable.'

'You've been here before?'

'Not long ago.'

'You met him?'

'Was his job we pulled. His orders.'

Blondie lights another cigarette from the stompie of the last. 'This is where he lives?'

'One of the places. Dr Gold moves around. Has a house in Cape Town for when he was in parliament. Another one in Pretoria. The farm he likes best's in the Free State. Has this koppie, more like a mountain, on it. Flat-topped mountain, you go up there you could be in another world. Something to see let me tell you. You think this looks good, you gotta see that place. Air you can drink. Big landscapes, big big landscapes. At night stars and stars to the end of the universe.'

'What sort of farm?'

'Cattle.' The Commander shakes his head. 'Not Angus or any of them. Not Frieslands. Nguni cattle, he calls them. Even breeds the bastards.' The Commander does his finger drum on the steering wheel. 'I don't know, something strange about Dr Gold, if you ask me.'

The Commander stops the Merc near the house. There's a black man standing at the front door. Smartest-looking black man Blondie's ever seen. Even wearing a jacket in the heat. Young too, about his own age, Blondie reckons. Says, 'Check those shoes.'

'Crocodile skin,' says the Commander. 'Very pretentious all that patchwork. Bloody awful.'

'Who's he?'

'Jacob Mkezi,' says the Commander, keeping his voice low. 'Dr Gold's man. Only Bantu security in the whole government. Comes from the Free State farm. We trained him. Special training in the security branch.'

They get out of the car, Blondie reaching in to lift the brief-case off the back seat.

'Kill the smoke,' says the Commander. 'Don't light another one.'

As they walk up the steps onto the stoep, Jacob comes forward. No smile, nothing in his eyes.

The Commander unholsters his gun, hands it over. 'Give it to him,' he says to Blondie.

He hesitates.

'Give it to him.'

Blondie obeys, pulls a pistol from his belt.

'And the briefcase.'

'You said ...'

'Give it to him.'

Jacob takes the guns and the briefcase, stands aside to let them enter. Inside it's dark, cool, smells of thatch. The ceiling of wood planks, a fan turning in the dimness.

'Wait,' says Jacob.

They wait not speaking, the day bright and harsh beyond the open door. Their eyes growing accustomed to the gloom. The room looks like a museum. Old farm implements on the walls. Rack of ball-and-powder rifles. Ancient cabinets, writing desks. Riempie furniture: chairs, benches, footstool bankies.

A door opens at the end of the room, a voice says, 'Thank you for bringing the briefcase.' There's a short man, stocky, carrying weight on his stomach. His pate bald, grey whispers of hair over his ears, approaching them. 'People call me Dr Gold,' he says, chuckling, shaking hands with the Commander, moving on to Blondie, lingering, his hand damp and soft in Blondie's grip.

'You are a surfer,' he says. 'So I'm told. Very nice, exhilarating, I would say.' He releases Blondie's hand. Turns towards a movement in the passage, says, 'Jacob, is all in order?'

'Yes, sir,' says Jacob.

'The briefcase was locked? The papers inside?'

'Yes, sir,' says Jacob.

Dr Gold smiles at Blondie. 'I was told you are discreet.' He lays his hand on Blondie's arm. 'There are no waves in Switzerland but we could use someone … discreet. Don't you think so, Jacob?'

Jacob says nothing.

'Well, think about it anyhow.' He backs off two paces. 'I appreciate your trouble, Commander, most sincerely. As they say, you've taken a great weight off my mind. I can return to Switzerland, relieved.' His hand flutters a goodbye. 'Oh, Jacob,' he says, 'fetch them a jug of lime juice. It is a hot day to be driving.'

12

Fish takes a shower, gets into a hoody and jeans, a pair of ankle-boots made of vegetable-dyed kudu leather he only wears in winter. Wanders through to the kitchen, toasts slices of bread under the grill. Actually, blackens slices of bread under the grill because he's thinking of his mother.

'You're thirty-three, Bartolomeu, you need to finish your degree. Get a proper job. In business. Play golf.'

'I'm thinking of it,' he'd said.

'Really, of what part?'

'Of finishing the degree.'

'I'm supposed to believe that?'

Yeah, he was thinking about it. Thinking that some law knowledge would be an advantage.

Which distracts him, which causes the toast to burn. Fish has to scrape off the singe into the sink. He smears on marge and peanut butter, drizzles syrup over this. Gets a Bialetti coffee pot going on the stove. Sits down at the table to eat. Through the open door he can see the *Maryjane* on her trailer, his long-board leaning against the boat. Maybe if the waves are down this weekend, he and Vicki can power out, put Mullet to rest. If Vicki can spring for the fuel. Bucks being what they are: scarce.

Talking of which.

He crunches down on a couple of slices of toast, finishes his coffee, spends the morning working the phone. Vicki first.

'You gonna feed me tonight?' he says for openers.

'I love you too,' she says.

'Brilliant,' says Fish, 'you promised. Yes?'

'Sounds like you're eating.'

'Only toast.'

He bites into a crust, spraying crumbs. 'So what time?'

'Six thirty. Seven latest. I'll get Giovannis.'

'Lots of the fancy stuff, hey. Chilli prawns. Octopus in that vinaigrette. Artichokes. Taramasalata. Calf liver pâté.'

'That's what you want?'

'Oh yes.'

'That's what you always have.'

'That's why I want it.'

He hears Vicki sigh, smiles to himself. 'Take the afternoon off?'

'Some of us have to work.'

Fish lets out a long 'Aaah, you wouldn't have anything coming up for me?'

After a beat, Vicki says, 'Please, Fish ...'

Fish going into the gap, 'It's cool. Sorry, sorry. I shouldn't have asked. It's only ... You know.'

'I know. Hang in, babes, it'll come right. Everybody's scratching.'

'Yeah. I guess.'

'Till later.'

'Sure.' Fish listening to the line go dead, thinking, talking to Vicki wasn't supposed to make him feel lousy.

He stands in the kitchen looking at the boat in the back yard: if he had spare cash for fuel he could maybe go out on the ocean, catch some fish for supper. If he had money for petrol. Can't be that difficult, fishing. Being on False Bay would be amazing. Alone, smoke some doob, pull in a couple of snoek. Talk to the seagulls. Toss Mullet's ashes over the side.

But work is what he wants. Phones a couple of the small firms doing insurance and divorce jobs, missing persons, has to listen to the gripes of hard times.

Investigators working as bouncers.

Investigators moonlighting as waiters.

Investigators doing factory security.

One guy freelancing as a car guard.

Bugger that, thinks Fish, no ways he'd be out there pushing shopping trolleys for the SUV ladies. No ways this side of the ice caps melting.

He boils up another coffee, sits there thinking, maybe he's gonna have to go back into paid employ. Join one of the security firms. Maybe that's what it's coming to. Have to swallow hard, have someone else telling you what to do. Not ideal.

Which is when he gets round to his mother's request. Three hundred and fifty rand an hour! Extortion. But when there's nothing else ... Fish wondering if he could stretch to maybe a thousand bucks worth. Powers on his laptop, types Prospect Deep into the google bar.

13

He's in the dock, the prosecutor on his case: 'Mr Mkezi, would you call your friend, the man who bought you the shoes, a known criminal?'

The judge watches him, the journalists watch him, the public in the gallery wait. Clifford Manuel glances at Jacob Mkezi from the huddle of defence lawyers, nods.

Jacob Mkezi stands straight, his hands crossed at his waist. A man attentive, unhassled.

'An associate.'

'In what sense would that be?'

'I'm sorry?'

The prosecutor smiles. 'Are you business associates? Do you belong to the same gym, perhaps? The same golf club?'

'I am a very bad golfer. Nobody wants to partner with me.'

There's a titter from the public gallery. The judge glances at them, instilling silence.

Below him Jacob Mkezi sees Clifford Manuel wag his finger.

The prosecutor shuts his smile. 'I think we all know your handicap, Mr Mkezi. It has been in the newspapers often enough. But that, as you know, wasn't my question. I want to know the nature of your relationship with this associate?'

'We had common interests.'

'In what, for instance?'

'Cattle.'

Another ripple through the back galleries. The judge ignores it.

Jacob Mkezi has his eyes on the judge, sees a twitch on the man's lips that might be amusement.

'We both kept Nguni cattle, on our farms.'

'If he bought you a pair of crocodile-skin shoes, this seems to suggest a close friendship?'

'He is a generous man.'

'Very generous. I wish I had friends like that.'

'Associates,' says Jacob Mkezi.

'You knew he was involved with organised crime?'

'I did.'

'Yet you still associated with him. Discussed cattle. Even sometimes enjoyed the odd luncheon together, didn't you? I have the payment chits.'

Jacob Mkezi looks at his lawyers, Clifford Manuel responding by nudging the advocate. The man lumbers to his feet. 'My Lord, this is going nowhere. We need to know who this mysterious man is?'

'Is he to testify?' says the judge to the prosecutor. 'I assume this is where you are leading?'

'Yes, M'Lord. I am.'

'Then maybe it is time to let us hear what he has to say.'

Jacob Mkezi frowns. His advocate turns from the judge to face his client, rolls his eyes.

'Certainly, M'Lord,' says the prosecutor. He's handed a piece of paper by a court orderly, reads it. Stammers, 'I ... Good God ...'

'What is it please?' says the judge. 'Can your share this?'

'M'Lord.' The prosecutor holds up the piece of paper, clears his throat. 'My intention, M'Lord, was to call a state witness at this point, Mr Mkezi's associate. We have sworn affidavits from him following a plea bargain. Affidavits which outline the nature of his relationship with the accused.'

'Apart from the lunch chits and the shoes?' says the judge.

Jacob Mkezi smiles. The judge deadpan.

'Oh yes, M'Lord. This man paid for overseas holidays for Mr Mkezi. Advanced him cash. Purchased artworks. This man was very generous in his relationship with Mr Mkezi. As Mr Mkezi has said.'

'This does happen between friends and associates.'

'That was for my witness to tell us, M'Lord.'

'Well, where is he?'

The prosecutor waves the piece of paper. 'I have been told he's passed, M'Lord.'

'He's died?'

'Yes.'

'When, for heaven's sake?'

'Last night.'

'Good grief.'

'He was shot, M'Lord.'

'Shot?'

'In a hijacking.' The prosecutor staring at Jacob Mkezi.

Jacob Mkezi impassive. His hands still, loosely crossed as they have been all morning.

'M'Lord,' says the defence advocate, 'if this witness has died we are unable to test his affidavits.'

'I am well aware of that,' says the judge. 'Perhaps, counsel, you can both see me in chambers.'

14

Fish stares at the screen of his laptop, thinking Prospect Deep is probably not a deal his mother should be brokering. Prospect Deep has big names attached to it. Prospect Deep is best left alone. He knows Estelle won't do that. Those names are going to fire her cylinders. For her those names couldn't get any better.

He can hear her: 'Mr Yan, Mr Lijun, this is one of the most promising investment opportunities we have in South Africa at the moment. You were right to come to us. This is a gold mine.' Which she'd follow with her tittering laugh, the one she keeps for schmooze moments.

Problem is those names attached to Prospect Deep give Fish the frights. Like when you're staring at a wave that's filled the sky, a wave that's curling. An Atlantic bonecrusher bred in the southern ocean. You're going to be pulverised. You're going down for a long time. Those kind of frights.

Thing is how to put Estelle off.

Fish's thinking about this when he hears footsteps drag across the back stoep, the scrape of the bergie chair, someone letting out a long sigh of relief. Someone with a high BO rating.

Fish closes the laptop, takes a look. There's an old bergie staring at him from the chair.

'Meneer,' says the bergie, 'you have some toast I can smell?'

'Maybe,' says Fish. 'Who're you? How'd you know about me?'

The old man grins. 'Nee, meneer, doesn't take long to find out.'

Fish nods. 'Okay. What's your name?'

'Colins.'

'Colin.'

'Colins. With a s.'

'That's your first name?'

'My only name.' Colins snorts back mucus, wipes his hand

under his nose. 'I can tell you something, gentleman.'

'That right. Like what?'

'For a piece of toast, gentleman. A piece of toast and marmalade. A cup of coffee too. Half milk, three sugars. Please.'

'You think I'm a cafe?'

'Agge nee, gentleman. People told me Mr Fish's the man. So here I am.'

Fish takes a swallow of his coffee, eyes Colins the bergie. Much like any other bergie, unkempt beard, his clothes grey, his backpack grey, his only other possession a huge manuscript of papers in a plastic bag.

'What's that?' says Fish.

'My life story.'

'Yes?'

'A bestseller, gentleman. For a rainy day when it's finished.' He looks at the coffee in Fish's hand. Rubs his stomach. 'Please, gentleman.'

Fish slides more bread under the grill, boils up an instant brew. He smears marge and marmalade onto the toast. Calls out to the bergie, 'You want a hit of Klippies in the coffee?'

'Jislaaik, gentleman, that's manna from the heavens. Thank you, gentleman. Sommer a large one, dankie please.'

Fish brings out the toast and coffee, goes back for his own mug. Leans against the *Maryjane*, far enough upwind of Colins.

'Where're you from, Colins?'

'No, gentleman, from here and there, just passing through.'

'Okay.' Fish stares at the man demolishing the toast.

'Can I ask you for some more, gentleman?'

'You haven't finished that yet,' says Fish.

Colins slurps at his coffee. Grins at Fish.

'Finished and klaar in another bite.'

'First what's it you're gonna tell me?'

Colins chews through a mouthful, washes it down with coffee, wipes his hand across his mouth. 'Gentleman,' he says, 'gentleman, I got here yesterday onna train no fare payable. People outside the bottle store tell me the mountain's safe, especially there by the old fort. They show me where to go on the corner at the parking lot where the fishermens park. You know, they got a locked gate there but no problem you can shift the fence, sleep in a national monument under the stars. Lekker like a crecker. Gentleman, it's a good place when there's no rains. These people they tell me about you. They tell me if I need it, you can give me a slice of bread.'

'That right?' says Fish. 'Which people are these?'

'You know, those people, gentleman. Just bergies.'

Fish nods. 'Ja, so?'

'So I find a nice place up there to sleep against a stone wall. There's a cardboard under the bushes, like they tell me, plenty for a man to make himself comfortable. You can lie there listening to the waves and you don't worry. You feel safe inna fort.' He laughs, spittle popping on his beard. 'I goes to sleep like a baby. Then I wake inna night with men talking. I think maybe it's anner people come to sleep there but I'm not worried cause I'm outta sight behind the wall. Only these men move some rocks, talking low low low, whispering. Nobody whispers up there, meneer, except skelms. Skelms up to bad things. Not my problem, hey, I'm not making a sound, absolutely tjoepstil. Next, they's gone. I goes back to sleep. This morning I take a look. What they's lefts in a plastic bag.'

He shuts up, finishes his coffee, holds the cup out to Fish. 'Some more, ag please, gentleman, won't you?'

Fish takes the mug. 'What was in the plastic?'

'You's not going to believe it, gentleman.'

'Try me.'

The old man slaps his thigh, laughs. 'You guess?'

'I dunno. Guns, diamonds, jewellery? Has to be something stolen.'

'Nothing like what you said.'

'Okay, what?' Fish thinking, enough with the games.

Colins crinkles his eyes. 'Horns from a rhinoceros.'

Fish gazes at the old man, the old man grinning.

'I'm not gonna believe you,' says Fish.

'Serious,' says Colins. 'We can go there after coffee.'

15

'Prost,' says Mellanie, raising her flute of bubbly. Real French bubbly, Moët, that brought Jacob Mkezi down five hundred bucks at Azura's, the Mandela Rhodes Place hot spot.

Mellanie sitting at the poolside table in a black military coat, her leggings tapering into leather boots, a scarf fluffed around her neck. She's a short and spiky blonde. The sort of blonde gives men pause. No lipstick, no nail varnish either. Mellanie reckons with saucy lips, you don't need colouring. Her lips have a natural juiciness.

'You got it,' says Clifford Manuel, clicking glasses with her.

Jacob Mkezi hesitates. 'Uh uh,' he says. 'Sounds like we're celebrating a hijacking. A man I knew died.'

'He was going to diss you,' says Mellanie, holding back her glass.

'Maybe,' says Jacob Mkezi.

'Some friend he was.' Mellanie getting into it.

'We had good times.'

'For associates.'

'Leave it, Clifford.'

Mellanie setting down her glass on the table. 'What I couldn't understand, Jacob. Could never see, was why you were friends? What'd you see in the man. He was bad news.'

'He's dead, leave it.'

'He did a deal to save his backside. He was going to hang you out, hang you out so far not even I could've done anything about it.'

'Doesn't matter now.'

'Heaven's sake, Jacob. What're you saying?' She shifts her eyes to Clifford: 'Help me understand this.'

Clifford Manuel shrugs, takes a sip of the champagne.

'He had family,' says Jacob Mkezi. 'A wife, kids who loved him.'

'There'll be insurance policies, Jacob. They'll be heading into more money than when he was alive. He was a crook, Jacob. A degenerate.'

'Everybody liked him. Even the president.'

'What you mean is he got his fingers so far up the arses of the big boys he was massaging their prostates. Different kind of like.'

Clifford Manuel clears his throat, dusts his sleeves. 'The essence here is the case has been dismissed. That's what we're celebrating.'

Jacob Mkezi is staring out over the rooftops, thinking seven floors up gives a great view of the city: what's left of the art deco, the new tower blocks, the hip in-fills, some old Victorian still squeezed in between. He sat here with the man, one long December lunch, eighteen months back. Talking sport, money, investments, among other matters. Sat here amid the black diamonds, the bright young corporates popping over to give him the power shake. Jacob Mkezi thinking, at the time, thinking, who didn't know this man?

'Jacob!' Mellanie waving her hand in front of his face. 'Come back.'

Jacob Mkezi turned lazy eyes on her. 'What?'

'The end of the case.' Mellanie holds up her flute.

This time Jacob Mkezi goes through the click ritual. Time to focus. He looks at Mellanie. 'You made it.'

'I said I would.'

'You weren't going to.'

Mellanie holds his eyes. 'Jacob, enough. We're not going there again.'

Jacob Mkezi doesn't know why he takes this attitude from her, but he does. It's what he likes about her.

'You're full of piss 'n steam,' he says.

She smiles. 'Always and everso.' Takes a cellphone from her handbag. 'We need to put out a press release. I'm going to say you're deeply saddened by this tragic murder …'

'I am.'

'… and regret that the truth will never be tested in court.'

'It's your scene.'

'And would like to state once again that the allegations are entirely without foundation.'

Jacob Mkezi drinks. 'You're the boss.'

He catches the sharp cut of her gaze. Hard to see affection in it when she's doing her job.

'Just so we're deejaying the same tracks, Jacob. Right?'

'Right.'

Mellanie's nails clicking at the BlackBerry keys.

Clifford Manuel reaches over, touches Jacob Mkezi on the sleeve. 'What happened with Tol Visagie?'

Jacob Mkezi says, 'We're on safari.'

'Good. Excellent.' Clifford Manuel finishing his glass. 'Let me know if you need anything.'

'Where're you off to?' says Mellanie.

'Not me, we,' says Jacob Mkezi. 'Both of us, you and me.'

Mellanie sitting back. 'I said I'd think about it.'

'And?'

'I've got a business to run, Jacob. Disappearing for a weekend takes arranging.'

'Fly-in. Five-star. On the Caprivi. What's to arrange?'

'No, Jacob. You think you can just snap your fingers.'

He snaps his fingers. 'I can. Pick you up at four.'

'In three hours' time?'

'Exciting, né?'

She stares at him. He holds her eyes until she smiles. 'You're something else.'

'Fixed up.' Jacob Mkezi signals for a waiter to fill their glasses. 'All I've got to do now is buy a toy for my boy.'

THE ICING UNIT, JUNE 1981

They arrive on the farm separately, the Fisherman from Port Elizabeth in his bakkie, Blondie from Cape Town in his VW Kombi, a sin bin complete with bed, camping fridge, a gas two-burner.

About an hour before sunset, the Commander and Rictus Grin get there in a police bakkie, unmarked. Haul three men from the back. The men shackled together in ankle chains, handcuffed. They lock them in an outbuilding.

With sunset the men in the outbuilding start singing. They sing through the night.

In the still cold night their voices are everywhere, as if the ancestors have arisen to join them.

In the morning they take the men into the veld. At an old antbear burrow they hand them spades, make them dig.

'A cigarette,' says one of the prisoners.

Rictus jams a cigarette between the lips of each prisoner, brings up a match. Says to the Commander, Blondie, the Fisherman, 'Any of yous want one?'

They do. The seven men stand smoking, staring across the grasslands.

When they're done, the one who asked for the cigarette says, 'Hey, mlungu, whitey.'

Blondie raises his eyes, says, 'You talking to me?' The man staring at him. Blondie staring back.

'Mlungu.' The man grinning, squaring himself.

Blondie hears Rictus shout, 'Hey, hey, watch it, watch it.'

Blondie catching the glint in the man's eyes. Sensing movement behind him. Sensing the one behind swinging his spade, the strike smacking Blondie across the back.

He staggers, goes on his knees, takes another blow. He sprawls. Sees through the dust the chained feet circling him. The men slamming down with their spades. He's got his head covered. He's curled against the beating.

He hears the shots, feels the men collapsing over him. Blood everywhere. Gushing. He crawls out, away, lies panting on the hard ground.

The Commander's bending over him, saying, 'You alright? Say something. Christ, man, say something.' The Commander's hands examining him. 'Talk. Say something, Christ, man. We need to hear you.'

Blondie sitting up against the pain. Drenched in blood. Hurting over his back, his shoulders, his arms, his side. Kidneys, he thinks, closing his eyes, like daggers in his kidneys.

The Commander saying, 'It's not your blood, boykie. You're not cut. No open wounds.'

Blondie sees the three prisoners on the ground, Rictus and the Fisherman standing over them, guns in their hands. One of the men not moving, three of them bleeding rivers.

'Still alive,' says Rictus. 'You want us to finish it?'

'Wait,' says the Commander. 'Let him straighten up. His pleasure, don't you think?' – pointing at Blondie.

Fifteen minutes it takes Blondie to stand, leaning on the Commander.

'Take it easy, okay. Go slow.'

One of the prisoners is sitting up, wild-eyed. The other two lie groaning.

Blondie walks towards them, takes the 9-mil Rictus gives him.

He shoots the two groaners first, head shots. Shifts the gun to the one sitting, the one watching him, the one who called him mlungu. Slots him in the face.

16

Fish follows Colins up the path on the lower slopes of the mountain to the old fort, branches whipping in his face. It's a short climb to low stone walls overlooking the bay.

'I've never been up here,' says Fish. 'Not much of a fort.'

'It's from the Muizenberg battle.' Colins crouched, shifting rocks aside.

'I read the info board too,' says Fish, watching the bergie haul out a plastic bag. Colins opens it, holds the bag for Fish to peer in. 'So you weren't lying.'

'Why was I supposed to lie to you, gentleman?' says Colins.

Fish takes out the bigger horn, runs his hand over the end that should be meaty. No flesh, no blood.

'Weird,' he says.

Colins steps away. 'You mustn't touch it because of the poison.'

'Huh?' says Fish, puts the horn down on the wall. 'What're you talking about? What's this poison?'

'Says so in the newspaper, gentleman.' Colins pulls a quartered page of newsprint from his jacket pocket. 'I read it this morning. Strues.'

Fish takes the page, flicks it open, reads the headline: 'Poison rhino horns poached'. Beneath that the story:

> A security guard was killed last night when thieves broke into the Iziko South African Museum in Cape Town and made off with 'priceless' white rhinoceros horns.
>
> The security guard, a foreign national, was fatally stabbed.
>
> The thieves are risking more than arrest and

prosecution: the horns are soaked in deadly arsenic and dichlorodiphenyltrichloroethane (DDT).

'Why didn't you warn me?'

'I did.'

'When it was too late. Shot, bru.' Fish puts down the clipping, scrapes his hands over the stones, wipes them on his jeans. 'This's DDT we're talking about. Sort of stuff kills everything.'

'Unforeseen consequences.' Colins saying it straight-faced.

'Unforeseen consequences.' Fish checks him out. 'You're fulla crap.' He squints down at the newspaper, reading:

> Museum officials have warned that there could be 'unforeseen consequences' if the stolen horns are ground into powder and marketed as an aphrodisiac or cure for fever.

Fish saying it again: 'Unforeseen consequences!' Reads:

> Iziko's director says museums and other heritage institutions all over the world have been targeted by criminals who supply 'lucrative markets with artefacts for various uses'.
>
> While the exact circumstances of the theft were still under police investigation, the director said evidence at the crime scene suggested that the theft had been 'carefully planned and … the exhibit was deliberately targeted'. Nothing else was missing. The priceless horns were displayed without incident for more than one hundred years.

Fish uses the plastic bag as a glove to pick up the horn, drop it back in with its shorter twin. He hands the bag to Colins. Points at the hole in the wall.

'You want me to put it back?'

'I reckon, my friend, what d'you think?'

Colins not saying anything.

'You think I should take it to the cops?'

'You's a private investigator. Probably there's a reward.'

'Probably,' says Fish.

The two men facing the sea, staring where once British gunships swung at anchor, firing cannonballs at the mountainside.

Colins clicks his fingers. 'You's wants to catch them?'

'Could be useful. A bigger reward.'

Colins laughs, settling the bag back in its hiding place, repositioning the rocks. 'Colins, private investigator.'

Fish says, 'Here's the deal.'

'What deal?'

'Listen, okay?'

Colins strokes his beard.

'I'm thinking those men you heard aren't gonna come back in daylight. They're gonna wait for tonight.'

Colins glances into the bush. 'Ja?'

'My problem is I'm helping a friend this afternoon. No ways I can sit here waiting. Understand? But you sit down near the gate to the path, you can watch for them. They're probably gonna be in a car. Rhino horn's not the sort of thing you want to carry through the streets. I'm gonna fetch you a cellphone. If they come, you call me. No hero stuff. You just phone me. Understand.'

Colins shakes his head.

'What? It's not alright?'

'Half,' says Colins.

'Half what?'

'Half the money.'

Fish thinks about it. 'Sixty-forty.'

'Half.'

'Look,' says Fish, 'it's sixty-forty, okay. I'm the person going to be in the firing line. Without me you've got nothing: sixty-forty.'

'You's a hard man, gentleman,' says Colins.

'I gave you toast and coffee. Served you, even.'

Colins waving this aside. 'They see me I'm in trouble.'

'They're not gonna see you. Like you said, you're a bergie. You're lying there at the bottom of the path, drunk, resting, sleeping, it doesn't matter to them. They come and fetch their package, if a bergie sees them it doesn't matter. Like you said, a bergie's not gonna tell the cops. Bergies don't even know about the burglary.'

'I do.'

'Yeah. Well, you got lucky.'

They head down the mountain, Colins grumbling about being short-changed.

Gets up Fish's nose. He rounds on Colins. 'Bro, we haven't been paid anything yet, so give it a break.'

17

Seven gets rid of the white chickee in his room, tells her he's hungry, tells her to make some food, spaghetti and mince.

The chickee says there's no mince.

'Poppie,' says Seven, putting a hundred note into her hand, 'Go to Checkers 'n buy some.'

The chickee pads barefoot out of his room, wearing her school dress, a chunky jersey.

'And, poppie, close the door.'

She does, banging it.

Seven sighs. Shouts, 'Yusses, what's your case?'

The chickee screaming back, 'I'm not your bloody cook, Seven. You want a black bitch, get one.'

Seven about to wind up a reply, lights a cigarette instead. Puts a call through to Mart Velaze.

Mart Velaze coming on short and sharp, 'Yes?'

Seven rolls his eyes. 'Howzit, Mr Mart, remember me, Seven. We's done business before. I got you good-time pilletjies for partying. You remember?'

'What's it, Seven?' says Mart Velaze. 'You don't call me, I call you. If this's a shit story, I don't want to hear it.'

'No, Mr Mart, everything's hanging, everything's fine,' says Seven. 'I got a little thing I'm selling, that's all.'

'I don't need anything.'

'You need this, Mr Mart. This's a big-time score. You need this like God needs a sinner for sure.'

'Of course.'

'You read the papers, Mr Mart? A man like you reads the newspapers.'

'Seven, no funny stuff.'

'Front page, Mr Mart. Onna front page.' Seven listens to the quiet. 'You there, Mr Mart?'

'I'm here. We need to end this call, Seven. Why don't we meet, same place as last time. Seven o'clock. Same time as your name so you won't forget.'

'Alright, Mr Mart. I'm there. Must I bring them?' But Seven's talking to dead air. He keys off his phone, sighs, 'Ja, Mr Mart, always the main man.' Shouts out, 'Jouma, we gotta go fetch the horns.'

18

'Nice car,' says Jacob Mkezi to Daro Attilane. 'You have the service history?'

'Yes,' says Daro. 'No problems there.' Daro in sunglasses thinking, he'd known it would be Jacob Mkezi he'd have made other arrangements.

He and Jacob Mkezi and Cake Mullins standing around this blue Subaru, complete with spoiler, parked on the driveway of Cake Mullins' Constantia home.

Jacob Mkezi's kicked the tyres. Walked round the car, running his hand over the wheel moulding.

'Nice condition. No scratches.'

'No bumps either,' says Daro. 'One owner. Older guy, a university lecturer. He looked after it.' Daro thinking, only way to play this is Mr Nonchalant.

'Strange car for a professor. Professor of what?'

Daro shrugs. 'Organisational management. Something like that, at the business school.'

'What'd he buy instead? A Merc? An old man's car?'

'Another one.'

'Another Subaru? Is that so?'

'Absolutely. Just without the spoiler.'

'Without the foil it'd be nothing. It'd look like any car. A Cortina. Some sort of Honda.'

'That's the thing. The looks don't count. It's under the hood that makes the difference. You put foot in this car, you feel acceleration, the exhilaration.'

Jacob Mkezi looks at him. 'What's that, advertising copy? Marketing spiel?'

'Happens to have some truth to it.'

Jacob Mkezi opens the driver's door, sits. 'What model?'

'2005.'

'Four years old. The prof didn't have it long. Why'd he sell it? What's the downside?'

'No downside. Seller fancied a newer model.'

'This professor?'

'Told me when he sold it that once you drive a Subaru, you can't drive anything else.'

Jacob Mkezi smiles. 'A very with-it professor.'

'Sometimes you get them.'

Jacob Mkezi swings the engine. It fires, the tailpipes guttural, throbbing. 'Sounds hot.'

'You want to take it for a spin?'

'Nah, I don't need to do that.' He points at the Hummer. 'Not my sort of car, you see. This's for my son.'

'He'd like it,' says Cake Mullins. Cake Mullins in slacks and a green shirt, a jersey draped over his shoulders. Macho Cake not letting the winter chill get to him.

Jacob Mkezi switches off the engine, pops the hood. He slides out, takes a look at the serious stuff. 'I don't know about these things,' he says to Daro. 'Engines've never been an interest of mine but when they're clean you know somebody's paying attention.' He nods. 'This is good.' Stands back dusting his hands to let Daro close the lid.

The men stand round the car gazing at it, saying nothing. Daro with his arms folded, alert. Cake Mullins blank-eyed, somewhere else. Jacob Mkezi hand to chin dragging out the minutes. Daro thinking, the games you play to make a sale. Damned if he's going to speak first.

'Alright,' says Jacob Mkezi looking over at Daro, 'I'll take it. How you want to do this? Cheque? EFT?' He takes a Samsung from an inside pocket.

'EFT's perfect,' says Daro. 'You don't want me to register it for you? Deliver it to you? All part of the service.'

'I got people who handle that,' says Jacob Mkezi, thumbing

his way through to his bank site. 'It can stay right here for them to collect. That okay with you, Cake?'

'No problem,' says Cake Mullins. 'A pleasure.'

Jacob Mkezi smiles at Daro. 'Sorted. You got beneficiary details for me?'

Daro tells him. Jacob Mkezi inputs while Daro and Cake Mullins make phone calls. Daro going through to Fish. Fish telling him, 'I'm right outside.'

Cake Mullins finishes his call, says to Daro, 'How'll you get home?'

'Lift's waiting in the street,' says Daro.

Jacob Mkezi laughs. 'Right from the beginning, you reckoned you had a sale?'

'Like to cover all bases,' says Daro, grinning.

Jacob Mkezi holds up his phone screen, 'You're a richer man, Mr Attilane.'

Daro's phone gives an SMS tone: a deposit notification.

'Wonders of technology,' says Cake Mullins. 'Anyone for a drink?'

Daro declines. Jacob Mkezi says, yes, a quick beer would go down. Shakes hands with Daro, he and Cake Mullins watching the car salesman walk up the drive, waiting while the entrance gates swing open.

Jacob Mkezi says, 'You've got CCTV up there, you record visitors coming in and out?'

'What'd you think?' says Cake Mullins.

'It's recorded.'

'For twenty-four hours. You want to see something?'

'Sure, Mr Attilane driving in.'

'No problem,' says Cake Mullins.

They go in through the garage with the Porsche Boxster, the Lexus coupé, to a small office with a bank of five screens.

Jacob Mkezi whistles. 'Serious paranoia, Cake.'

'Caution,' says Cake Mullins. 'It pays off.' He taps at a keyboard, brings up some images from half an hour earlier, shows the Subaru turning in to stop at the intercom post. The front window slides down, Daro Attilane leans out, takes off his sunglasses, speaks into the buzz box. Cake Mullins's voice comes on welcoming him. Daro Attilane looks up at the camera, resets his sunglasses.

'A recording of that would be handy,' says Jacob Mkezi.

Cake Mullins takes beers from a bar fridge, pops the beer caps, hands a bottle to Jacob Mkezi. 'Can be done. Any chance you're going to tell me why?'

'Not really, no,' says Jacob Mkezi. 'Guy looks familiar, that's all. One thing I will tell you, I want that girl, Manuel's girl, working for me.'

'Vicki Kahn?'

'Yeah, Vicki Kahn.'

'She's smart, Manuel says. He's willing to give her up.' Jacob Mkezi sips from the bottle. 'But what's her story, Cake? What's her story with this gambling thing?'

Cake Mullins tells him she's a serious card player. Very good. Compulsive. Addictive personality. Can't stop when she's in the zone. Got herself into a major problem, then quit. Went for counselling, joined Gamblers Anonymous.

'Interesting,' says Jacob Mkezi. 'I need to get her onboard. Organise a game.'

'She won't play.'

'Persuade her, Cake, persuade her.'

19

'There's a bergie,' says Jouma.

'So what, doesn't matter. Bergie's probably drunk. Old toppie like that can't remember the last drink.'

Jouma parting the fence for Seven to climb through. Seven taking the lead up the mountain path.

Their car's in the parking area next to a fisherman's bakkie. The bergie's lying eyes closed against the sun in the grass.

Jouma's antsy. 'You's mad, my bru. Everyone can see us.'

'Which everyone?' Seven stopping halfway up the path, turning on Jouma. 'You see anyone?'

Jouma spits into the bush, his breathing heavy. 'Not now. When we go off.'

'When we go off the horns gonna be in the car boot. Yusses, Jouma, what's your case?' He goes on slower to the stone wall, waits inside the fort for Jouma. Jouma's out of breath, stands bent over with his hands on his knees, gasping. 'You gonna get them?' says Seven. 'Or yous just gonna stand there. We's not got all day.'

When his heart's quietened, Jouma moves aside the rocks to get the plastic bag. 'Someone's been here,' he says.

'Ag nonsense, man,' says Seven. 'They's still there. Someone'd found them they'd be gone.'

'They were the other way,' says Jouma.

'You can remember that?'

'I'm telling yous.'

'No, man, my bru, you's wrong. In the dark you's not gonna know that.'

Jouma stands with the horns wrapped in the plastic bag. 'What about the poison?'

'Ja, what? All you gotta do is wash your hands. No piepiejolling in the car.' Seven making the jerk-off gesture with his fist, laughing loudly. 'Come'n, we's gotta go, the man is waiting.'

He turns, there's the bergie from the car park taking pictures of them on a cellphone. Seven blinks, can't believe this. This old bergie with the grey beard holding up a cellphone, the cellphone going bzzzt, click. Twice. He raises a hand in front of his face. Springs towards the bergie.

'No, my bru, what you doing? What you doing? No, my bru. You's in the poo, gimme that.'

The bergie's not answering, the bergie's making off down the path, Seven after him. The bergie going it for his age. Not the boozed-up old wreck he looks, ducking, twisting, jumping down the pathway.

But Seven's younger, Seven's stronger, Seven has him in ten paces, grabs him by the jacket, pulls him down. Shouting at him, 'Gimme the phone.' Trying to wrench it from the old man's grasp. Leaning over, smacking blows into the man's spongy face. The bergie kicks upwards, catches Seven in the balls. It's not a striker's kick, more a soft shoe shuffle, still makes Seven suck in air, grimace. The bergie scuttles backwards into the bush, getting onto hands and knees to crawl beneath the branches.

Seven dives after him, fastens hold of his ankle, yanks, the bergie falling on his face.

The bergie spitting out sand, howling, screaming for help.

Seven panting, coughing. 'You's dead, my bru. Stone dead, morsdood.' He drags him back, straddles him, pinning the man's arms beneath his knees. 'Yous thinks you's a clever, hey? Yous can take pictures with a cellphone. You's a stupid, a moegoe, my bru.' He reaches round for the knife in his back pocket, flicks out the long blade, lays it against the bergie's cheek. 'Let it go there inna sand.' The bergie squirms. Seven pushes in the blade's tip through the cheek skin, pulls it out. 'Fok, bru, the phone.'

The bergie twists, throwing off Seven. He's on his feet, crashing down the path. Seven's up, after him. Stabs the bergie in the back, the bergie grunting, pitching forward with the thrust. Seven pulling out the knife, the blade smeared. The bergie's stumbled off the path, staggers a few paces, falls. The cellphone's knocked from his hand. Seven stands over him, the bergie gazing up at him, blood flowing from his cheek.

'Yusses, bru, what yous doing?'

Seven seeing the fear in the man's eyes. Same fear he saw in prison when a man was to die. Fear like a small dog, tjanking yip, yip.

'You's a stupid, my bru. Yous should of stayed inna blue train.'

Seven with the knife in his fist, plunging it down, once, again, again, into the man's neck, the blood spray arcing about.

When the man's body stops twitching, Seven finds the cell-phone, smashes it against a boulder. He glances up at Jouma, clutching the plastic bag, watching. 'What yous looking at, hey?'

'The bergie's killed.'

'Yous think there was another way?'

20

Daro Attilane's quiet in the car driving back to the showroom. Fish's on at him about cracking some frosties to celebrate, isn't every day he makes a sale, cash on the nose just like that.

Doesn't get much joy and laughter from Daro. All Daro says is, 'About time I had a sale.'

Fish rolls his eyes, thinks what's eating him?

The rest of the route they drive in silence. Ten minutes later Fish pulls up at the showroom. Switches off, looks across at Daro. 'Hey, Daro, what's the problem?'

'Nah, nothing,' says Daro. 'Young Steffie's on my mind, that's all.'

Fish considers this. The two men still in the car, facing the two vehicles on the showroom floor: an Audi A4, a Benz Kompressor.

'And?'

'And this gangster Seven in the ghetto. He's giving the police forum a hard time. I told you. Everybody knows he's supplying the kids, there're girls, teenage girls, going in and out of his place all hours, no troubles in the world.' He sighs. 'The cops are supposed to raid him this weekend. Fat lot of good it'll do.' Daro opens his door, gets out.

'You gonna ask me in for that beer?' says Fish.

'Next time,' says Daro. 'Thanks for the lift.'

Daro Attilane watches Fish pull off. He takes a beer from the bar fridge, sits down at his desk. There're two pictures on it in silver frames. One of Steffie. The other of his wife, Georgina. He arranges them both in front of him on his blotter. Takes a swig of beer, his eyes on the two women in his life. He's looking at them but who's on his mind is the man in the crocodile shoes: Jacob Mkezi.

THE ICING UNIT, OCTOBER 1984

The Commander, Rictus Grin, the Fisherman, Blondie. An MK soldier. A terrorist to the four men, caught in a Johannesburg township with a cache of AKs, grenades, Taurus 9-mils, enough ammunition to cause widespread grief. What they've been told to find out is where's the rest of the terr's unit?

He's told them where he was trained, where he crossed the border, who he reports to. He's talked about his parents, his brothers, his years growing up in Soweto. They've got him naked, sitting on a hard-backed chair in an outbuilding. Oil stains on the concrete floor. Some of the windows broken. Pile of old tyres in a corner. Bird shit streaking the walls.

By the third day he has cracked ribs, a broken humerus which the Commander has set in a makeshift splint. His left eye is swollen shut. His lips are split. There's a gash on his forehead. The Fisherman's extracted three teeth: two bottom right (molars), one top left (a lateral incisor). Across his back are tiny wounds where Rictus has inserted the point of his stiletto a few millimetres. He is confused because he hasn't slept. He's shivering with cold.

The Commander, Rictus and the Fisherman have been playing good cop, bad cop. The Fisherman and Rictus are the bad cops. The Commander does the nice stuff. Gives the terr Cokes, cigarettes, talks to him about his family. Tells him about his own daughter. Feeds him because the terr's wrists are in handcuffs, the handcuffs chained to a ring in the floor. During his shift the Commander cleans the wounds the Fisherman and Rictus caused.

Blondie's the silent observer. Doesn't wince at the man's pain, doesn't smile at the banter. Stands there watching, thinking, why can't the munt spit it out? Save everyone a helluva lot of strife. Blondie's uneasy on the farm. After the first time. To pass the hours he sits in the farmhouse reading magazines. Stacks and stacks of mags from the 1960s when the house was lived in: *Personality, Huisgenoot, Farmer's Weekly, Scope.*

Despite his unease Blondie walks in the veld. Climbs up to the vulture colony on the koppie. Can sit there for hours watching the birds riding the thermals, great wings brushing their shadows over him. On the krantz is a spot called a 'vulture restaurant', where local farmers dump carcases, offal, stillborns. The restaurant a litter of bones. Without the carrion, Blondie's heard, there'd be no colony. Would be a pity to lose the birds.

Morning of the fourth day, the terr dies. Without blabbing on his unit. The Fisherman and Rictus drinking coffee at the open door, taking in the view at sunrise, hear him sigh. They glance at one another.

The Fisherman says, 'Ag, nee, dammit, man.'

'Bugger,' says Rictus.

They turn round. The terr's head's slumped forward, he's shat himself.

The Commander isn't pleased. 'Arseholes,' he tells them. 'What'd I tell you: keep him alive. At any cost.' He does the finger search for the terr's pulse. 'Fuck.' The three men standing looking at the naked corpse when Blondie comes in.

'He's dead?'

'What's it look like, hey? Bloody what's it look like?' says the Commander. 'Bloody arseholes.' Pointing at the Fisherman and Rictus. 'You don't have to tell the brass. You don't have to stand there, tell them, sorry, General, the terrorist pegged. Before he could say anything.' The Commander pacing about the room, hands flying. 'We're supposed to be good. Get the job done, get the goods. That's what we've done, that's what they expect. We get results.' The Commander grabbing at Rictus's jacket. 'This one was important. He was important. We could've turned him. Made him an askari. Better, sent him out there, back to his unit. But no. No, you know better. Push him over the edge. Arseholes.'

He heads to the door. Swings round. 'Get rid of him. Okay, just get rid of him.'

'Where? You want us to bury him? Burn him?'

'Feed him to the bloody vultures,' says the Commander.

Which is what Blondie's delegated to do.

'Why me?' he says. 'I'm outta here.'

'Just do it,' says the Commander. Wags a hooked finger at the other two. 'Get the body into the bakkie.'

Rictus grumbles. Toys with his rings.

The Commander comes back. 'What's that? What's that? Who caused this scene? Tell me. Huh? Huh? Who caused this scene? Crap, man! Just get it out of here. Hose the bloody place.' He throws a bunch of keys at Blondie. 'When you get back, lock up the house, leave the keys under the pot.'

Blondie drives up the track onto the krantz. The vultures are still on the cliff face on their nests, waiting for the thermals. At the restaurant it's quiet. Almost silent. No insects. No birdsong. He looks about: scattered bones, white, clean. No carcases. Doesn't seem the vultures have been fed in a while.

Blondie hauls the body off the bakkie, lowers it gently to the ground. Drags it among the bones. For a moment he stands, looking down at the terr. The man groans, a flicker at his good eyelid.

Blondie steps back, thinks, shit. Crouches. Says, 'Hey, man. Can you hear me?' He picks up the guy's wrist, feels for a pulse. Maybe. Maybe not. He lets it flop back. Stands, with his shoe nudges the terr in the ribs. 'Hey, hey.' No response.

Blondie walks back to the bakkie. Fires the engine, remembers being told vultures could devour a sheep carcass in a couple of days. Make it disappear.

21

Fish decides on the Muizenberg station parking: short walk to where Colins is playing stake-out, shorter walk to the bottle store. The car guard's at his window before he's switched off.

'I like this car.' A beam of Congo teeth. 'Red is very strong.'

Fish taps the accelerator, gives the engine a roar.

The car guard keeps up the smile. 'I like the sound.'

'It's cool, yeah,' says Fish, switching off, getting out.

The car guard running his hand over the bodywork. 'I have not seen one like this.'

'Perana V6.'

'Perana? I don't know, Perana.'

'You know cars?'

'In Kinshasa my car was a Mustang. I made it from photographs.'

'You built a Mustang? In the Congo.'

'It looked like it.'

'My friend,' says Fish, 'you're in the wrong job. You know Basil Green Motors?'

'They can give me a job?'

'They made this car. 1969.'

'They can give me a job?'

'They're in Johannesburg.'

The car guard shrugs. Says something in French. 'I will go there.'

'Excellent,' says Fish, moving off.

He gets to the gate up to the fort, no Colins. Phones Colins. His call goes to voicemail. He's standing there wondering should he risk going up? Should he come back? His phone rings: his mother.

'Bartolomeu, what've you got to tell me?'

'About what?' says Fish, playing forgetful.

'Prospect Deep. You remember. The research you're doing for me.'

'Jesus, Ma. I can't just drop everything.' Not wanting to go there yet without more info.

'You went surfing this morning.'

Fish thinking, she's trying her luck.

'Don't even think of lying to me. You did, didn't you?'

Fish can lie. He's a pretty good liar. Has to be, comes with the territory. Actually, what got him started on lying was his mother. Every time he lied to her as a kid she bought it. He reckons there's something in his voice that convinces her. Convinces most people. This time, though, he sees no point in lying.

'I did. It's my exercise. Like you go to the gym.' Estelle a water aerobics addict. Most mornings, four times a week, Saturday too, she's there at seven thirty for the early-bird class.

'That's different. It's formal and organised. Only children surf, Bartolomeu. You've got to grow up.'

Fish has been through this many times. When he turned twenty-one she said, 'You're of age now. No more surfing. Time to be an adult. It's what your father would've wanted.' That's when she came out with the gun. The heirloom: Astra Model 400 with wooden grips chambered for both 9mm largo and 9mm parabellum cartridges. Very nice. His father had shown it to him, let him hold it, given him the provenance: Grandfather Pescado had acquired it fighting for the internationals during the Spanish Civil War. When things went pear-shaped Avô scurried back to Portugal, shipped out for Luanda, Angola, hopped boats, ended up in Cape Town.

When his mother gave him the gun, a sort of coming-of-age present, Fish believed it hadn't been fired in decades. First thing he did was take to the range at the Glencairn quarry. The pistol fired as if the targets were Spanish fascists. Nice heft. Not much jump when you were used to it.

Fish often wondered, if his father hadn't gone terminal with the coronary, would Estelle have hassled him about his lifestyle? He thought not.

But here she was again telling him grown men don't surf, and … And. And only drunks, drug addicts and emotional retards end up playing Sherlock Holmes.

'You just hired me to do some investigating for you?' he says.

'Research, Bartolomeu. There's a world of difference. No one dies when you're doing research. Brings me back to my question: when?'

'When what?'

'When're you going to let me know about the gold mine? My clients are Chinese. They eat with chopsticks. They eat fast. They do everything fast. Please, Barto, I need the info. Tomorrow. Sunday latest.

'Monday,' says Fish.

'First thing.'

'Cool.'

'And don't say that, Bartolomeu. You're too old for that word.'

As always she was gone without a goodbye.

Fish pockets his phone, finds he's walked all the way back to his car. The car guard nodding at him.

Fish says, 'You see a bergie earlier with a large plastic bag?'

'Bergies all carry large plastic bags,' says the car guard.

'Older man. Had on a grey coat.'

'Bergies all have grey coats,' says the car guard.

'Okay,' says Fish, 'any bergie of that description come past you since this morning?'

The car guard shakes his head. 'No, sir, monsieur.'

'You'd notice?'

'Of course.'

Fish nods. Hoping Colins has taken a position up there under the bushes out of sight. Turned off his cellphone against unwanted calls. Clever thinking. Colins saw money. Desired it.

Fish's about to get into his car, he remembers he needs booze. At the bottle store runs two bottles of Villiera bubbly, a six-pack of milk stouts, one 750 ml bottle of Smirnoff vodka and a six-pack of tonics through his MasterCard.

'Straight or budget?' asks the teller.

'Budget,' says Fish. No reason why the bank shouldn't pick up the tab. What his father had always said: 'Pay the latest you can, son, you might drop dead in between.' Fish reckoned in his line of work this was sound advice.

22

Jacob Mkezi next to Mellanie in the back of his Hummer says to Mart Velaze driving, 'There's a car I bought standing over at Cake Mullins' place. A Subaru. Gangster-looking job but someone has to drive them. It's for the boy. I'm hoping you could arrange for him to collect it tomorrow. Maybe take him over there yourself, I'd appreciate it.'

'No problem,' says Mart Velaze, eyes flicking to the rear-view mirror, making contact with the dark shades.

'Get someone to sort out the licensing too next week?'

Mart Velaze's shaved head nodding in the front.

Mellanie turns to Jacob Mkezi. 'D'you know where it is, this lodge, where we're staying? Will there be coverage?'

Jacob Mkezi laughs. 'Hey, sugar, this's a holiday. Relax.'

'Some of us need contact, Jacob sweetie.'

'I don't know,' says Jacob Mkezi. 'No idea. Probably not. It's in the bush.'

'Most of Africa's in the bush but there's cellphone coverage.'

'Less than you think.'

Mellanie says into her phone, 'Take that as a no. I'll be in touch from the lodge phone when we get there. They must have a landline.' She disconnects. 'I don't even know why I'm doing this.'

'For me.'

'Jacob, do you know, have you even the slightest idea, of the sort of issues I'm dealing with?'

He smiles at her. She's back at her BlackBerry keying in numbers.

Mart Velaze says, 'Does he know about the car? Lord, I mean?'

'Uh uh. It's a surprise, for his birthday.'

'When's that?'

'Tomorrow.'

Jacob Mkezi stares at the traffic. Bumper to bumper but it's moving: Cape Town tailbacks. He looks at his watch, sits forward. They should've been at the airport already. 'Are we going to make this?'

'I've spoken to them at the plane. It's okay, they can wait.'

Jacob Mkezi relaxes. 'Two other things, Mart. Next week, Monday, Tuesday, early next week, go and see a guy, Daro Attilane, who runs this car dealership, Exclusive Motors. I got the Subaru from him. He's a nice guy, very professional. I want you to take a look at him, that's all, for a confirmation. See if you match him up to a photograph I've got. And then phone Cake Mullins, say I'm out of cellphone range, ask him to set up a card game with Vicki Kahn.'

'Sure,' says Mart Velaze. 'I can do that.'

Three hours later in the dark the Beechjet's approaching the landing strip that once upon a time saw Mirages, Hawker Hunters, Hercules cargo planes, Daks touching down on it. Once upon a time in a secret war. Mellanie leans across, shakes Jacob Mkezi awake.

He opens hooded eyes, yawns.

'We're here. Buckle up.' She snaps closed her laptop, slips it into a bag at her feet.

Tol Visagie crouches in the aisle between them. 'There's an hour's drive still when we're down. In a Land Rover, it'll be comfortable.'

Mellanie sighs. 'It'll be pitch black.'

'Ja, sorry,' says Tol Visagie. 'Can't be helped, hey?'

'As long as there's whisky,' says Jacob Mkezi.

'There'll be that when we get there.' Tol Visagie grins, touches Jacob Mkezi lightly on the knee. 'The best.'

Half an hour later they're driving through the night in silence. Some crackle on the radio receiver, some mumble between Tol Visagie and the driver that's fed back to Jacob Mkezi and Mellanie as wildlife hype. Two hyenas spotted on the road when the driver came through earlier. Also a big herd of elephants, twenty, thirty with young in the river reeds. Lions killed a giraffe two nights ago outside the lodge.

'Exciting,' says Mellanie.

Jacob Mkezi smiles at her sarcasm, says nothing.

Tol Visagie glances at her but she's invisible in the dark, her head back against the rest, her gaze into the night.

Occasionally there are spots of firelight in the distance, villages, now and again the red glare of eyes caught in the headlights.

'Impala,' says Tol Visagie. 'There're hundreds of them.'

'Wouldn't have guessed,' says Mellanie. Only Jacob Mkezi hears her, stretches out a hand to squeeze her knee.

'Don't,' she says, prizing loose his fingers.

'Sisi,' says Jacob Mkezi, 'relax.'

The lodge is luxurious. Stone, wood, thatch, leather, polished slate floors. Skulls of tuskers flanking the entrance doors. The lighting from paraffin and gas lamps. Attendant reception staff in khaki, welcoming them with schooners of sherry.

'Your room's a stand-alone unit, river-facing,' says Tol Visagie. 'You want to freshen up first?'

'I do,' says Mellanie, as a man picks up her luggage, says to please follow him. Mellanie casting a glance at Jacob Mkezi. 'You coming?'

Jacob Mkezi drains off the sherry. 'No. I want a whisky.'

'You could at least wash your hands, Jacob.' Mellanie not waiting for a response.

Jacob Mkezi laughs at the surprise on Tol Visagie's face. 'Women. That woman, particularly. You have to love them.'

'Ja, man, it's why I've never married,' says Tol Visagie showing him towards a bar counter on a wide stoep, only others at the bar a couple murmuring to one another at the far end. 'That whisky?' He signals the barman.

'Why not?' Jacob Mkezi looking round.

'Johnny Walker black?'

'Sounds good?'

Tol Visagie orders two whiskies.

'Where are all the guests?'

'This time of the evening, in the lapa eating.' Tol Visagie arcing his arm to indicate the other side of the building. 'Meals are served in a reed enclosure, round a fire. I like it. A high dark sky with stars and a fire. Very African.'

They clink glasses, walk to the edge of the stoep.

'Out there,' says Tol Visagie, 'is a river bed. When the river's flowing it reaches the Kunene. Right now it's pooled. Wait till you see it tomorrow.' Tol Visagie going on about the wonders of the place, the abundance of birdlife.

When he's finished Jacob Mkezi says, 'Why're we here, Tol?'

Tol Visagie sips his drink, gazes off into the night. 'Let's leave it until tomorrow, rather, if you don't mind? I'd rather not talk about it now. I just want to take you there and show you something, then we can talk.'

'Very mysterious. I don't like very mysterious.'

'Only seems so but it's not. In a way it's quite ordinary. But …' He doesn't finish.

'But?'

'Nothing. Tomorrow you'll see.'

'This's not how I do things.'

'You're here, Mr Mkezi. You came without knowing anything. A couple more hours isn't going to matter. Really.'

'I hope not.'

They turn back to the bar. The couple has gone, there's a man lounging against the bar counter, watching them.

'Former Commissioner Jacob Mkezi,' the man says. 'When you see Mr Jacob Mkezi then you must watch out. Then you know something is going on.'

Jacob Mkezi squints at the man. 'Do I know you? Have we met?'

'A long time ago. Lusaka, in the old days. I was a junior then. My name is Vusi Bopape.' Vusi Bopape drinking from his bottle of beer, not straightening up, lounging there without of-fering a handshake. 'I heard your news today, the news about your court case. About your associate's death.'

Jacob Mkezi keeping up the hard stare. 'Nice to meet you again, Vusi. You having a holiday here?'

'Honeymoon,' says Vusi Bopape, tapping the bottle lip against his teeth. 'We arrived earlier.'

'Congratulations.'

'My wife's gone to bed.' Vusi Bopape draining off the last of his beer. 'Time for me to follow. Perhaps we can have a drink tomorrow, Mr Mkezi. To remember old times.'

As he leaves Jacob Mkezi says, 'Why'd you say that, Vusi, about me? That something is going on?'

Vusi Bopape grins. 'You're a mover and shaker. Everybody knows that. I was just making a joke.'

Jacob Mkezi and Tol Visagie watch the man saunter off, handing his empty beer bottle to a waiter.

'It seems like Bopape wasn't surprised to see me,' says Jacob Mkezi.

23

'You're the ones did it?' Mart Velaze laughs. 'I heard about it on the radio. Cape Talk. Really! You guys!'

'Ja, Mr Mart,' says Seven, grinning. 'It's good, hey?' Jouma beside him showing the gap in his teeth, his head bobbing like a toy dog.

Mart Velaze looks at the horns lying on the table, pulls on a pair of rubber gloves.

'You don't need gloves,' says Seven. 'They's clean.'

'They're poisoned, I read about it. You better wash your hands.' Mart Velaze examines where the horns were sawn off. 'Hell, man, this's a rough cut. You've damaged them.'

'No, they's fine.'

'Why?' Mart Velaze glances at the gangster. 'Why'd you do this?'

'Because there's money in horns.'

Mart Velaze shakes his head. 'These were in a museum, Seven. You know what museums are for? Cultural heritage. Keeping our cultural heritage safe.'

'No problem,' says Seven, gives Mart Velaze his theory about an artificial horn.

'Ah, that's crap.'

'No, it's true's. They can do that.'

'Not the point,' says Mart Velaze.

Seven shuts his mouth, stares at his feet. 'They's worth a hunnerd thousand.'

'You killed a guard.'

'Ja, we had to. He tuned us grief. But he's a Mozambique, a alien.'

'Doesn't matter.'

'Happens in the townships all the time. 'N we didn't burn him.'

'He was dead quickly, Mr Mart,' says Jouma.

Mart Velaze stands back, crosses his arms. 'Why'd you bring them to me? What'm I supposed to do with them?'

'You can help us. You said you could help us with things.'

Mart Velaze has met them at a warehouse. Nothing in the building except the table, a broken motorbike, some tins of paint. Place belonged to a yacht builder, put together his dream boat here, sailed it out of Cape Town harbour with a keel of solid gold. Never looked back. Nobody knew, except Jacob Mkezi. And by association Mart Velaze. Jacob Mkezi collecting a commission in the Caymans.

Mart took over the warehouse for occasions like these. Quiet industrial park off a motorway. Excellent knock-and-drop location.

He looks at the horns, looks at the two men. Seven and Jouma squirming.

'You've given me a big headache,' he says.

'Ag no, Mr Mart,' says Seven. 'S not like that.'

'It is like that, my brother. Just like that. A big headache.'

'We can take them away ...' Seven begins, Mart Velaze holding up his hand, 'Stop, stop, stop. I'll sort it, you hear me?'

The two men nod.

'You leave them with me, I'll sort it. But I don't want any flak. No phone calls, no hassle, not a peep.'

'Okay, Mr Mart. No problems, Mr Mart.' Seven touches Mart Velaze on the sleeve. 'Hows about an advance?'

Mart Velaze puts the horns back into the plastic bag. 'I'm not a bank.'

'Just something. Ten thousand.'

'You think I've got that, here?'

'Five thousand.'

Mart Velaze digs in his pocket, takes out a clip of notes, peels off five. 'This'll have to cover it.'

'That's min, such a little,' says Seven. 'We's leaving you a hunnerd thousand, you give us five hundred.'

Mart Velaze folds the rest of the notes, fastens the clip. 'Take it or leave it.'

'Highway robbery.'

'You want it or not?'

Jouma nudges Seven. 'No, we take it,' says Seven. 'What can we do?'

'You can wait,' says Mart Velaze. 'Patience is a virtue, né?'

He ushers the men out of the warehouse, locks it. 'Maybe I've got a job for you next week. Twenty thousand rand. You could be rich manne soon. Somebody from your hood. Maybe somebody called Daro. You know him?'

'On the forum?'

'That could be him. Sells cars. I'll be in touch.'

Seven and Jouma don't crack a smile, get into their car. Mart Velaze watches them pull off. Wonders what he should do? Slip the horns back to the museum. Bring Jacob Mkezi in on the deal? He pulls off the gloves, drops them in a bin.

24

Fish's done a number, cleared all the debris off the table: CDs, herb sticks and pips in the pearly-abalone ashtray, speeding fines, unopened accounts, books, laptop, car keys. Swept the floor, washed up.

More: whisked out two candles from the bottom of a drawer, snapped each one in half. Melted wax onto saucers, plugged the candle stumps into the wax. Laid the table for two, with the Boardmans cutlery and crockery he bought when Vicki came on the scene. Placemats too. Wine glasses. Put a candle dead centre of the table. Puts the others on the window ledge, a cupboard, the sink.

Selects some CDs. Jim Neversink, his new discovery, Laurie Levine, his all time standby, Dixie Chicks. Something for Vicki: Alison Krauss and Robert Plant, *Raising Sand*.

Vicki comes in on a waft of perfume that gets Fish deep-breathing. It's the smell of her he reckons he could track down in a crowd. Raises a heat on his palms. Stirs other places too. He's rooted, stands there gazing in wonder.

She's toting the Giovanni takeaways, white wine, her laptop in a sling bag over her shoulder, a briefcase.

'It's fine, Fish,' she says, 'I can manage' – bending to slide the food and booze onto the table, noticing the candles. She's well impressed. 'What's this? Candles. Babes. I like it.'

Fish snaps a grin, takes the wine from her.

'I'll have a glass of that,' she says, 'in the bath.'

'Hey! This's a sleepover?' Fish can't believe his luck.

'I thought so. It's the weekend.'

'May as well join you,' he says, 'in the bath.'

Vicki holds up a hand. 'Uh uh, dude. My time. A candle and

wine's what I want. You're dessert. Meanwhile, keep the food warm in the oven.'

'How about this?' says Fish, taking the champers from the fridge.

'You bought that?'

Fish grins.

'It's methode cap classique.'

'Says so.'

'That's expensive.'

Fish shrugs. 'What're credit cards for?' He breaks the foil, loosens the wire cap.

Vicki staring at him, amused, lips open, her eyes dancing. 'We're celebrating something?'

'Yeah,' says Fish. 'Us.'

Vicki laughs. Her gentle laugh that shows the pinkness of her tongue. 'My ever-romantic Fish.'

'That's me.' He puts his thumb to the cork. 'You gonna say no?'

'Bring it to me, in a flute. I'll call.'

When she does she's lying there covered in bubbles, steam rising. A brown knee raised. Her hair up, her shoulders wet, shiny. She reads his mind. 'You're not coming in.' Clicks her fingers. 'I'll have that.' Pointing at the glass in his hand. As she reaches up, her left breast lifting from the foam, the nipple dark as a roasted hazelnut.

Fish swallows. He could stand there staring at it all night.

'The bubbly.'

He hands her the glass.

'Hey,' she says, 'eye contact would be good.'

He looks at her. Thinks, bugger dessert.

'Babes.' Drinks. 'Cheers.' The wine glistening on her lips. 'Now let me have some me-time.'

Fish sits it out with glass of MCC and Laurie on the snazzy Sony sound system, thoughts of being dessert uppermost in his mind, thinking how he'd start with her boobs, work his way down.

Roll under her, let her ride the pace. She liked that. Probably my favourite position, Fish decided: women on top. You could just lie back, lust on their boobs, watch their faces go all mushy.

Vicki slops into the kitchen, hair's still up, wearing one of Fish's jerseys, a pair of his tracksuit pants. He knows there'll be nothing on underneath. He can see her nipples pushing at the cable knit. What he wants is to run his hands into the elastic top of the pants, feel her bum. Has a sip of wine to stop himself.

Vicki saying, 'Let's eat. Get the food, babes. I'm starving.'

They eat. Vicki chatting through the mouthfuls. What about this meeting Jacob Mkezi? The next day he walks? Polite man, had said something about knowing her aunt. Then this hijack killing of the state witness. Clifford completely schtum on that score. What a coincidence! Like, it was really a hijacking! Who d'they think they were kidding? Just that Jacob Mkezi didn't seem that sort of man. Probably it was all happening while they were having drinks at the Cullinan. And then this guy from her past, Cake Mullins, on her case about a poker game. No matter how much she tells him she's off the cards, Cake's nagging about a game. About some person really wanted to play her.

Fish listening to her, coming in on the mention of Cake Mullins. 'The second time his name's come up today. I did a pick-up for Daro at this Cake Mullins' place.'

'In Constantia somewhere?'

'Very nice house.'

'That's Cake.'

Fish coming back to the cards story. 'You won't? You'll stay out of that?'

'Of course. I'm in the programme, Fish, you know.' Vicki peeling a prawn, finishing the bubbly. She pops the prawn, chews. 'Tempted though.' Watches Fish looking at her unsure if she's having him on.

She leans over the table, holds his hand. 'Only joking, babes. No need to get all narrow-eyed.' Lets go of Fish's hand to select another prawn. 'How's your life?'

'Interesting,' says Fish. Tells her about bergie Colins and the rhino horns and the arrangement they've got.

'Godfathers, Fish! You left them there? You didn't let the police know?' Vicki sitting back, frowning.

'No. Can't trust them.' Fish opens the wine Vicki brought, fills their glasses. 'They could screw up something like this. Or they lose the horn. You know what I mean, someone walks off with them.' He takes down a swallow. 'It happens all the time these days.'

'Like it didn't happen before.'

Fish shrugs. 'I suppose.'

'Lots of times. How'd your dead friend end up selling dope otherwise?'

'Perk of the job.'

'Exactly. So what happens if bergie Colins walks off with them?'

'He's not going to. He could've already.'

'Or the bad guys kill him. They killed a guard in the museum.'

'There're not going to. He's a bergie. They won't even see him.'

'This's true.' Vicki reaches across, takes his hand.

Fish looks at Vicki looking at him. There's that spark in her eyes. A twitch to her lips. Does that thing with her tongue against her teeth. Touches his earring. Says, 'Come, I've got another idea.'

Fish grins. 'Cool.'

THE ICING UNIT, DECEMBER 1985

They're in a convoy of two cars, a Merc and a Cressida: the Commander and Blondie in the Merc, the Fisherman and Rictus Grin in the Cressida. They crossed the border at sunset into Swaziland, hit Mbabane in the dark. Now they're in a suburb: close to the midnight hour, driving slowly, checking out the houses. What they can see of the houses through the gloom and shrubbery.

Blondie says to the Commander, 'You know this street?'

Quiet street. Treed. No cars parked against the kerb. Lights on in some of the houses, most of them in darkness.

'I do,' says the Commander. 'Been here once before. On a recce, couple of months back.' He stops. The Cressida coming up close behind them. It's hot, still. A thunderstorm earlier's left the ground steaming in the headlights. 'That's it.' The Commander pointing into the darkness.

'Which one?'

'Two houses down. The one with the fancy gate posts.'

'The tall white jobs?'

'Those.'

Blondie peers about. 'Big houses.'

'They need it, all the terrs they got going through.' He looks at Blondie. 'You ready?'

Blondie holds up his Uzi.

'They're gonna have AKs.'

'Let's go.'

'Hang on. I'm gonna get closer,' says the Commander. Switches off the headlights, glides the Merc towards the gates, the Cressida pressed in behind them. Stops. 'Okay?'

'What about guards?'

'Shouldn't be any.'

'Shouldn't?'

'Mostly they don't bother.'

'Mostly?'

'Mostly.' The Commander smiles. 'Nothing to worry about. If they're not asleep, they'll be pissed.'

'Let's cook.'

The men get out, leave the car running. The Fisherman and Rictus joining them.

Dogs bark. The men wait until the barking stops. Till the only sound is the soft idle of the cars.

The smell is of damp vegetation, frangipani, wet earth. Petrol fumes.

They pull on balaclavas, leather gloves. All of them with Uzis. Pistols stuck in their belts. Rictus's got a stiletto sheathed up his arm.

The Commander nods. 'No names, no talking.'

He waits until they've all signalled agreement.

They start up the driveway. The house is in darkness, only light on is over the front door. In the driveway's a small bakkie, skedonk of a vehicle, bashed and dented.

Blondie and the Fisherman sidle round the back, wary of dogs, Blondie ahead, his torch beam sweeping the garden. Not so much a garden as an orchard of fruit trees. Nothing moves. His shoes scrape on the concrete path. He tries the handle on the back door. It's unlocked. They're into a scullery, sinks line the wall, stacked with plates, pots, spoons, a heap of potato peelings on a board. A bin of booze bottles.

'Been a party.' The Fisherman whispering, flashing his torch over the debris. 'Could of cleaned up first.'

Blondie ignores him, moves into the kitchen. Pots on the stove, more dirty plates, glasses, mugs, a nightmare mess. Heavy smell of stewed meat. There's a door to his right, partly open. He pushes it, peers into an empty passageway. Listens. Imagines he can hear the sound of people asleep: the house breathing.

Then a voice. A voice saying, 'Who're you?' A voice shouting. Other voices.

Somewhere else in the house.

And the burp of Uzis. Lights coming on at the end of the passageway. The crack of another gun. Men screaming.

Blondie sees figures appearing in the passage. He pulls off a spray: a short burst, eight, ten rounds, the shells pinging against the walls. The figures go down. Cordite catches in his throat.

The Fisherman's charging past him, firing single shots. At the end of the passage Blondie takes the bedroom to the right. It's in darkness. He can make out beds, bodies. Someone sitting up. A person standing at the window. Opening the window, trying to get out. He shoots. The figure at the window collapses. Puts shots into the beds. Hears the cries. Fires again.

The Fisherman's shouting at him. 'Let's split, let's split.'

The two of them crash out of the passageway into the lounge. Blondie sees movement in the corner: a man with an AK, coming up behind a chair. The man covered in blood.

He swivels the Uzi, one-hand firing, watches the man picked up, slide down the wall. The Fisherman laughing.

Ahead of them making for the gates the Commander holding Rictus, Rictus limping, bleeding from the leg.

In the car Rictus's moaning, the Commander telling him it's a flesh wound, in the muscle, no blood vessel damage. Cutting away the trouser leg, staunching the bleeding with wads from a first aid kit.

Telling Blondie go first right, second left to the main road. Blondie squealing the tyres on the corners.

The Commander says, 'Slow down, okay. Take it easy. We don't need swagger from the traffic cops.'

On the dark road other side of the border post, Blondie driving the Benz, his eyes focused on the road, says to the Commander, 'You didn't say there'd be children, women, in the house.'

'Weren't supposed to be.'

'Weren't supposed to be?'

'Simple as that, weren't supposed to be.'

The Commander alongside him in the passenger seat, Rictus lying propped up at the back. The Fisherman behind them in the Cressida.

'There were.'

'I didn't know that. Okay, I didn't know that.' The Commander lighting a cigarette. 'I was told it's terrs. Some going out for training, some coming back to cause trouble. That's what I was told.'

'Kak intel.'

'We did the job.'

'Women and children.'

'We did the job, okay. Leave it. There were terrs in the lounge. We got them.'

'They got me.' Rictus from the back. 'Weren't supposed to be sleeping in the lounge.'

The Commander swivelling in the seat. 'Enough. We do these jobs, nobody knows what's gonna happen on the day. On the day everything can be different.'

Rictus snorts. 'Fokken was. Big Bantu waiting for us with a gun.'

'There's gonna be hell about his,' says Blondie. 'Those kids. All over the newspapers.'

'So what. Kids today, terrs tomorrow.'

'All over the newspapers.'

'What, all over the newspapers? Nothing about you. Nothing about me.'

'Kids. Kids.'

'Was a raid. A strike on a known centre. Terr units from that centre, come here, kill, bomb Wimpy bars, bomb bus stops, cause major kak. We're fighting a war, boykie. In case you forgot.'

The Commander crushes out the butt.

'Their problem, they let women and kids sleep there. They know the risks. Their problem. You wanna blame someone. You blame them. Cowards, hiding behind the women. Using kids as shields. What's that tell you? Dogs. All out no one's innocent. We're fighting dogs.'

25

Tol Visagie, fresh-faced, pressed khaki shorts, Save the Rhino T-shirt, trail sandals, comes striding across the slate towards Jacob Mkezi and Mellanie eating breakfast on the lodge's stoep. Mellanie into the muesli and yoghurt; Jacob Mkezi facing a full English.

It's eight o'clock, the stoep's empty, the safari guests still out on the morning bush ride. No sign of Vusi Bopape.

'Sleep well?' says Tol Visagie. 'You have a good meal last night?'

'Where'd you go to?' says Jacob Mkezi.

'Lovely meal,' says Mellanie. 'Lovely sleep, when Jacob wasn't snoring. Reminded me why we have different homes.' She waves a spoon at the river bed, an old buffalo walking across the sands. 'This is different.'

Tol Visagie pulls up a chair. 'Better than the city, hey?'

'In many ways.'

Jacob Mkezi speaks through a mouth of bacon. 'Where'd you go last night?'

'Heaven's sake, Jacob,' says Mellanie. 'Give the guy a break.'

'To check on something,' says Tol Visagie.

'Something you're going to tell us about?'

'Ja, this morning, something I'm gonna show you.' He signals a waiter for coffee. 'When you're finished, we're off.'

'Where to?'

'Up the road a bit, and off to the side. On the way I've got a favour to ask both of you?'

'Which is?'

Tol Visagie crosses his legs, keeps his gaze fastened on the old buffalo standing now in the warmth of the sun. 'It's a bit of a cheek, I suppose. The thing is this, I'm the judge for a local beauty contest. It'd be better if you were judges too. Make it look more professional, more serious. I've asked the organisers and they'd like you do to it.'

'A beauty contest. Man, Tol, what's your case?'

Mellanie licks yoghurt from her lips. 'That's hectic. What's the title they're after?'

'Miss Landmine Survivor.'

Jacob Mkezi laughs. 'No. Uh uh. No. You've got to be joking.'

'Excellent,' says Mellanie. 'Awesome. I like that. I like that. It's really, really fantastic. A fantastic opportunity.' Turning to Jacob Mkezi. 'This is brilliant, Jacob. This is truly brilliant.'

Tol Visagie stands, takes the mug of coffee from the waiter. 'The one we're going to's not the final, that's judged in Luanda. This's just the local one, for the province.'

'It's in Angola?'

'Ja, not a problem, Mr Mkezi. Honestly. People go across the river all the time. All day long, backwards and forwards. I've got a permit.'

'Tol, we're talking about a border.'

'Just a detail. A line on a map. What happens on the ground's different.' He smiles at them. 'See you at the Landie in twenty minutes? That okay?' And he's gone.

Jacob Mkezi says, 'I'm not doing this. Are you out of your mind?'

'You will do this, Jacob,' says Mellanie. 'This is perfect. Just the sort of publicity you need.'

An hour later they're across the river at a low-water drift into Angola. Couple of clicks down a dirt road to a small town, posters for the Miss Landmine Survivor contest stuck on the buildings: Everyone has the right to be beautiful. Not a building in the town that isn't bullet-pocked.

'There're seven contestants,' says Tol Visagie, 'from Cuando Cubango province. Some of them stepped on mines when they were children being chased by soldiers raiding their villages. Some of them stepped on mines in the fields. Couple of days ago

I heard a woman trod on a toe-popper near her village. Took her leg off below the knee, whap. Second time in two months I've heard that sort of story. You go anywhere along the Strip, there's thousands of them, mines, still lying in the sand, waiting. Bouncing Bettys. Jumping Jacks. Toe-poppers. Sprinklers. Weird names like that. You've got to wonder who decides what to call them, hey? Some advertising agency somewhere?'

Tol Visagie stops the Land Rover at a church. Men in suits, women in dresses are gathered in the shade. 'The girls'll be inside,' he says. 'This's a helluva thing for them. Like a leg-up, without being funny. The two you pick go to Luanda for the final. The winner there gets a custom-made prosthesis, Norwegian technology.'

'Thanks,' says Jacob Mkezi. 'All I need is to be choosing someone with the best war wound.'

'It's a beauty contest, Jacob,' says Mellanie. 'It's nothing to do with the girl's wound. You look at her face, you look at her tits, you look at her figure. You like pretty girls, don't you? So here's your moment, Mr Mkezi.'

The crowd surges around the car, singing, welcoming 'Doctor Tol'.

'They like you,' says Mellanie.

'I do some medical work when I'm here,' says Tol Visagie, cracking open the car door.

'You're a vet.'

'Studying to be a doctor. What I know is better than anything else they get.'

The three slide out of the Land Rover into the morning heat that's heavy and blinding. Mellanie letting out a whoosh, like she's been hit. Jacob Mkezi raising his arm to squint against the sun.

They're mobbed by the crowd, people shaking their hands talking at them in Portuguese. Tol Visagie responding, passing on people's greetings to Jacob Mkezi and Mellanie, the townswomen taking their hands, leading them into the church, singing.

It's as hot inside, the air stale.

Up at the holy end, seven lovelies in gowns sit on a bench, two steps above the crowd. A makeshift catwalk balanced on plastic beer crates extends into the hall.

The sight of the girls causes Jacob Mkezi to whistle. They're beauties, slim, groomed, not one of them older than thirty. Not one of them with two legs. Not one of them looks like the heat's troubling.

'What'd I tell you?' says Mellanie. 'Pretty girls are pretty girls.' To Tol Visagie she says, 'Where'd they get the gowns?'

'Sponsored,' he says. 'Part of the deal with the organisers. The girls get to model in them and bathing costumes.'

'Oh nice,' says Jacob Mkezi.

A large man in a corduroy jacket, sweating, mopping his face, does the opening, a prayer included. Tol Visagie and Jacob Mkezi and Mellanie getting plenty of name mention in both. Tol Visagie supplying a whispered translation. Then the man sits. A young man in a pink shirt, low-cut jeans, springs up, punches a boom box into life: *2001: A Space Odyssey*, the girls peeling off the bench, stomping across the hall on sticks and wooden crutches, their half-legs swinging. A girl on two metal crutches with no legs at all.

'Oh, Lord,' says Jacob Mkezi.

'Oh, Lord nothing,' says Mellanie. 'They're having a scene. Look at those ladies go.' Mellanie standing to applaud.

The crowd in the hall loving it, clapping, whistling, some women ululating.

After a couple of turns the girls parade one by one, smiling at the judges. Mid-walk they stop, stand still, lovely and young. At a quick glance you couldn't tell they were missing a foot, half a leg.

The MC turns down the music, runs through their names, tells the audience it's swimming-costume time. Which gets men whistling. The girls crowd behind screens to change.

Mellanie says to Jacob Mkezi, 'This's so amazing. The best contest I've been to. Pity I can't tweet it.' She takes cellphone photographs anyhow. 'I need you with the girls, maybe afterwards. We can Facebook this.' Mellanie turning to photograph the audience.

Pink Shirt flips tracks, brings up 50 Cent's 'So Amazing' on the boom box.

The girls hobble out in a line: the first one's got both legs blown off at the knees, her stumps tapering. She's hanging between the aluminium crutches, balancing there no problem, the biggest smile across her face.

'She's got a good bod,' says Mellanie, 'down to the knees.' Glances at Jacob Mkezi. He's riveted. The other girls are following. Mr Pink Shirt calling out their names. 'They've all got good bods.'

The young women stand shoulder to shoulder on the catwalk looking down at the audience. They're wearing black full-length costumes. Their bodies glisten in the heat, voluptuous: thighs, mounds, the belly curves, breasts, the soft lines of their shoulders. Slowly they turn, hop back to the bench. Jacob Mkezi has his eyes fastened on their bums.

Especially the long-legged girl with the short dreads, her left leg gone at the foot. She's an eye for him too, he thinks.

Now they do the catwalk one by one: the short-dreads girl last. She's got a roughly carved blackwood stick to lean on, is hesitant, vulnerable with each step.

Mellanie leans across to Jacob Mkezi. 'Look at her skin. Don't you just want to touch it? I know women spending thousands to have their skin look like that. It never works.'

Jacob Mkezi's got his hands crossed over his lap. She lifts his hand to hold it, brushes against his crotch. Grins at him. 'You enjoying this, sweets?' Putting pressure into the palm of her hand.

'Stop,' Jacob Mkezi, hisses in her ear. 'Don't.'

Mellanie draws her hand away, slowly, caressing. 'We could've done with this last night, big boy.'

'I said, don't.'

She straightens, smiling. 'Kinky, sweets, kinky. I love it.'

The costume parade ends, Pink Shirt punches up Nat and Natalie doing 'Unforgettable'. The audience clap, whistle, yell as the girls disappear behind the screens to change.

Tol Visagie shouts against the noise, 'Over to you, Mr Mkezi. All yours.'

Mellanie singing in his ear about the thought of him doing things to her. She glances at his crotch. 'Ah, it's gone. Just in time.'

Jacob Mkezi stands, turns to face the people, raises his arms for quiet. All you can hear are Nat and Natalie. The man in the pink shirt turns them low. Jacob Mkezi waits for the girls to come out, take their places on the bench. He asks for a standing ovation for them. Tol Visagie translating.

Then he does smarm: oh what beautiful women.

Then he does history: oh what a dreadful war.

Then he does inspiration: oh what courage.

Then he does humble: oh what an honour.

Then he chooses: Miss No Legs. Miss No Foot.

Going up to touch both of them. Mellanie moving in with her camera for the shots: Jacob, arm around Miss No Legs. Jacob, arm around Miss No Foot, his hand close to her breast. Jacob with arms around them both. Jacob among the bevy.

There's laughter and tears, the audience squeezing through the church door into the day's heat, Jacob Mkezi supporting Miss No Foot.

Leaning against their Land Rover is Vusi Bopape.

'Excellent choice, Mr Mkezi,' he says, coming away from the SUV, dapper in khaki chinos, a white cotton shirt worn loose, sandals. 'My favourites too.' Vusi Bopape, raising the hand of Miss No Foot to his lips. Turning to Mellanie, introducing himself.

'Ms Munnik, I like your work.'

26

Knead, Saturday morning. Fish's being treated. Vicki's driven him in her MiTo, now she's buying him the French toast number and a cappuccino. Watching him take it down like it's not food, it's fuel. She's halfway through her own, he's eyeing that too.

'We can order another one,' she says. 'I want this.' Shielding her breakfast.

Fish catches the Nigerian waitress's eye, points down at his plate, holding up a single finger. She smiles her pixie smile, gives him the thumbs up.

'Done,' says Fish, cramming in the last mouthful.

He and Vicki are sitting on the stools at the window counter checking the beach scene. The parking's the usual SUV motor show: Grand Cherokees, Discoverys, X-Trails, CR-Vs, Prados, Benz ML300s, BMW X5s, Nissan double-cabs, the beautiful people strutting their stuff. Kids zipping into wetsuits to go ride a ripple that's got most everyone else phoning the hotline for the surf spots.

The news is surf's down around the peninsula. A cold front threatening late Sunday, Monday. Till then, chill, drink beer.

From where he's sitting Fish can see the ridge on the lower slopes of the mountain, the fort hidden there under alien growth. He's tried Colins on the cell twice, ended in voicemail. It's nagging at him.

He points a fork at the ridge. 'Reckon we should go take a look,' he says.

'For your bergie friend?'

'Just to make sure.'

'He's probably sold the phone to buy booze. Probably sold the horns too.' Vicki takes a swallow of cappuccino, stares at him over the froth. 'What were you thinking leaving them there?'

'Colins was watching.'

'Colins is a bergie.'

'I've used bergies before. Bergies're good for stakeouts.'

Twenty minutes later they're at the locked gate in the paling fence, staring upwards. The mountain above in clear light.

'And now, smartarse, how do we get through that?' says Vicki. Vicki in skinny jeans and a grandpa vest, hands sunk in the pockets of her fleecy jerkin.

'No problem,' says Fish, pulls aside the loose section. 'Slide through.'

'Just as well I don't have big boobs,' says Vicki, ducking through the opening shoulder first.

'Not my type,' says Fish. 'Perky tits're what I go for.'

Vicki snorts. 'I noticed.'

They trudge up the path to the stone walls, Fish in front. In his belt he's packing, in lieu of the family heirloom, the old Astra Police he inherited from Mullet in his belt. A six-shot revolver that Mullet said had got him out of shit more times than were worth counting.

He's all ears, hears nothing to get his pulse racing, nothing to settle his anxiety either. At the entrance to the stone enclosure he stops Vicki, goes up alone into the fort. It's empty. No Colins. No rhino horns hidden behind the rocks.

'Not cool,' says Fish, a prickle of perspiration breaking out despite the winter chill. 'Not cool at all.' Casting about for footprints, any sign.

Vicki hears him, waits him out. Watches him reading the scene. This side of Fish's something she doesn't see often. The fluster.

Fish's all over the place, going, 'Shit, shit, shit.' He looks at her. 'I buggered this up. Bloody amateur. Bloody Jesus Christ what an arsehole.'

She says nothing. Keeps her eyes away from him on the sea: a long view down the beach, kids riding the kiddie waves, walkers dotted along the low-tide sands. She's not going to comfort him, say, Don't worry, babes, it'll be alright. Mommy'll make it better. She can see the little boy in him, the guilt on his face.

'Let's go,' says Fish. 'This's just so stupid. This's making me feel sick.'

Some way down the path he stops, points at some broken brush to the side. 'That's recent.' He crouches to look closely at the sand, rubs a handful through his fingers. Leaves a blood smear on his skin. 'Shit's happened here. See.' Holding his hand out to Vicki. 'Blood.' He straightens. 'That boulder. What's that next to it?'

Vicki's closest, she reaches over. 'Bits of plastic. Could be the cover of a cellphone.'

She's examining it, Fish snatches it from her.

'Let me see.'

Vicki biting her lip to keep her temper.

'It's black. The phone I gave him was black.' Fish smoothes away sand, finds more pieces of casing. 'This's it. This's the phone for sure.' He glances up at Vicki. 'Check around, the rest has to be here.'

'Please,' says Vicki.

Fish frowns. 'Please what?'

'Please is what you say when you want some help.'

'Ah, bloody hell, Vicki, not now, alright? This's a problem we've got here.'

'Yes, now.'

Vicki stands staring down at him, thinking, You say the wrong word and I'm outta here. Sees the flush on his face, his eyes gone hard. Holds his gaze. Waits, one, two, three, four.

'Please,' says Fish. 'Alright. Please.'

Vicki breaks the eye lock. 'I'm not your skivvy, Fish Pescado.' She crouches next to him. 'Remember that. Don't forget it, ever.'

Fish nods.

She tucks strands of hair behind her ear. 'You can say sorry. Men're allowed to say that.'

He snorts. 'Alright, sorry. But this,' he points at the ground, 'means they got Colins.' Fish searching through the sand.

Vicki pulls back, raises a hand. 'This what you're hoping to find?' Holds up the SIM card still clipped into the casing. Blows the sand off it.

27

'Who's he?' says Mellanie. 'This Vusi Bopape. Who's he?'

They're in the Land Rover, she and Jacob Mkezi with Tol Visagie at the wheel, driving away from the town, some children running beside the SUV. The beauty contestants and the crowd gathered in the shade outside the church door. Everyone watching them leave, waving.

To the side, Vusi Bopape's also staring after them, his hand up shading his eyes.

'We should've stayed for the food,' says Jacob Mkezi. 'That was wrong, going.'

'I explained,' says Tol Visagie. 'They know you're a busy man. That you did this as a favour.'

'Doesn't matter. It wasn't polite.'

'And Vusi Bopape, rocking up like that?'

'It's strange. But we don't know his business.'

'A man on honeymoon comes out alone?'

'What's happening, Tol? What's happening that you're not telling me?'

'I'm going to show you.'

The children give up playing escort, fall back as the Land Rover leaves the town. Lowland grass and thicket savannah ahead.

'At last.' Mellanie chirping again, 'Who's he? For heaven's sake will one of you tell me who he is? And what you're talking about?'

'He's a guest at the lodge,' says Jacob Mkezi.

'He's a snoop,' says Tol Visagie.

'Why? What's he doing out here?'

'That's what Tol's not telling us,' says Jacob Mkezi. He twists in the passenger seat to look back. 'The mystery man's not following.'

'He doesn't have to,' says Tol Visagie. 'I reckon he knows where we are.'

Jacob Mkezi frowns, glances at Tol Visagie. 'You're saying he's got a tracker on this car?'

'Ja, he has to have.'

'What the hell for? You're being very strange, Tol. What's going on?'

'Look,' says Tol Visagie, 'there's a waterhole on the way back to the lodge. It's off this road. We're gonna go there and park for a while. Wait. See if he pitches up.'

'And if he does?'

'Then we're eating a picnic lunch, watching the birdlife.'

'If he doesn't?'

'Then I'll show you.'

'Ah,' Jacob Mkezi throws up his hands, 'come on, Tol. Stop the game. Just tell me.'

'I can tell you what this is, sure I can tell you. But it's not going to be the same as seeing it,' says Tol Visagie. 'You need that first impact.'

Mellanie leaning forward, 'Am I any part of this?' – neither of the men answering her.

They go on in silence, the dust swirling behind the car, clouding out the rear-view. Tol Visagie's driving fast, stones clattering against the chassis. The landscape's empty, the bush on either side's hot and still, 35°C on the car gauge. Inside it's cool, the aircon set at eighteen degrees. The kilometres click past.

'You see if there's a car behind us,' says Tol Visagie to Mellanie eventually. 'We're getting near the border.'

'This waterhole, is it this side or the other?' says Jacob Mkezi.

'Angolan side.' Tol Visagie pointing into the bush towards a distant hill. 'About five or six kays, other side of the koppie.'

'Why'd I think that?' says Jacob Mkezi. He swivels round. 'Anything?'

'There's no one behind us,' says Mellanie. 'Not that I can see through the dust. Are you going to tell me yet what's going on?'

'If I knew.'

Tol Visagie turns sharply onto a track hardly visible in the long grass. It leads downhill between thickets to a dry floodplain, through dense vegetation, sandy drifts that have no tyre marks on them.

'You better hope the sand's not soft,' says Jacob Mkezi.

Tol Visagie fights the wheel. 'I know this track. It's okay.'

The koppie comes ahead, the track going round it to the north, then east to a vlei that gives on to deeper water. Some buck along the mud edge, drinking. Otherwise nothing. Tol Visagie stops beneath the trees, kills the engine.

'If I'm right he knows where we are. Maybe he'll come find us, maybe he won't. We'll give him an hour.'

'Thanks,' says Mellanie. 'That's what I really need, an hour out here in the heat. We could be back at the lodge with a drink.'

'There's cold beer,' says Tol Visagie. 'Sandwiches.'

'And then what?' says Jacob Mkezi. 'If he doesn't pitch up, then what?'

'Then we take a short walk. Not far.' He waves his arm to the south. 'Not far from here at all.'

An hour later he swings open his door, says to Jacob Mkezi, 'Let's go.' To Mellanie says, 'You stay here, in the Landie. I'm sorry, hey.'

'I'm going with you.' Mellanie opening her door, getting out.

Tol Visagie turns to Jacob Mkezi. 'I'm sorry, Mr Mkezi, I can't have Miss Munnik with us. That's the deal, alright?'

'Like hell you can't,' says Mellanie. 'If you think I'm going to sit out here, you can think again.'

'Fifteen, twennie minutes, that's all.'

'Doesn't matter.'

'She can come,' says Jacob Mkezi.

'I'm not sure. I'm not sure I want that.'

'Non-negotiable,' says Mellanie.

'Please, Mr Mkezi, Miss Munnik. Do me a favour, won't you?'

The three of them standing at the back of the Land Rover, prickly in the midday heat.

Jacob Mkezi shrugs. 'Your call.'

'I'm going with you.'

'There you have it, Tol.'

Tol Visagie opens the back of the SUV. 'I don't like it. The more people that know this, the more the risk.' He slides a Remington 700 out of a canvas rifle sleeve.

'Nice gun,' says Jacob Mzezi. 'You don't see them often.'

Tol Visagie works the bolt back, raises it, presses four cartridges into the magazine, the fifth into the chamber, pushes the bolt handle down. 'Present from a Yank after his safari.' Tol Visagie leaving it there; Jacob Mkezi thinking it's not the end of the story, but not pressing it. The vet shrugs into a backpack, hands floppy hats to Jacob Mkezi and Mellanie.

Mellanie says, 'I'm not wearing that.'

'Your burn,' says Tol Visagie, throwing the hat back into the car. He slams closed the rear door, remote locks the vehicle. Grunts, 'Come'n,' heads towards the koppie, the scattering of black rocks at its base. Jacob Mkezi follows, Mellanie behind him, saying, 'Christ, Jacob, what's his case?'

'Leave it,' he says. 'You can stay in the car.'

'Yeah, like that's going to happen.'

At the base of the koppie, they thread up through black rocks to a cut overgrown with a mosaic of thickets. Tol Visagie pushes through, calling out 'Mind the branches' – the branches whipping back into the faces of Jacob Mkezi and Mellanie. Mellanie swearing, putting her hand to the sting on her cheeks. 'Chrissakes, Tol, watch it.'

Tol Visagie holding back the last bush for them to step through into a small clearing, a rock face rising in front of them. Heaps of bones, huge skulls, skeletons draped in old skin piled about.

Jacob Mkezi sucks in his breath. 'What's this place? Somewhere animals came to die?'

Mellanie says, 'Hectic.'

'It's amazing, hey?' says Tol Visagie. 'Comes as a surprise. You step outta one reality into another. From outside you wouldn't say this koppie's got a hole in it.'

'What're these bones?' says Mellanie.

'I told you you had to see it.'

'You,' Mellanie giving heat to the word, 'wanted me to stay in the car, remember?'

'Ja, okay …' Tol Visagie turns to Jacob Mkezi. 'Impressive, hey?'

'You brought us here to see this?'

'This and something else.' Tol Visagie steps over bones towards a gap in the rock wall. 'Come.'

'Now where?' says Mellanie.

The gap in the rock is narrow and low. Tol takes off the backpack, pushes it into the opening. Goes down on his knees in the dust. 'You've gotta squeeze through.' He unclips a torch from his belt, shuffles into the opening.

'Ah, no,' says Mellanie. 'Why'd I do this?'

'Your choice,' says Jacob Mkezi, not smiling, kneeling. 'Beauty contests and caves all in one day.'

He and Mellanie follow Tol Visagie into the cave, Mellanie swearing, breaking a nail as she scrabbles through. The entrance is short, opens into a large chamber.

'Check this,' says Tol Visagie, standing, clicking on the torch.

'What the hell're those?' says Mellanie.

'Rhino horns,' says Tol Visagie. 'Maybe four hundred, five hundred rhino horns. Those're their remains outside, some of them.'

'Those're rhino bones?' says Mellanie.

'Ja,' says Tol Visagie. 'They must've had like a factory going here.' He keeps the light on the horns stacked in a five-metre column sloping back against the cave wall. 'I dunno. I haven't counted exactly. That's a guess based on the depth of the column. It's a lot of horn. What're you think we're talking, Mr Mkezi? Twenty-five, thirty million US?'

Jacob Mkezi runs his hand over the horns, they're dry, dusty, he smacks his palms clean. 'They've been here a while.'

'I reckon,' says Tol Visagie. 'About twenty years, thereabouts.'

'These're worth twenty-five million dollars?' says Mellanie. 'These're just sitting here worth twenty-five million dollars!'

'They could be worth that.' Jacob Mkezi caressing the horns with his fingers, rubbing a tip. 'Locally, you'd get ninety, maybe a hundred million rand right off.' He snaps his fingers. 'Pass me the torch.' Tol Visagie takes a spare Maglite out of his backpack, hands it over. Jacob Mkezi bends close to peer at the horns: there's no mould on them, no rot. He gives the torch back to Tol Visagie. 'When'd you find them?'

'Two weeks ago. By accident. I was over here tracking an old buffalo, we had a radio collar on it. Thought I'd go up on the koppie to check out the area, and found the bones, then this huge stack of horns.' He runs the beam up and down the column.

'They're war stock,' says Jacob Mkezi.

'Ja, I scheme. They have to be. This was UNITA territory, Jonas Savimbi land. He probably traded them with us for guns and ammo. Food, medicines, God knows. Don't you think? I mean this was like a bank for him.'

'Could be. Question is, why're they still here?'

'They got forgotten.'

'You think so?'

'Has to be like that.'

Jacob Mkezi plays the torchlight over the cave walls: it's a sizeable chamber, the column of rhino horns almost reaching the ceiling; the floor space big enough to park two SUVs. 'No San painting?'

'I looked. There's three circles, that's all, nothing fancy.'

'These them?' Jacob Mkezi picks out the forms near the entrance, vague, ochre in the torchlight.

'Ja. Doesn't mean anything to me. Bushmen were into weird stuff.'

'Like a kid's done it,' says Mellanie.

'Who else knows?' says Jacob Mkezi. 'Apart from Cake Mullins.'

'No one.'

'And how'd Cake get in on it?'

'I know Cake. He was up here a lot about ten years ago.'

'I'm sure he was.'

'I know what he was doing, dealing, trading, middleman stuff. He didn't tell exactly what, but you find out things in the bush. In the bush nothing's secret. Someone's always watching. You think you're in the middle of nowhere, not a soul in sight but, no, no, my friend, there's eyes in the bush.'

'Go on.'

'After Cake stopped coming, we kept in touch. Once, twice a year he visited for old times' sake. To keep his hand in, he said. He'd meet people, drive around. I'd take him with me into the bush, to the villages when I did clinics. Cake helped with money.'

'Generous.'

'Ja, he's like that.' Tol pauses, listens.

'What's it?'

'I thought … No, it's nothing.' He flashes the light onto the rhino horns. 'When I found these, I phoned him. He came up to have a look and he said to speak to you. He said you're the only one could handle this sort of thing.' Tol Visagie stops again. Listens. 'It's a vehicle. I think we better go.'

28

Fish slides open the back of his phone, clicks out his SIM card, fits the other one. Nokia gives its good-to-go jingle. He checks the call log. Nothing went out. Two messages in voicemail, both from him, both asking Colins to phone him.

Fish says to Vicki, 'He's dead, Colins. They killed him. The bastards.'

'Supposition.' Vicki making a show of looking around under the bushes. 'I don't see a dead body.'

'They've dumped him. Could've dumped him anywhere. Bergies die every day. Too much booze. Too much meths. Heart attacks. Knife fights. Who cares? What's one more?'

Vicki places all the bits of the phone on the boulder: the smashed screen, the broken keypad, the battery, shards of plastic casing. 'This phone had a camera?'

Fish nods. 'I reckon he took photographs. Thought he was being smart. Problem is pictures go to the phone memory. Then again, I know someone who knows cellphones. If the memory's not smashed he could take a look.'

Fish gets his phone working, dials, the call going to voicemail. He leaves a message. 'Not ideal.'

'I know someone too,' says Vicki. She tries her contact, scores a hit.

'Let's go,' says Fish. 'One stop first on the way.'

This's the cop shop along the road, up in the old primary school building.

Fish flashes his PI card at the desk jockey. The man's drinking a Fanta orange through a straw, holding the can in his left, his right making slow calligraphy with a flat-nib pen. His eyes flick up, his lips take a suck on the straw. He swallows, stands the pen in an ink pot.

'How can I help?'

'Beautiful writing,' says Vicki.

'I like it,' says the constable. 'My granny wrote like this.'

'So did my aunt,' says Vicki. 'I've still got a couple of her letters.'

Fish tucks away his card, says, 'You have any bodies brought in this morning?'

The constable frowns. 'Bodies?'

'Dead people.'

'Only a bergie.'

'Right,' says Fish, leaning closer to the constable, speaking softer. 'Look, do me a favour, let me see the corpse?'

The constable sucks at his Fanta. 'She's gone already, to the mortuary.'

'She?'

'Mad Martha. You know the crazy woman, slept there by the synagogue.'

'There's no dead men?'

The constable frowns at him. 'You got a problem with that?'

In the MiTo, Vicki says, 'So maybe your Colins is alive.'

Fish shakes his head. 'Long shot maybe. Maybe your whizz-boy can help us.'

29

Tol Visagie leads them out the cave, into the clearing. Pauses there to listen: the engine grind of the oncoming vehicle less distinct in the open. He gestures at them to follow, heads through the cut, then angles behind the black rocks towards the south. They can hear a vehicle in low gear approaching, then the engine idling, then silence. Tol Visagie keeps moving until the koppie hides them from the newcomer. He's not following any path but moving down a bank towards the soggy vlei ground. They're hidden in riverine bush, can see the SUV stopped some distance from theirs. A door opens, Vusi Bopape gets out, lets the door click closed.

'You still think I'm joking about the tracker?' whispers Tol Visagie. 'How'd he know to come here?'

They watch Vusi Bopape scan the vlei through binoculars. Turn around, gaze at the koppie. He takes a rifle out of the vehicle, slams closed the rear door. Again he scans the vlei, turns, walks towards the koppie, stopping when he reaches the black rocks.

'An AK,' says Jacob Mkezi. 'Interesting.'

'That gun?' says Mellanie. 'That's an AK? What's he doing with that?'

They watch him hesitate, listen, pan his binoculars along the high ridge.

Tol Visagie looks at Jacob Mkezi. 'You want to say hello?'

'To a man with an AK? Why'd I want to do that?'

'He knows we're here. Somewhere. He probably thinks we're watching him.'

'Let him keep thinking that. For the moment.'

'You sure?'

'I'm sure.'

'Jacob ...' Mellanie waves at a cloud of midges buzzing her.

'Jacob, this isn't a boy's game. Why's that man here? Why's he got that sort of gun?'

'I don't know. Okay? I don't know why he's here, I don't know why he's carrying that gun.'

'In the bush you need some sort of gun,' says Tol Visagie. 'The AK's not a bad option.'

'And you wanted me to stay in the car! You knew about this guy, and you wanted me to stay in the car! Heaven's sake, Jacob, where's your head?'

They watch Vusi Bopape return to the cars, walk over to theirs, make a slow circle looking in the windows. He tries a door. Glances back at the ridge.

Taking his time he wanders across to his SUV, stows the rifle, lights a cigarette. He perches on the driver's seat, staring up at the koppie. Smokes leisurely, rolling the ash off the cigarette against the side of the door.

'He reckons we're up there,' says Tol Visagie. 'We can surprise him.' He points north along the vlei edge at an animal path that leads towards the water. 'If we go that way for another two hundred metres we can come behind him. The bush is thick, he won't see us.'

Jacob Mkezi nods. 'Let's do that.'

Mellanie sighs. 'You men lead such exciting lives. Never stop playing cowboys and Indians.'

They walk quickly along the sand path to the edge of the bush. Beyond is vlei grass. Beyond that, sun glinting on sheets of water.

Tol Visagie leads them up the bank onto the edge of the clearing. Calls out a greeting.

Vusi Bopape swivels to face them, frowning.

'That's surprised him,' says Tol quietly.

Vusi Bopape now coming towards them, arms open. 'I took a chance you'd be here. Too good a place for Tol not to show you.' He grins at Jacob Mkezi. 'Wonderful birdlife on the vlei.' Takes Mellanie's hand. 'Hello again. As I said last time, I think you're one of the best. Né, Mr Mkezi? Even if you are standing in the rain, Ms Munnik can convince you the sun's shining.'

Mellanie pulls free her hand. 'Cut the bull.'

'And then she can also be a straight talker. Is that not right, Mr Mkezi?'

Jacob Mkezi doesn't respond, brushes past Vusi Bopape. 'Time we got back for lunch, Tol,' he says.

Vusi Bopape standing amused, watching them. 'There's no need to be like that. Relax. We're in the bush. The Angolan bush, having time off.'

'For a man on his honeymoon, maybe you should be with your bride,' says Jacob Mkezi. 'New wives don't like being left alone.'

Vusi Bopape laughs, winks. 'Something you'd know, Commissioner.'

Jacob Mkezi spinning on him, hard-eyed. 'I've retired. I'm not the commissioner any longer. Cut it.'

Vusi Bopape steps back, holds out his hands. 'No offence, Mr Mkezi. Just a joke. You know, just a funny between friends.'

'Look.' Jacob Mkezi gets in his face. 'I don't know who you are. I don't know what's your problem. I do know I'm seeing too much of you. Understand, my friend. A little privacy, all right?'

'All right.' Vusi Bopape knocks a cigarette out of his twenty pack, lights it with a Bic. 'No offence.'

'Right, no offence.' Jacob Mkezi shakes his head, gets into the Land Rover, Mellanie following. 'I were you, Mr Bopape, I'd get back across the border.'

Vusi Bopape gives a half-salute. 'I'll be doing that. Right behind you.' To Tol Visagie he says, 'Nice gun, the 700.'

'Ja.' Tol Visagie unloads the Remington, slides it into the rifle bag. 'Helluva coincidence you found us here as well, Mr Bopape?' He slams shut the rear door.

'Not really,' says Vusi Bopape. Stands there watching them pull away. Waves before they disappear between the trees.

30

'This one's useless,' says Fish, flapping the printout. 'It's fuzzy. All you can tell is maybe it's the fort.'

'You can see a face in this one,' says Vicki. 'Not sharp but sharp enough.'

'Let me look,' says Fish.

They're going down the stairs of a block of flats, the sort of block of flats students colonise. The sweet smell of doob ubiquitous. The walls papered with posters of gigs, movies, parties, plays, exhibitions. Voices in harmony somewhere.

Fish thinking wasn't so long ago he used to live in places like this. Like the boykie they'd just seen: strong BO, cigarette breath, a patchy beard, jeans sagging round his arse. His flat a midden of hi-tech junk.

'How'd you come by this guy?' Fish asked Vicki, while they waited. He and Vicki squashed on a two-seater couch.

'She works for my uncle,' the boykie had answered.

'Who, Cliffie?'

'Yeah, Cliffie.' The boykie laughed. 'He'd like that. Being called Uncle Cliffie.'

'Really?' said Fish. 'Clifford Manuel?'

'Yes, Clifford Manuel,' said Vicki. 'Let the guy work.'

The boykie did. Finished the job in no time flat. For which Vicki'd forked out two hundred.

'Not great pictures,' he said as he gave Vicki the printouts. 'Nothing I can do about that.' Offered Fish the broken phone. 'You want this?'

'Of course,' said Fish, not keen to have nerdy types frootling around in his old cellphone. 'Could come in handy.'

'It's stuffed.'

'Doesn't seem to be. You got the pictures out.'

The boykie lit a cigarette, scratched at his beard. 'You got secrets in there?'

Before Fish could reply, Vicki had him out of the flat, pulled the door closed behind them. Started down the stairs.

'Interesting family Cliffie's got,' Fish'd said, catching up with her. 'Come'n then, let's see the pictures.'

Two flights down they stop on the landing, Vicki angles the printout to the light. A dull light through milky windows.

Fish squints at it.

'There's a thing, look who we've got?'

'Who?' says Vicki.

'Seven.' Fish taps at the face. 'The pharmacist of Muizenberg.'

Jacob Mkezi and Tol Visagie, perched on stools, clutch bottles of beer in a bird hide, the view over a vlei. Not much going on: a heron stalking the verge, two Egyptian geese on the water. The hide's not far from the lodge, close enough they can hear the murmur of voices on the veranda.

Tol Visagie's been on the pitch about the rhino horns, Jacob Mkezi listening, keeping his thoughts to himself.

'I'd say a fifty per cent deal would be fair,' says Tol Visagie.

Jacob Mkezi considers this. Stares at the heron, sips his beer, says, 'There're big logistics. Major arrangements to be made. You know that.'

'I know that.'

'These things cost.'

'I realise, ja.'

'Even before a buyer's lined up.' Jacob Mkezi leaves it there. Takes another swallow of his beer. It's still cold, the bottle wet with condensation.

'It's just that,' says Tol Visagie. 'It's just that there's a helluva lot I can do with the money. Get a clinic started and funded. Pay for another medic, nurses, maybe even interns. This'll ease people's health problems out here. We can maybe save lives from the landmine detonations. In many cases save limbs. You see what I'm saying? There's nothing for these people. They get malaria, they die nine times outta ten. They get hepatitis A and E, meningitis, typhoid, a bunch of fevers, rabies. They die. They get HIV from the truckers. The kids are born with it, or they get it at birth or breastfeeding. A clinic could stop this.'

Tol Visagie turns to Jacob Mkezi. Shifts his stool.

'Getting a clinic on the go's expensive.'

Jacob Mkezi keeps his gaze on the heron. The bird's perfectly still, focused.

'This sort of clinic is expensive. The paperwork, the plans, architects, even before the bricks and mortar. Then equipment, medicines, maintenance, upgrades, running costs. They eat away at budgets, Mr Mkezi. I've seen it.' He lifts his bottle, doesn't drink. 'Fifty-fifty'd be fair.'

'You going to put all your fifty into the clinic?'

'Most of it, ja. Some of it I'll need personally.'

'Sure.'

'I've got no pension. No investments. Nothing for old age. And that's not far off, Mr Mkezi. Twenty years or so. Maybe a bit longer if I go to sixty-five. Without this, I'm in the shit. Truly.' Tol Visagie drinks. Waits for Jacob Mkezi to say something. Jacob Mkezi keeps watching the heron.

'The sort of jobs I've had there's never been the opportunity. Bush vets get paid peanuts. Enough to get by, have a holiday now and again. Buy a car. You see what I'm saying? Being out here I never bought a house in the city. Now I can't afford one.'

The heron strikes fast, its head snaking down. Jacob Mkezi lifts his binoculars, sees the heron's stabbed a frog.

'You catch that?' he says to Tol.

Tol raises his binoculars, says, 'It would make a difference to me. Give me security. A clinic'd give people health security. We could maybe call it the Jacob Mkezi Clinic if you wanted. Something like that.'

'Amazing,' says Jacob Mkezi. 'You don't often see a bird do that.'

The heron drops the frog, stabs again.

Jacob Mkezi stays riveted.

'So fifty-fifty?'

'It's eating bits, stabbing them off.'

'I could go sixty-forty.'

Jacob Mkezi puts down his binoculars. 'I've never seen that.

That was fascinating.' He swigs his beer, eases off his stool. 'I think I'm going to have to pass on this one, Tol. Sorry.'

Tol Visagie stares at him. 'What? You're not …'

Jacob Mkezi shrugs.

'You don't mean it. You saw them, the horns. You saw how many there are. You know how much they're worth. You don't mean it. Please, Mr Mkezi, I need your help.' He puts a hand on Jacob Mkezi's arm. 'Please.'

'It's the risk, Tol. The risk.'

'Seventy-thirty.'

'Stop.'

'Seventy-five, twenty-five. I could do that.'

'Let me think about it,' says Jacob Mkezi.

THE ICING UNIT, MARCH 1986

They've been on the pass an hour, the Fisherman and Blondie, sitting in a stolen BM with the doors open, drinking the last of the beer.

It's hot. The bush ticking with insects, flies buzzing them. Blondie walks to the road edge, unzips for a piss. Below, the ground slopes off through boulders, aloe clumps, euphorbias, spekboom thickets towards a ravine dark with forest. Beyond, the escarpment drops into haze.

A week ago, when the Fisherman got the message that the job was on he checked out the pass, decided this spot above the U-bend was best. A clear view from the rocks down the twists and turns. For bloody miles. You can see them coming up a long stretch to the snake bends where they'd do it.

The plan's simple, he tells the Commander: as the trade union boys come round the last bend, Blondie forces them over the edge. There's no barrier, they roll down the slope, plunge into the ravine. They go into that, finish 'n klaar. Home James.

This's simplicity, he tells Blondie.

Blondie thinks it's mad. What if the car doesn't bounce into the ravine? Gets stuck in a stand of aloes. What then?

The Fisherman says, 'Don't question, china. Just do it, okay.'

Blondie keeps stone-faced.

Now the Fisherman glances at his watch: 3.42. 'I better go check.' He takes the binoculars, scrambles up the incline to his lookout. Stands there scoping the scene.

Blondie shields his eyes, squints into the bright sky, shouts, 'See anything?'

No response. Then: 'Ja, there's dust. Far away, about ten kays.'

Could be anyone, Blondie thinks. Not a car's been over the pass the time they've been sitting there.

'Two cars,' shouts the Fisherman. 'Definitely, ja. Two cars. The other one about a kilo behind.'

'What colour?'

'Could be anything.' A beat. 'Light colour. White. Ja, white.'

The unionists are in a white Corolla. That much they know.

'There's the flare.' The signal that the plan was on. The Fisherman smacks his thigh. 'We're on, boykie. This's it, hey.'

The Fisherman worked it out, told the Commander where to let off the flare. 'There's a farm gate on the left,' he said. 'All sorts of stuff stuck on it. Keep-out notices, buck horns, sheep skulls, the name of the farm's Vergenoeg. When they get there, fire the flare. They won't see it, I will. Even if they do, what's it mean? Some farmer playing silly buggers. Nothing they're gonna worry about.'

Blondie takes some cans of waste oil out of the BM's boot, empties the slime over the gravel a couple of metres out from the bend.

Mad bloody plan, he thinks. The sort of plan could get himself killed. The Fisherman's idea. They drew straws, he pulled the short one.

The Fisherman's reassurance: 'The driver will brake, swerve, skid, won't even touch you. Trust me.' Giving into a crazy cackle hew-haw laugh as if he knew better.

Blondie hurls the empty cans into the ravine.

The Fisherman's yelling, 'Start up, start up. They're crossing the drift. Come'n, man, start up.'

Blondie mumbling, 'Keep your hair on,' as he tries to fire the car. The engine turns but won't catch.

'Shit's sake,' screams the Fisherman. 'They're coming, man. They're coming fast.'

All Blondie hears is the naaah, naaah, naaah of the engine. Maybe the battery's dying. He glances up at the Fisherman on the rocks. The oke's doing a dance, like he's being bitten by ants. He's pointing down the pass, his mouth working overtime.

Blondie sticks the gear in reverse, lowers the handbrake. Keeps turning the key as he rolls. There's about fifty metres of straight before the next bend. Shit happens, he doesn't make the turn, he's into the ravine backwards. Though which way you go into the ravine doesn't matter at that point.

The car gathers speed.

The starter motor swings naaah, naaah, naaah.

Up on the rocks, the Fisherman's jigging about.

Blondie feels sweat clammy in his armpits, damp on his face.

The car rolls, Blondie drops the clutch, the motor coughs, the wheels skid. Dust swirls in the window. The dry grit on his teeth.

Ten metres, fifteen metres, twenty metres.

The car's rolling, the starter motor swinging naaah, naaah, naaah.

About halfway to the bend, he drops the clutch again, the motor catches, the BM lurching backwards. Blondie stands on the clutch, the brake. The engine doesn't stall. The car stops. He hauls up the handbrake, juices the engine.

The Fisherman's waving him up with both hands. Desperate.

Blondie shifts into first, wheelspins on the gravel, thinking, mad plan, this isn't a plan, this's suicide. He fishtails, straightens, calms the car. Creeping back to the top bend. He can see the Fisherman's shouting, can't hear a word. The Fisherman pointing downwards at the bend.

Blondie eases the clutch out, glimpses sunstrike on the windscreen of the car coming out of the bend. A white car. White Toyota Corolla. Three guys in it. He accelerates at them.

Sees the alarm on the driver's face. Sees him yank the wheel leftwards. Sees the car swerve towards the edge. Sees the wheels skid on the oil patch. The car sliding, sliding.

Blondie brakes. Sees the Corolla upend, disappear over the edge.

He's out of the BM, got the can of petrol from the boot. As he dreaded, the Corolla's slammed up stuck against some boulders, hasn't pitched into the ravine.

The Fisherman's bloody plan.

Blondie scrambles over the edge. The Fisherman's with him, the two of them slipping down the slope to the car.

It's wrecked. Crumpled.

The driver's slumped against the wheel, the only one moving's in the back seat. He's saying, 'Help me, help me.'

There's blood on the windows.

The Fisherman grabs the can of petrol from Blondie, pours it over the car. Blondie flicks a match. Through the flame crackle he can hear the man screaming, banging on the window.

They climb back to the road, Blondie and the Fisherman, watch the car burn. Can't hear the man's screams any longer. Five minutes, the Commander and Rictus Grin pull up. Rictus's driving, does a cautious about-turn on the narrow pass. The Commander stands with Blondie and the Fisherman, watching the fire.

'All done,' he says.

'Ja,' says the Fisherman. 'Thought there was supposed to be four.'

'The VIP didn't pitch,' says the Commander. 'No big deal. Follow us. We ditch the BM in Somerset East, take the long way back to the Bay.'

Going down the pass, Blondie says to the Fisherman, 'That's kak, what you were saying earlier. About babies looking like their fathers.'

What the Fisherman said was, 'First thing a man checks when his child's born, does it look like him. The first year everybody says, the kid's the spitting image of you. They all say that. Oupas, oumas, friends, everyone. What they're telling you is it's yours. That your wife wasn't screwing around. Cos if it didn't look like you, you'd say, get rid of it. You would, hey? You wouldn't want some other oke's sperm fertilising your wife's eggs. So the kids pop out, they look like you. For the first year, then they look like their ma, if they're girls. You know why? Because we screw around. That's what we do, all of us, men and women. That's what we meant to do. Naturally. A natural attraction.'

Now the Fisherman sitting up, turning to Blondie. 'You reckon I talk shit? Why's that?'

'I don't know the history, okay, not down to the century but I'd guess, mirrors weren't everywhere two, three hundred years ago.'

'Twak. Bull.'

'No really. I'd say if you weren't rich you didn't know what you looked like. You yourself, I mean. Unless you had a bucket of water handy.'

'So what?'

'So. Yusses, if you don't know what you look like, how d'you know your baby looks like you?'

'Because everybody says so.'

Blondie takes his hands off the wheel, holds them up: help-me-Lord fashion. 'Maybe they're lying. Ever thought about that? To keep you happy. To stop you causing grief.'

'Rubbish,' says the Fisherman. 'Sometimes you talk absolute shit.'

32

Vicki follows Fish's directions into Muizenberg ghetto at Killarney Road, first right into Church, stops the MiTo opposite a semi in want of paint and TLC. Some of the windowpanes boarded up.

'Won't be long,' says Fish.

'Uh uh, I'm not waiting here. I'll come with you.'

'Not a good idea.'

'Not a good idea sitting here either.'

'Gonna be two ticks. Just want to see if he's there.'

Vicki sighs. 'You're not going in alone.'

'I'm not going in. Place looks shut up anyhow.'

The semi's got a small patch of dirt in the front that's a cesspit of bottles, bloody tissues, condoms, tins, doll parts, syringes. Some weeds straggling through. The gate's long off its hinges, the pathway's cracked concrete, faded red. On the stoep two chairs, their seats burst open. Reminds Fish of old tomatoes, rotting.

The door's the 1930s style: panes of dimpled glass, every one cracked, two replaced with wood. A security grille fronting it, unlocked. To the side, dangling through a hole in the ceiling's a length of string with spark plugs weighting it. Fish pulls the string, hears pipes clanging in the house. No human stirrings. He jerks the string again. Keeps the pipes banging.

No movement.

He cups his hands over his eyes, squints through the glass. No flickering shadows inside.

Turns to Vicki in the car, shrugs. 'Nothing doing.'

Nothing doing the next day either when Fish calls. Late afternoon Vicki's headed back to her city pad, Fish's at a loose end: wanders over the vlei bridge into the warren. Some people about, mostly the street's empty, the houses shut.

Two girls are ahead of him clanging the pipes at Seven's

crack house. They glance at Fish, ask, 'You know where he is?'

Teenage girls. Fourteen, fifteen, both in sheepskin boots, tight jeans, cutaway tops with their bra straps showing. The white one thin, her shoulder blades etched beneath her skin. The black one dumpy, her stomach falling over her belt. Gives Fish the shivers just to look at them. Fish in a jacket zipped to his neck.

'No idea,' he says.

'You got any stuff?' says the thin girl.

'Stuff?'

'You know, doobie?'

The girls jiggling in front of him, naked arms pimpled with cold.

'No,' says Fish, 'I've come like you.' Leaving it there vague.

The fat girl, tugging at her friend's arm. 'Let's go.'

The thin girl whining, 'He hasn't been here all weekend.'

Fish watches them slope off towards the beach, follows at a distance. They score from a car guard, run giggling to smoke among the bathing boxes.

Easy as that, thinks Fish. Why'd they bother with Seven?

He's standing there on the sea wall, eye on a small brown swell. An offshore wind's holding it down. The ocean looks cold, depressed. Forecast is a front'll pump up the waves overnight, put some life into this murky soup. Already the sky's clouding over.

As Fish turns away, he stops, notices a family: mom, dad, teenage daughter playing frisbee on the low-tide beach. It's Daro, Georgina, their Steffie. He can hear their laughter, enjoyment. Makes him smile.

33

His cellphone wakes him: one o'clock Monday morning. Mart Velaze lies there without looking at it, considering, should he answer it? This time of a Monday morning could be a range of people: Jacob Mkezi heading the list.

Except he spent much of the hour ten o'clock to eleven o'clock on the phone talking to Jacob Mkezi. Not talking, listening to Jacob Mkezi telling him some weird adventures of the lost rhinoceros horn fairytale. Like Jacob Mkezi had been in a parallel universe for the weekend. Walking with Indiana Jones.

Telling him, first thing in the morning arrange lorries to collect rhino horns from a cave. A cave in some hills. Some hills where? Mart Velaze had managed to get in.

'I don't know, Angola, somewhere,' Jacob Mkezi snapped back. 'And maybe fly the freight straight out. Get a cargo plane, an Airbus, a Beluga should do it or an Antonov, the small one, the turboprop. They're good, they can use a smaller runway.'

Like Jacob Mkezi was on magic mushrooms.

'We'll talk in the morning,' Jacob Mkezi said. 'Make it nine. My place.'

Mart Velaze hummed, then bit down. 'It'll have to be later. I'm meeting your car dealer first thing. That guy Daro Attilane.'

He could hear Jacob Mkezi clicking his tongue, recalling the Daro Attilane request. 'Oh, ja, him. Okay, that's important. Meanwhile, get some people putting this thing together. No don't. I'll do it.'

Now Mart Velaze lies listening to his phone. Looks at the time on the bedside clock, looks at the pulsing screen. Lord Mkezi written there. First the dad then the son. Mart Velaze sighs, sighs deeply, connects.

'Bra Mart,' says Lord. Two words, they're enough, for Mart

Velaze to know Lord's freaking out.

'Yes, Lord,' he says. 'What's it?' Knowing it has to be major crap this time of a Monday morning.

'I hit someone.'

'More detail, Lord.'

'Just now.'

Mart Velaze taking a stab at it. 'You were racing?'

A sob from Lord.

'In the new car?'

The new car that wasn't yet registered which if anybody had got the plate number would go straight back to Daro Attilane, the paper trail ending at the office of former police commissioner Jacob Mkezi. Nice one, Lord.

A sob from Lord.

'The person you hit, what can you tell me?'

'Nothing,' says Lord.

'You left the scene?'

A sob from Lord.

Mart Velaze thinking, thank the Lord for that. Says to Lord, 'Keep the car garaged. Don't tell anyone. I'll sort it.'

Lord sobbing, 'What about my father?'

'I'll sort it,' says Mart Velaze.

He does. Finds out which hospital admitted the victim. Finds out the guy's in a coma. Finds out his name's Fortune Appollis.

He phones Clifford Manuel. It's now three in the morning, he doesn't give Manuel any advantage. Says, 'Clifford, we're dealing with some problem here.' Outlines the situation, says, 'Who've you got can work pro bono for the victim? Keep that side covered? I'd like it to be Vicki Kahn.'

'Yes,' says Clifford Manuel. 'She could help you.'

'Don't tell her anything. Brief her like it's a genuine one.'

34

Fish and Daro paddle their longboards through a rising sea to the backline, sit on the ocean watching the sun come up behind tattered clouds.

They let a set slide under them to get the feel of the swells.

'It's building,' says Fish.

On the peak there's a sense of the wall dropping away, a pull and suck in the water.

'Not as big as Thursday.' Daro's facing the shore, watching the back of the waves feather then drop down in white water. The peak's breaking right. You're fast you can get a long ride ahead of the soup.

'Getting there,' says Fish. 'Be even better this afternoon.' He angles his board towards Daro. Says, 'I was at Seven's place. Twice. Saturday and yesterday. You must raid him again, Daro.'

'I know,' says Daro. 'The weekend raid didn't happen.'

'There were kids there, teenagers, wanting to buy stuff. Like he's running a takeaway.'

'I know.'

'You have to surprise him.'

Daro's nodding his head, holding his hands up. 'I know this,' he says. 'I know this.'

'You don't want Steffie rocking up at his door.'

'You say anything to him about Steffie?'

'I didn't talk to him. He wasn't there.'

'So why ...?' Daro leaves it hanging.

'Something else came up with Seven's name on it. The shithead's bad news. You've got to move him out. Lock him up.'

'I know.'

'So then? You've got the forum, pull some weight. Force the cops down there.'

'Not that easy.' Daro's got an eye on the incoming, points over Fish's shoulder.

Fish glances back. Sees the ridges on the sea, rising up. He flattens, starts stroking shorewards to catch the first swell. 'You still want me to arrange a talk, I can do that,' he shouts. Doesn't hear Daro's answer.

The wave's under him, pulling him onto the wall. Fish feels the take, slides onto his knees, hesitant, gripping the board's rails, bottoms out too far back, the wave closing on him. First wave, and a wipe-out. He surfaces, goes back for more.

35

Vicki Kahn has set up office at Knead. Outside on the pavement beneath a roaring gas heater. On a morning like this, a paradise morning, who wants to be inside? Even though it's in the winter shadow, you want to be outside breathing ozone air.

She likes Knead, Knead's the smart place, especially when the surf's running. Half-naked boys traipsing through to get to the surf shop at the back, flat washboard stomachs. Firm young flesh. The sort of flesh you'd love to caress your hand over, just for the feel. Instead of her palms, she runs her eyes.

Sexy pastime. One Fish isn't averse to either, checking out the girls, that is. Their wetsuits skin-tight over their thighs, dangling down from the waist; their skimpy bikini tops just doing the job. Fish giving them the sneaky eye.

'You're leching,' she'd tell him.

He'd blush. This man blushing. So sweet. Then he'd retort, 'So why's it okay for you?'

And she'd grin at him, reach out, give his thigh a feel.

She plonks down her handbag, laptop, iPhone, car keys. Keeps on her coat with the fur collar. Real fur collar. None of this faux stuff for Vicki. Some animal might have worn it once, but now it's her turn.

Vicki orders cappuccino from the Nigerian waitress with the pixie smile. Asks, 'My boy out there, I assume?'

'For about an hour.'

'Time he came in.'

She powers up her laptop, plugs in a 3G flash drive. There's an email from Clifford Manuel.

'Further to the Fortune Appollis case, I'd appreciate it if you'd keep me in the loop.'

I'd appreciate it – Clifford-speak for You will. In the loop – Clifford rolling with the hip lingo.

How much in the loop did he want for a pro bono? Detail by detail? Briefing memos? What?

He phoned her at seven thirty, said, 'Can you handle a pro bono?' Implication: you will.

'Sure,' she replied. 'I'm going to get points for this? It'll show up in my bonus?'

'Of course.'

Clifford Manuel giving her the brief, saying, 'See what you can do.'

Then sending the email. Keep me in the loop. Why? Fortune Appollis was nobody. A bystander. An ordinary youngster from an ordinary family. A kid out watching the thrills of urban racing. Why were the fortunes of Fortune Appollis of even the vaguest interest to Clifford Manuel? Vicki Kahn clicks her black fingernails on her laptop, stares up at the mountain, bright in the winter sun.

Sees a beautiful apparition in a wetsuit, barefoot, dripping, standing next to his board like it's a shield, grinning at her.

'Fish,' she says, 'get dressed' – wishing she could say undressed. 'I've got a job for you.' Calls to the waitress, 'Bring him the breakfast. The one with bacon and sausages. And a cappuccino.'

THE ICING UNIT, SEPTEMBER 1987

Paris is Blondie's job. The Commander handles him. Rictus Grin is the point man. The Fisherman does surveillance.

The Fisherman takes a short stay in Gay Paree. After two weeks, he decides a bomb is best. He flies home, reports to the Commander. His scheme: the target's car is parked outside her apartment. A Peugeot 505, still looking good. Mostly she uses it for joyriding out of the city. Connect something to fire on ignition would be the answer. Over to the explosives man, Blondie.

Blondie gets a manual of the 505, works out a plan. Compiles a shopping list. Five grams of P4 he reckons should do the trick. A military detonator from East Germany. Wiring sufficient to carry the charge. A plastic funnel, five-centimetre diameter. Same colour as the dashboard would be best.

Rictus flies to Berlin. Checks into a pension in Kreutzberg. Next morning makes a deposit in US dollars at a branch of Deutsche Bank AG, checks through Check Point Charlie for a day tripper excursion with a straggle of Americans.

Not the first time Rictus's been through. He gets a kick out of the grey, decaying, bullet-smacked buildings of East Berlin. Likes to see people scurrying through the streets, eyes cast down. Frightened as the rabbits in no man's land behind the Wall. Rictus sees this and grins. Convinces him he's fighting the good fight. Communism's a kak story.

He wanders through Mitte, feels like the day after World War Two ended. Takes a tram to Prenzlauer Berg. Climbs the hill to an apartment block drab as dripping washing. Up two floors to the arms dealer. Grim man never smiles. Rictus has dealt with him before, twice. Always the same protocol: the Kraut has the hardware on his kitchen table. Rictus inspects it, hands over the bank deposit slip. This detonator's so small he slips it into his pocket. Grins at the grim spectre.

'*Auf Wiedersehen.*'

The man doesn't respond.

The following day Rictus trains through to Paris. Long tedious trip via every small town and Frankfurt. Rictus hates trains. Hates sitting in the compartment with people who smell of sweat, eat garlic salami rye bread sandwiches. Swill it down with lager. At Frankfurt he changes trains, almost misses the connection looking for the platform.

In Paris, Rictus sources the PETN – pentaerythritol tetranitrate – from a black trader in Clichy-sous-Bois, other side of the ring road. Cocky Senegalese floppy offers him a bankie of heroin as a thank you for the business. Rictus grins. Tells him nicely, not his scene. The man raises his eyebrows, considers Rictus, holds up a finger. Says something in Frog Rictus doesn't understand. Next thing he's cracking open a wooden box with a claw hammer, whips out a Johnny Walker black. Rictus takes it gently in his hands. The two of them standing there, grinning at one another.

Heading for the subway, the whisky and the PETN in a plastic bag, Rictus reckons it's a toss-up between Prenzlauer Berg and here. Clichy-sous-Bois being another reason to keep the Bantu bastards down. Give them a building they turn it into a location. Overnight.

In a small supermarket, Rictus locates a funnel. Colour: off-white.

Next day the Commander and Blondie fly in, check into separate hotels, two-star joints on the rue du Faubourg Montmartre. Blondie hasn't been in Paris three hours, the Commander takes him to Les Deux Magots. It's a Sunday. A sunny Sunday. Parisians out getting the last of the summer's golden rays.

'Sartre mean anything to you?' the Commander asks, as they stroll up Boulevard St Germain. The Commander affecting the European style, his jacket coat-hangered on his shoulders, empty sleeves flopping about.

Blondie shakes his head. 'Yeah, I've heard of him.'

'Fitzgerald? Hemingway?'

'Of course. I've read Hemingway. *A Farewell to Arms*.'

'*For Whom The Bell Tolls*? *The Old Man and the Sea*?' The Commander showing off. Long thin cigarillo between his fingers.

'Uh uh, something about a gun.' Blondie clicks his fingers. '*Have Enough Gun*.'

'That's Ruark. Robert Ruark. *Use Enough Gun*. Airport stuff. Ruark's not Hemingway.'

'About a guy called Harry Morgan.'

'Harry Morgan?'

'That was his name. The main man.'

'Morgan's in Hemingway.'

'So, okay, he's a Hemingway guy, he was the honcho.'

'Hell, man. You've been surfing too long.'

'*To Have and Have Not*.'

The Commander stops, squints at Blondie. 'You're taking the piss?'

Blondie shakes his head again. 'No, man. I'm not, I'm serious.' Giving the Commander the full eyeball, holding the twitch out of his lips.

The Commander keeps up the stare. 'Sometimes I don't know about you.'

They sit down, the Commander orders Pernods.

'Great place, hey?'

'Sure,' says Blondie.

'Same place where Hemingway sat.'

'Really?' says Blondie, eyeing the French birds. Almost like they were creatures of a higher order. Long legs, tits, attitude. Cigarettes and perfume. Sitting there in the sun. This bird two tables away in a linen jacket, nothing underneath. She leans forward he can see her boob. Perky shoo-shoo boob with a raisin nipple.

'One thing you got to appreciate,' the Commander says to

Blondie, 'you've got a loo to sit on. Used to be the Frenchies were squatters.'

Blondie hauling himself back from his ogling.

'What's that?'

The Commander laughs. 'Randy sod.'

Blondie grins, blushes.

'Something else? The dolls.'

'No kidding.' Blondie's eyes alive, glinting. 'Far out.'

'What I was saying,' says the Commander, 'about the loos ...'

'Yes,' says Blondie.

'... The first time I came here, the loos were a hole in the floor. These two places in the ceramic for your feet, you squat over a hole.'

'Shit.'

'You said it.'

The waiter sets down their aperitifs.

'What's this?' says Blondie. 'Gin? Vodka? I don't do spirits.'

'Taste of Paris,' says the Commander.

The waiter holds a jug of water, the Commander nods at him. '*S'il vous plaît.*' Sounding to Blondie like 'Seeboplay.'

The waiter splashes water into the glasses.

'It's gone milky,' says Blondie. 'Look at that.'

The two men clink glasses, sip at their drinks. The Commander smacks his lips, Blondie pulls a face. Says, 'Takes some getting used to.'

'You'll do that,' says the Commander. 'Get used to it. Tomorrow you'll be wanting one first thing.'

'You reckon?'

'I do, boykie. I do.'

They do some catch-up talk, the Commander telling Blondie about his daughter, now thirteen years old. Deals some photographs of her out of his wallet. No photographs of his wife. Photographs of the daughter alone, no mom in any of them. Blondie thinks about it, the Commander's never mentioned a wife. He's this single parent raising a daughter by himself. Helluva thing.

The Commander says, 'We've got the stuff for you. You're sure about the P4?'

'It's stable.'

'Czech?'

'Isn't it always?'

'My plan is tomorrow night, we, you, do the job. You reckon she's not gonna see the funnel?'

Blondie shakes his head. 'Think about it. You start your car, you know where the key hole is, you're looking through the windscreen while the motor swings. You've got your head full of stuff: where you're going, who you're going to see. The last thing you'll notice is something under the dash.'

The Commander nods. 'Okay. I'll go with that. How long, to do it, the job?'

'Bout four, five minutes. All that's got to be done is hook up the wires. Glue the funnel to the dash.'

'Won't drop off.'

'Uh uh.'

'Even after a week?'

'Serious surfboard glue I'm using.'

The Commander smiles. 'I shoulda known.' He sees Rictus talking sign language to the waiter, pointing at them. He comes over, sidling through the tables. Sits.

'Bloody Frogs, don't understand simple English.'

'It's France,' says the Commander.

Rictus grins. 'No excuse.'

They all laugh, order another round of Pernods.

The Commander says, 'Where're the goodies?'

'Don't need them,' says Rictus. 'Job's done.'

The Commander's face goes rigid, he leans forward. 'What're you saying?'

'Job's done. Mission accomplished.' Rictus grinning, cocky. Holding up a hand of flashy rings.

'Job's done? What d'you mean job's done?'

'Job's done.'

'How?'

'I got an opportunity, I took it.'

'Bloody hell.'

'I'm clean. No trail.'

'You're sure.'

'Ja. Of course. No problems.'

'Bloody hell.'

The drinks arrive. They shut up while the waiter splashes in water. When he's swirled away, the Commander says to Rictus, 'Where? Where'd it happen?'

'The Metro. Montparnasse. About forty minutes ago.'

The Commander shaking his head, 'Bloody, bloody, bloody …'

'No. Relax, man, relax. I'm clean.'

'How?'

'I was following her. She's in front of me, big Sunday crowd, pushing 'n shoving to get on the train. I thought: do it. Do it now. Stiletto in, stiletto out. Walk on by. I got on the train, she didn't. She's standing there on the platform holding her side, sort of swaying.'

The Commander takes the rest of his drink in a swallow.

'You sure she's dead.'

'Pretty much. Midline in deep. Fatal. Most cases it's fatal.'

'Most cases?'

'Long as you don't miss.'

'Meaning?'

'You gotta cut the aorta, the thoracic portion. You do that she bleeds out.'

'Before medics get there.'

'Long before.'

The Commander stands. 'You better be right.' He adjusts his jacket over his shoulders. 'Where's the bomb stuff?'

'My room.'

'Let's get it. In case. Hell, man, we had a plan, you shoulda stuck to it. This could've cocked up everything.'

'The coolie's dead.'

'She bloody better be.'

36

Fish, wearing jeans and a black T-shirt under a blue hoody, leans in for a quick smooch with Vicki, her naughty tongue in his mouth. His hand goes over hers, pinning it to the table.

He likes the tongue bit.

Vicki pulls back, jerks her hand out from under his. 'You're frozen.'

'Yeah,' says Fish, sitting down, 'it's chilly out there.' He leers at her. 'This's early. Why'd you go back? You could've stayed.'

'This's not what you're thinking.'

'What's it I'm thinking?'

'You're thinking a quickie.'

Fish shakes his head. 'Uh uh. Not a quickie.'

Vicki stays with a wry face. 'Trouble with you, Bartolomeu Pescado, you've got a one-track mind.'

Fish swipes a slice of toast through egg yolk, forks it into his mouth, 'You haven't?'

'I compartmentalise. My life's ordered, sorted.'

'Is that so?'

'It is. That's the way it is.'

'Miss Lawyer.' He grins at her, goes head down back to his food. 'Sorry: Ms Lawyer.'

Vicki finishes her cappuccino, dabs with the paper serviette at her top lip, says, 'Fish, serious. For a moment.'

'I'm dead serious. Always.' Fish wolfing the last mouthfuls. 'I could do that again.' Signalling to the waitress for another, slurping at his cappuccino.

'Listen to me first.' Vicki tapping her laptop screen with a black fingernail. 'Please.'

'Yes ma'am.'

'We've got a client we're taking on pro bono.'

'Wow, Vics, Cliffie's being very generous.'

'Fish.'

Fish eyeing her over his cup, getting off on the light in her eyes, her straight face. Scheming, come on, Vics, what's the real vibe here? Thinking, God she's stunning. Those cheekbones. Those brown eyes. That latte skin. He reaches over, runs the back of his hand down Vicki's cheek. Lovely. Silky.

'Fish.'

'Vicki.'

'Will you listen to me?'

'All ears.'

'We've got this client, Fortune Appollis. Twenty. Nice ordinary Cape Flats family. Dad's in the printing trade, mom's a shelf-packer. Fortune's at tech, graphic design.'

'Cape Flats: Mitchell's Plain? Cape Flats: Delft, Belhar, Bonteheuwel?'

'It makes a difference?'

'You're the Athlone girl, you don't come from the wild parts, you'd know.'

Fish loving the frown Vicki's giving him.

'What's that supposed to mean?'

'I'm teasing.' Reaching for her hand.

'You leave Athlone out of it.'

'Athlone's major. All those larney lawyers.'

Vicki putting the no-kidding look on him. Fish getting a kick at the beauty of this woman.

'Are you going to listen to me?'

'Of course.'

'Then do so.'

Fish leans back, opens his arms, expansive. 'All yours.'

'Good. Now focus. My client ...'

'... Fortune Appollis ...'

'... Fortune Appollis is into cars. Urban racing, specifically. Not doing it, he's not got the money, but following it. Like the drivers have got fan clubs. Even on Facebook. You know, these kids. Post goes up on Facebook, or they get a Mxit SMS about where it's happening, when it's happening, and they drift over to watch. For the thrill of it.'

'The cops pitched up, Fortune got arrested.'

Vicki shakes her head. 'Fortune got injured. Badly. A driver lost control, ploughed into the bystanders. Well, into a bystander.'

'Fortune Appollis.'

'Exactly.'

'And now the driver's disappeared. His car's disappeared. Nobody knows anything. And the Appollis family's facing medical bills.'

'Big time.'

'And he might die.'

'Exactly.'

The waitress slides in Fish's second breakfast. He squints at her. 'Can I get a coffee? Americano instead?'

'You don't want the cappuccino?'

'Too much foam.'

She shrugs. 'First time I've heard that one.'

'Special favour,' says Fish, giving her his boy-grin.

When she's gone Vicki says, 'Stop it.'

Fish chews down on a large bite of toast and egg and bacon. 'What?'

'You know what. Now listen. He's in ICU. Unconscious. He's bad. Probably not going to make it.'

'The cops?'

'Opened a culpable homicide charge. So what?'

'They'll find him, the racer.'

'Maybe. More likely maybe not.'

'You think I can?'

'Sure. It's why I'm asking.'

'You haven't.'

'Not in so many words.' Fish catches her glance. 'It's a job. You need the work.' She sets up an index card against his cup. On it, Fish reads two addresses. 'What's that?'

'All we've got. First one's the Appollis' contact details. Second's where the accident happened.'

'That's it? No witnesses.'

'That's it.' She purses her mouth. 'When the medics got there, the bystanders took off.'

'This's not a lot to work on.'

'Sorry. But it's money. The stuff you don't have much of.' Vicki closes down her laptop, gathers keys, iPhone, handbag. 'Got to rush.' Kisses him on the cheek. 'Later. After work, my place?'

Fish chews, swallows. 'What about a proper kiss?'

Vicki's refreshing her lipstick. 'Oh no, not that egg mouth.' She beeps open her MiTo, gives Fish an air kiss. 'Don't worry about the bill, I've paid.'

'I love lawyers on expense accounts.'

She pulls a face.

37

Mellanie's there, BlackBerry to her ear, pacing the floor, talking loudly. Mart Velaze would rather Mellanie pissed off, but that doesn't look likely to happen any time soon. He's facing Jacob Mkezi from the far end of the man's ten-seater dining room table. Jacob Mkezi at the head eating segments from a halved grapefruit with a silver spoon. Telling Mart Velaze over and over about this cave of rhino horns like it was some mystical experience.

He breaks off. 'Why're you here? You said you couldn't make it.'

'It's Lord,' says Mart Velaze, glancing at Mellanie. She's engrossed, not part of their talk.

Jacob Mkezi doesn't look up, keeps at his grapefruit. 'Lord's in trouble? He's totalled the car already?'

'Something like that.'

'How'd I guess? Give the boy anything, he wrecks it. When?'

'Last night.'

'He phoned you?'

'Ja.' Mart Velaze shifts on his chair. 'Ja. Must have been after one, almost two o'clock.'

'He doesn't phone me. He phones you?'

'He knows I fix things. For you.'

'He knows you fix things. He doesn't think his father fixes things.'

Mart Velaze's is about to speak. Jacob Mkezi holds up the grapefruit spoon. 'Stop. Leave it. Lord is what Lord is. My son but not my son.' He pushes away the eaten fruit, dabs at his lips. 'Thank you, Mart. I appreciate what you do for both of us.' Lifts a silver warming lid from an English breakfast, sniffs the aroma. 'One thing useful the English gave us: bacon and eggs.' He starts in. Through a mouthful says, 'How bad?'

'A spectator was knocked down.'

'Dead?'

'In a coma.'

'And the car?'

'Dented. Scraped. Will need some panel work. It's not too bad.'

Jacob Mkezi chews through a couple of forkfuls. 'Which hospital?' Mart Velaze tells him.

'I can't have this coming back.'

'It won't.'

'Nothing. Not a word. Nothing in the press, no whispers. You keep it dead quiet.'

'I will.'

'I'm not joking. This thing must go away. Whatever you have to do. Make it vanish' – Jacob Mkezi blows a puff of air – 'Poof.' Looks down the table at Mart Velaze. 'You'll sort it?'

Mart Velaze nods.

'Whatever you think best. Do it. I don't care. Just no come-back.' He forks a mushroom. 'One other thing, you know someone called Vusi Bopape?'

'No.'

'Not national intelligence? Some other spookery?'

'Never heard of him. You want me to check him out?'

'You could. Why not? Might be useful to know.'

Mellanie sits down, pulls a grapefruit towards her. 'What's that I heard about Lord?'

Jacob Mkezi laughs. 'You were on the phone, talking.'

'So? What'd I miss?'

'Lord had an accident.'

'Typical,' says Mellanie. 'Buggered up his new car, no doubt. What'd I tell you would happen?'

38

Fish, at Knead, finishes his breakfast, his coffee. Leans back, watching two chicks suiting up. Both wearing black Speedos. Probably better than them standing there naked, he reckons, imagining the hidden boobies, taking in the tummy swell, the hips. Costume cut high like that meant bikini wax, gives Fish gooseflesh. The thought of hot wax, the tear of hair ripped out. The way Vicki prefers it. Almost a Brazilian.

'Why'd you do that?' he asked her once.

She shrugged. 'Body art. It's what we do with our hair.' She pointed at his groin. 'Not much you can do with that tangle.'

Which got Fish flushing, Vicki riding his embarrassment. The way she did, teasing him.

But he's cool with that. Vicki's not angling to move in. Not throwing a hissy fit that he doesn't love her, that he's selfish, that he doesn't talk, that she feels locked out. Vicki doesn't do any of that stuff. Vicki Kahn gets that little smile on her lips says, 'I've got to go, dude.' Gets in her fiery Alfa MiTo, zips off.

Lets him chill with Shawn, Jesse Sykes, Alison, the new local he's discovered, Laurie Levine.

He brings his mind back, refocuses on the women chatting, students probably, zipping one another's wetsuits, lovely as impala bokkies. Picking up their boards, heading for the water.

A short spliff. That'd make this a perfect day, Fish believes. But he's not one to smoke in public. He pulls off his hood, feels the winter sun warm on his head.

Not a bad start: a surf, a breakfast, a job. A paying job.

The waitress with the pixie smile, says, 'That all?'

'Sure,' says Fish. 'I'm good' – patting his stomach, standing.

'She paid,' says the waitress, 'your girlfriend.'

Fish grins at her. 'What I call WEE,' he says. 'Women's economic empowerment.'

Next thing on this lovely morning, he's got the professor calling. Fish's sitting in his inherited Isuzu, tapping his fingers on Fortune Appollis's card, staring at the sea. Still wondering if he shouldn't do another surf before starting the day. Considering how a trip to see a guy in a coma in ICU is hardly a wow activity.

Jim Neversink's on his CD player: 'Skinny Girls are Trouble'. Fish hearing Jim's lament. Thinking the skinny girl could be Vicki. No it couldn't.

His cell rings. 'Prof Summers' on the screen.

Thumbs him on, doesn't even say a word, the professor's up and away, 'Fish. Two baggies. There any likelihood you can provide?'

'No reason why not,' says Fish, thinking, the prof must've smoked up all weekend.

The prof says, 'I know what you're thinking. It's not like that. I lost what you brought me.'

'I'm not thinking anything, prof,' says Fish. 'When're you in?'

'Today?'

'Maybe,' says Fish. 'Certainly tomorrow.'

The prof saying, 'Who's that playing?'

Fish watches the two young women hit by a hard break go into the wash. Sucks in his breath. 'Jim Neversink.'

'Interesting. Not Mozart but interesting.'

'I'll make you a copy.'

The professor laughing as Fish thumbs him off. His phone rings, like someone saw him end the conversation. His mother, Estelle.

Fish hesitates, just for a second, but he hesitates. He could press her to voicemail. He looks at the ocean, at the horizon stretched across the bay connecting Hangklip to the peninsula, at the waves so perfect. Takes a deep breath. Keys her on.

'It's eight thirty-five in London, Bartolomeu, nine thirty-five your time. I thought I'd save you the cost of the phone call. Tell me you've got what I want. That you're about to email your report.'

'It's not that easy,' says Fish.

He hears his mother sigh. Imagines her in some Victorian rental, in the kitchen at a little table with her laptop open to her Gmail account. She'd have a cup and saucer to the right, a pot of green tea under a cosy on the nearest counter. There'd be a notepad and a pencil. She was probably tapping the pencil on the pad.

'What's not so easy? Explain it to me.'

'Where are you, Mom?' he says.

'I'm here, Bartolomeu, in London waiting for some information from you.'

'Where in London?'

'What d'you mean where in London.'

'I don't know where you stay when you're there. You've never told me.'

'You've never asked.'

'I'm asking.' Fish watches a surfer shredding a wave. The sheer exhilaration of it. Doing that would be way better than sitting here with Estelle on his case.

'You can call me Estelle now,' Estelle said to him when he turned thirty. 'Calling me Mom at your age is silly.'

But he couldn't call her Estelle, not in person. That didn't work for Fish. He wasn't getting on first name terms with his own mother.

'I don't think so,' he said.

She shrugged, 'Suit yourself.'

But he calls her Estelle in his head.

'I'm in Bayswater this time,' she says. 'A very nice flat, very comfortable in a leafy mews. Thank you for asking. Now what's your problem?'

'I need more time,' says Fish.

'You've had all weekend. All you had to do was make some phone calls.'

'I've left messages,' Fish lies. Stares out the windscreen at the high tide running up the beach, licking the bathing boxes.

'Bartolomeu, this is important to me. These Chinese investors have come to me. The company I work for. I can't let them down. We have to show that we want foreign investment. That we're not about to nationalise our major assets.'

'Find them another mine.'

Again he hears his mother sigh. 'They want this one. For whatever inscrutable Chinese reason they have, they want this one. But I need to know what I'm dealing with, Barto. I must know what Prospect Deep's about before I make the approach. I don't want anybody taken for a ride. Not us or the Chinese.'

Maybe they want it because of who owns it, Fish thinks. Says, 'I'll get back to you. Soon. Promise.'

'When? This afternoon?'

'If I can. Tomorrow—'

Is about to say, Tomorrow would be better. But she's gone, leaving Fish with a bad feeling.

39

From the deck of his mountainside house, Daro Attilane surveys his kingdom: below, the slow curve of the vlei as it slides towards the ocean, on the horizon the mountains of the Hottentots misted back against the sky. In between, the warren and the Cape Flats with their drug dens and their gangsters, the townships and the shacklands of desperate people.

Always when Daro looks at this view he sees what can't be seen.

'Paradise,' says his wife Georgina, bringing out their coffees. 'On mornings like this.' Georgina in exec black for her exec job in the city, managerial placements. Georgina the headhunter.

Daro doesn't want to mention what lies in the distant haze or point out the three crack houses below them. 'Paradise,' he says.

They sip their coffees, side by side.

'Good surf?'

'The best.'

From their deck they can't see Surfers' Corner but they can see the sweep of the beach beyond the vlei mouth, the swells like ribs in the ocean.

'Did you mention to Fish about …' Georgina taking it for granted Fish would be there. Wouldn't actually be on a job. Slacker Fish surfing, not much in the way of a care in the world it seemed.

Daro told her he was in the investigation business. Specialised in finding people. Mostly for insurance companies. Sometimes men who'd run away from their wives. Wives who'd run away from their husbands.

But she saw him as a surfer. Thirty-something, no sense of responsibility. The sort of guy would hang out on a beach at three o'clock in the afternoon checking the surf. What Daro found in him she couldn't understand.

'I did mention it.' Daro with both hands wrapped round the mug for warmth. 'He's going to get hold of this woman he knows, she was a drug addict. She does talks to kids now. Seems she's got a peg leg from shooting up. Which she takes off to show them.'

'Nice. The kids'll enjoy that.'

'If it scares them out of drugs, I don't care how she does it.'

'Daro,' says Georgina, 'Steffie was experimenting, it's what kids do. We all did. It's part of growing up. Be thankful she did it here at home, not in some club.'

'If she liked it she'll do it again. Not dagga but pills, Ecstasy, coke, there's a drug store out there they can pick from.'

'Steffie's not like that.'

'I don't think so either. I just don't want her going down that road.' Daro glances at his watch. 'Dammit! I'm going to be late. I've got a client.' He finishes his coffee.

'This's good. A prospective sale?'

'Let's hope so.' He kisses her, feels her hand on his cheek.

He's halfway down the stairs, she calls out, 'Hey, Daro, did you say anything about that gangster? The one you think's dealing.'

He stops, looks back at her.

'You know, the one with the number name?'

'Seven.'

'Him. Did you say anything to Fish?'

'I mentioned him, once.'

'But not to do anything.'

'What d'you mean?'

'If Fish goes messing around it'll come back on the kids.'

'Fish's not going to do that.' At least he doesn't think so.

40

The surf's still an option but Fish's feeling flat after talking to his ma, decides maybe not. Time for a bit of action. Work her out of his system. He fidgets around under the driver's seat of the Isuzu, pulls out the old Z88 he inherited.

Another police gun. Licence applied for. Could take years for the cops to clear the backlog of applications.

Now, standing at the open door of his bakkie like a TV hero, Fish sticks the pistol into his belt behind his back, flops his hoody over the bulge. Slams shut the vehicle door, tweets the remote. Sets off, unhurried, down damp Sidmouth over Atlantic into Killarney, goes right at Church. Three men on the corner – Congolese, Nigerians, Rwandans – talking, catch something in Fish's face that moves them on. Fish smiles. Wants to say, Brothers, relax, I'm not the xenophobe, a whitey's not going to hurt you.

At Seven's house, takes the short path to the front door. Nothing's changed in the cesspit. He pulls the string, hears the pipes clank. Hears shuffling in the corridor behind the door. A voice says something, nothing Fish recognises as speech.

'Where's Seven?' he says.

Again the alien language.

'Just get Seven.'

The shuffling goes away, returns.

The voice says, 'Fok off.'

This time Fish understands the drift. Says, 'Ah, no. Don't cause grief so early. Give him this, okay.'

'What's it?'

'Money.'

A bolt slides back. A lock turns.

Fish shakes his head, sometimes you don't even have to try. He opens the security grille, reaches behind his back for the gun.

The door squeaks open, Fish shoulders it hard. He's in. The scrawny gangbanger sprawled in the passageway, snarling at him, toothless. Not a pretty sight this early.

The house is a fridge, stinks of dead rats under the floorboards too. And something else, drains, toilet blowback. Fish gags. Says, 'Jeez, you need Marvellous Maids.'

Toothless squirms away, eyes on the Z88.

Fish bends down, puts the barrel into the dental gap. 'Which room?'

These old houses, the front door opens into a long passage with rooms off either side. A sitting room, kitchen, bathroom at the end.

Toothless points vaguely into the depths.

Fish straightens, studies the drool-glisten on the barrel. Bends again, uses the guy's T-shirt to wipe off the spit. 'Now look at you, you've pissed yourself. Must learn to hold your fluids, bru. Didn't mommy teach you?'

Fish finds Seven in the third bedroom, sprawled on a bed, a girl in the crook of his arm, her head on his chest. A schoolgirl. Probably not sixteen. Probably should be at school.

'Ah, Seven,' says Fish, 'not kosher, bru, not kosher.'

The girl screams at the sight of the pistol in Fish's hand.

'Who're you?' says Seven, hand scrabbling under the bed for hardware.

'Doesn't matter,' says Fish. 'Best leave the weaponry, hey. You don't want a hole in your arm.'

Seven pushes the girl off the bed. She's naked, runs shrieking past Fish. Seven glares, mouth open to show his teeth. He's got perfect teeth, ruby studs in the front two.

'Nice teeth,' says Fish. 'Falsies.'

'Still bite,' says Seven. 'Love bites. What's your case, whitey?'

'And look at you' – Fish pointing at his chest – 'nice tats. A main man in the Twenty-Six gang. A main gang, hey. When're you going to change your name?'

Seven frowning.

'Call yourself Two or Six. Two's good. Completely "toe".' Fish waving his hand across his face. 'The Afrikaans "toe". As in stupid.'

'Fok jy, ' says Seven.

The two men doing the stare, not breaking it. Seven's eyes reminding Fish of a tuna's: flat black. His face all bone and hollow cheeks. Men in the prison gangs no longer humans, in Fish's reckoning.

'Ja?' says Seven. 'Wha'ju wan, Mr No Name whitey?'

'Nothing much,' says Fish, stepping close to the bed, so close he can smell sour sheets. 'Thing's like this, I've got this picture here of you' – he flips a folded copy of the printout at Seven. 'Check it out.'

Seven unfolds the page. Looks at the picture. Says, 'Not me.'

'Don't give me that shit,' says Fish. 'It's you. I know it's you. Guy taking this picture is Colins, the cellphone he used was mine. You're up there, at the fort, to collect two rhino horns. Two rhino horns you stole.'

Seven laughs, his teeth moving sideways. 'You's looney, whitey. What you been smoking?'

'Where's Colins?'

'Dunno Colins.'

'You kill him?'

Seven gives him the hard black eyes. 'I've seen yous. At the beach. Surfing with Daro the sparrow. Daro's forum. Daro's gonna have his wings clipped. You gotta watch out, Mr No Name. Yous don wanna be on the list as well.'

'What list?'

'Daro's on a list.'

'Whose list?'

'Big business.'

Fish racks the pistol. 'Where's Colins? Where're the horns?'

'Strues, whitey.' Seven makes a gun of his right hand, puts it to his forehead. 'One time. I tell you, ek sê. Daro's gotta watch out. That's what happens on the forum.'

'Bullshit.'

''S not bullshit, Mr No Name. Cross my heart.' Seven drawing the sign over the rising sun tattooed on his chest: six sun rays. Below it the number Twenty-Six either side a gun, his badge of membership in the Numbers gang, the gang that really ran the prison system.

'Big business, what they calls organised crime. The manne think you's a problem' – he snaps his fingers – 'you's dead.'

'Crap.'

'Don't believe me, nothing I can do. What the larneys say, time will tell. You'll see. Seven's got connections, all the way. All. The. Way. Into big business, government.' Seven cackling. 'Pellie-pellie with the high-ups.'

Fish lets him subside, taps at his foot with the pistol.

'You listening?'

Seven staring at him with those tuna eyes.

'Nod.'

Seven nods.

'Where's Colins?'

'Don't know Colins.'

'Where're the horns?'

'What horns, whitey?'

'How far you want to push me, Seven?' Fish moves the muzzle up Seven's leg, over the tattoos to his shoulder. Asks the questions again. Gets repeat answers. 'One more time, okay, then I'm coming back with cops, forum, all the friends you don't want to see.' Fish puts the Z88's stubnose next to Seven's arm, pulls the trigger. Big, big explosion. Cordite, burnt skin, the bullet ripping through the mattress, smacking into the floor. Seven clutching his arm, rolling off the far side of the bed, howling. Swearing at Fish that he's gonna get him. Eat his heart alive.

Fish walks out, passes Toothless standing in the doorway, drool hanging from his lips.

THE ICING UNIT, SEPTEMBER 1987

'Why?' Dr Gold wants to know of the Commander and Blondie. The question so softly asked Blondie's not sure he heard it.

The Commander shrugs. 'Orders.'

'Not my orders.' Dr Gold wheezing.

'Yours aren't the only orders we get,' says the Commander. 'Tell me again what happened.'

The Commander tells him about the planned bombing, Rictus Grin's decision to knife the target.

'That was unprofessional.'

Neither the Commander nor Blondie respond.

'She was my contact.' Dr Gold pausing to catch his breath. 'She was a clever woman. Very thoughtful. She knew we had to talk, her people and ours. That we couldn't go on with the war on the border, the war in the townships.' He gazes at them with rheumy eyes, looks away, stares out the window at the lake. The water grey, cold green tinges on the mirror surface. A ferry in the distance approaching. 'You don't know where your orders came from?'

The Commander shakes his head.

'These days I cannot trust anyone. Not on my side, not on theirs.'

Dr Gold wears pyjamas, is dressed in a towelling gown, his feet in slippers. He leans on the window sill for support.

Softly he says, 'It is beautiful among the mountains, don't you think? You can see why the Swiss feel secure. They believe they are protected by all this high rock.' He pauses, his breath ragged. 'When you can't see far your world is smaller, you are content. A chocolate-box world.' He wipes at his mouth. Turns back to confront them.

The Commander and Blondie have flown in from Cape Town on Dr Gold's orders.

'I want you to tell me what happened,' he shouted at the Commander on the phone a week back. 'In person. I want you to tell me who ordered this. You'll come here and tell me. And bring Blondie.'

It is ten days after the Paris hit. They watch Dr Gold, a thinner Dr Gold than the last time they saw him, a sick Dr Gold shuffle from the window to a chair, panting, wheezing. He takes shallow breaths, his mouth open. 'Who gave you the order? I want a name.'

'Not possible,' says the Commander. 'You know that.'

'You are my men.'

'We're Security Branch.'

'You are killing me,' he says. 'You and them, the blacks. Poisoning me. You both want me dead.'

Blondie glances at the Commander: what's he talking about?

The Commander steps closer to the sick man. 'Nobody wants you dead.'

'You all do.'

'What d'you mean by you all? You mean us? You mean we want you dead?'

Dr Gold shakes his head, gasping his breath back. 'My friends,' he says. 'I mean my old friends in the cabinet. My brothers. The generals. They are the ones poisoning me. They have the poison, you know. They have tried it out.' He looks from the Commander to Blondie. 'In Angola, there on the border with the terrorists, they tried it out. When they caught the blacks they put the dust on them. In a few days they were dead.' He tries to snap his fingers, the dry skin rasping. His fingers as soft as lizards. 'You get weak. And then you die. Like I am weak.' He points at a glass of water beside his bed. 'Water. Please.'

The Commander hands him the glass.

'They put it in my clothes. Them and the blacks. They want me dead because I know what they are doing, the cabinet ministers and the generals, they are selling out. Making deals with the blacks. And for this they want my money. They need my money. They want me to die.'

Blondie's not into this. He's desperate for a cigarette. Can't leave the hospital soon enough. The man's really sick, you can smell him. Whiffs of his breath that stink of wet dog. Worse, the man's meshuga. Paranoid. Whatever's happened to him, cancer, stroke, hell knows what, Blondie's not happy about hanging around a dying man.

He hears the Commander saying, 'No one's trying to kill you.'

Dr Gold laughing. A husky dry laugh. 'I thought I would be safe here, in the mountains of Switzerland. But even here they come with their poison in the night.' He stops, stares at the lake.

Blondie nods his head towards the door. The Commander lets the silence play out. Blondie taps his watch.

'Doc,' says the Commander, 'we've got to leave.'

Dr Gold flips a hand. 'Go.' He looks up at Blondie. 'Not you.'

The Commander raises his eyebrows, smiles, heads for the door of the private ward, mouthing, 'All yours, boykie.'

'What's it?' says Blondie when they're alone.

Dr Gold beckons him closer. Blondie crouches next to the sick man's chair.

'Run,' says Dr Gold.

Blondie trying not to smell the stench of the word.

'What d'you mean run, Doc? I don't understand.'

'Before they kill you. Run.'

Blondie stands. 'Okay, Doc. Thanks, I'll do that.' He backs away. 'Get better, hey.'

'I mean it,' says Dr Gold. 'Run.'

Outside the Commander and Blondie sit in their hire car, smoking, watching the scene. Day patients. People come to see the sick and dying. Doctors and nurses laughing. Behind the hospital a slope of houses, behind them pine trees. Back, high above it all some mountain rising into cloud.

'What'd he say?' the Commander wants to know.

'Told me to run.'

'Yeah. From who? To where?'

'He just said, run, before they kill me.'

'The man's gone cuckoo.'

They smoke down their cigarettes, crush the butts.

'You think the doc's right about the Swiss?'

'About the Swiss what?'

'Feeling protected by the mountains.'

'They sat out the Nazi war, didn't they? In their mountains.'

'I hadn't thought about it that way. Or about what far horizons do, if the doc's right.'

'Why d'you think the bushmen hotnots smoke so much dagga? You've got all that space in your head, you're going to see humans with animal bodies.'

'I suppose,' says Blondie, lights up. 'You reckon he's right about being poisoned?'

The Commander shrugs. 'Wouldn't be the first time a politician's been dispatched, as we well know. But nah. I think he's sick. Paranoid. Something's eating his brain.' He stops, nudges Blondie. 'Looky there. My oh my. See who's here.' Pointing at a black man, hurrying into the hospital.

'Who's that?'

'Jacob Mkezi. The man the doc wanted taken out. Remember?'

'The mountain job? Those union guys in the car?'

'The very one. Jacob Mkezi was supposed to be with them.'

Blondie blows blue exhale against the windscreen. 'I never understood that. Why he wanted him killed.'

'Betrayal. That's why. He basically educates the guy, gives him a job, then Jacob lights out for the struggle. Becomes an MK commander. This pisses off the good doc. Obvious.' The Commander opens the passenger door. 'That's how I see it. Would piss you off, don't you think?'

He's out of the car, heading for the hospital entrance. Blondie shouting after him, 'What're you doing?'

The Commander half-turns. 'Stay there. Be right back. Just need to check this out.'

Blondie's got no mind to go after him. The whole trip's been a waste of time. But it's on the doc's tab so what the hell. Couple of days in Switzerland's alright. Only thing bugging Blondie is the doc's suggestion, run before they kill you. What's that supposed to mean? Who's the they for starters? Paranoid old coot. Completely delusional. Thinking he's being poisoned by his own people and the terrs as well. Chrissakes. But it's still worrying.

There's the Commander coming out of the hospital, shaking his head. He gets in the car, laughing.

'How about this. Jacob's pulled up in a chair, chatting with the doc, knees to knees. No hard feelings there I'd say. The way they're sitting they could be the best of friends, like an advert for racial harmony.' He holds up a small Kodak. 'I've even got a piccie.'

'You got that? Did they see you?'

'Come on! What d'you think I am?'

'Just asking.'

'Makes you wonder what all that business was about, wanting him killed. From killing to making up in a couple of years. A funny story, hey?'

Back at the beach, Fish's hyped. Cursing his bad luck. Cursing Colins for a stupid bastard. For trying to play the hero. Knows it for sure now: Colins is dead. Has to be. The horns fenced. Seven being a member of the Twenty-Six gang, into money big-time, he'd have moved them quickly. Could be on a plane to Vietnam, China, Yemen, wherever. Talk about a balls-up. Major. Worse, nothing he can do about it. Can't tell the cops. What's he going to tell them: some half-arsed story about super-sleuth Fish's plan to catch the horn thieves? Yeah, that would really fly. Not.

Colins is a guilt. A notch in his conscience.

Then Seven's blab about Daro on a hit list. An organised crime hit list? What was that? Some drug syndicate pumping their muscle? Gangster big talk. Probably bull 'n brag. Probably Seven upping his own reputation.

'Nah,' says Fish to the seagulls, 'the prick's cooked. Been using too much product.'

Fish gives the waves another hesitation: maybe. Except the tide's drawing out, the swells flattening.

You got the best of it, he thinks. Balances on the low wall dividing beach from walkway, sighs for Colins, sighs because sometimes everything seems fucked up. The guilt tweaks.

He finds a band of bergies at the railway bridge, men, women, dogs, sitting in the sun, mashed faces watching his approach.

'My larney,' they greet him. Hustle for a cigarette, a two rand for bread, grin at him. Mr Fish the bergie's friend they call him.

'Where's Colins?' he asks them. 'A new guy.'

Gets shaking heads, raised shoulders, hands flapping like pigeons.

'No, Mr Fish,' they say, 'Colins is gone.'

'Gone where?'

'To the Lord God in his heaven.'

'He's dead?' says Fish.

'As a snoek on the slab.'

Fish rocks on his heels, keeps his gaze on the band, no one meeting his eyes.

'How'd he die?'

'Nay, we's only know he's dead, Mr Fish. We's found his book.' One of the women pulls out a plastic bag of manuscript pages, a bag Fish recognises. She hands it to him.

Fish remembers: Colins's life story. 'Where'd you find it?'

'There by the fort.'

'Really,' he says to them. 'You hear anything you let me know.'

'Of course, Mr Fish. Of course, always.'

Fish turns away, stops, turns back to them. 'The cops know he's dead?'

'The cops know nothing, my larney. The cops're mos a closed chapter.'

Fish drops the Isuzu at home, takes the Perana. Listens to Jim down Prince George Drive, through Lavender Hill, the gangster flats draped with washing, passes Zeekoevlei, Princess Vlei onto the highway. Singing with Jim to keep down his sad thoughts of Colins: 'Can I rely on the Western world ...' To the left, the mountain chain in sharp etch, to the right brown fug over the townships. Under his foot, raw power.

Singing with Jim: 'Just being by my side you'll be playing roulette ...'

First stop on Fish's schedule, the hospital. Check out how the client's doing. What's his condition? What's his prognosis? You never know, guy might've popped out of the coma. Might be sitting there eating jelly, busting to tell him who the dicers were. You never know, you could get lucky.

Fish knows his way round the hospital. Spent almost a week there recuperating from a gut shot. Well, not so much a gut shot as a muscle wound at his waist. Hard-nosed bullet went clean through his side.

During that time kept it from his Ma. It helped she was in London on one of her buy South Africa trips. To this day she doesn't know he's taken lead. Doesn't even suspect his life can get so hairy. Like gunfight hairy. Was his dead partner Mullet got him to hospital after the poachers opened fire. Thank God for Mullet. Poor bugger.

The best part of that ordeal? Tripping on some drug, some painkiller for a while, after he'd smooched up to one of the nurses. In the pre-Vicki days, of course.

The worst part: the pain, the food. Taking a dump. You didn't want to push down on your stomach muscles. Pure, pure agony. He blocked solid in no time. Hated the enemas. Even when the morphine nurse stuck them up. Those surgical gloves she wore, like he was meat.

Fish's got a theory about hospitals, white coat plus a black attaché case and no one sees you. Especially not security. The stethoscope's an added extra, non-essential. The black attaché case's in the boot, the white coat he lifts from casualty. So much chaos there no one notices. Then he's up the lifts, squeaking down the corridors on his Adidas Gazelles. Strides into ICU, nodding to security, nurses, anyone who needs nodding to.

Bends to a nurse. 'Fortune Appollis?'

The nurse shakes her head, points to an empty bed.

'What?' says Fish. 'The patient died?'

'Gone to another hospital,' says the nurse. 'This morning.'

'I see,' says Fish. 'Matron didn't tell me.' He brings up the briefcase, riffles through some papers. Glances at the sister. 'You know which hospital?'

'Constantiaberg,' she says.

He holds up a piece of paper, one of Vicki's letterheads. 'Here it is.' Flicks it twice, nods to the nurse.

Back at his car, still white-coated, he phones Vicki.

'Constantiaberg,' she says. 'They can't afford a private hospital.

Ma and Pa Appollis don't have that sort of money. They're never going to have that sort of money.'

'Makes it a bit more difficult.'

'What?'

'Getting the info.'

'Technicality, Fish. For a man like you.'

'Yeah, yeah,' he says.

'It's why you're on the case. Don't waste time.'

She's gone, Fish's left staring across the parking lot, over the roofs, away to Hangklip ghosting at the end of False Bay. He digs up the index card Vicki gave him with the Appollis address: finds Samson and Daphne Appollis live in Beechcraft Street, Mitchells Plain. The map tells him right down at the coast, an area where every street's named after an aeroplane: Junkers, Heinkel, Alouette, Halifax.

Fish sheds the white coat. Shrugs into his leather jacket. The one he likes to use for interviews. Gives him that serious investigator image he doesn't mind using.

In the car Fish cranks up Neversink. He fires the Perana, just loves the gurgle of the pipes.

42

High up a city bowl tower block, Vicki Kahn looks south towards Hangklip, only she can't see the hanging cliff of rock low on the horizon. Toys with her cellphone, wonders if she should call Fish back, ask him to pick her up. Maybe she needs to be with Fish for the Appollis interview. Tap tap of the cellphone in the palm of her hand, until she decides, no, better to let Fish have his head. Better to keep Clifford Manuel in the Appollis loop as he wanted, though she can't get the nag out of her mind about his interest on this.

Why? she's thinking, clipping up the stairs to Manuel's office. What's it about the family Appollis that stirs Clifford Manuel? Or maybe he's checking on her? Not a thrilling thought. Maybe this is about performance, points, billing hours, equity in the firm. A chilling thought.

With not a heave to her breath after the stairs, Vicki Kahn mouths at Clifford Manuel's PA, Is he in? – pointing at the half-open door. The PA's on the phone, doesn't stop her flow, nods, flutters her hand.

Vicki sticks her head round the door, says to Clifford Manuel, 'Got a minute?'

Clifford Manuel, hands linked behind this head, staring at the harbour ten storeys below, swivels round in his huge leather chair. 'Of course.'

'Fortune Appollis's been transferred,' says Vicki, watching Manuel take this in. Not a twitch to his lip, no tell at his eyes, only his hands unclasp, drift down to the desk. 'To the Constantiaberg.'

'I see.'

'You wanted to be kept informed.'

'I did. Thank you.' His fingers reknitting. 'The parents tell you?'

Vicki taking two steps into the room, stopping behind a chair fronting Manuel's desk, her hands resting lightly on the chair back. Manuel not asking her to sit. 'Our investigator, Fish Pescado. He phoned from the hospital.'

A nod from Manuel. 'The Constantiaberg?'

'Groote Schuur.'

'So he hasn't seen the patient?'

'Not yet.'

'But he's going to?'

'I'm sure. I don't know what his moves are.'

Another nod from Manuel. 'Good. Good. Maybe a rich relative has come to their assistance.' Manuel looking at her, Vicki locking on his eyes one, two, three beats, glancing away. Back, away. Manuel fixed on her.

He smiles. 'He any good, your friend Pescado? The art connoisseur. He's the one wears an earring?' Clifford Manuel touching his own earlobe.

She glances down at her hands, long fingers, the black varnish of her nails. 'He finds people. He's done what we've asked for, in the past.'

'You think he's up to this?'

Vicki meets his eyes. The challenge in them, a glint of predator. Notices his mouth, his slightly parted lips, the glisten on his teeth.

'What? Finding out who's paying the bill? Of course. He's good. He'll sort it. Before lunch, I'd imagine.'

'Excellent.' Manuel still with that smile. 'Let me know how he gets on.'

Vicki wants to say, Why? Why're you so interested? Is it the case or me? Thinking, Do I need this? Leaves with, 'Naturally' – turning away.

She's almost at the door, Manuel says, 'Oh, and Vicki …'

Vicki glances back, over her shoulder.

'I like your hair. The short style suits you.'

'Not a bad cut you've got either,' she says. 'Very now. Very executive.'

Hears him force a chuckle, she's out of there before she says anything else. Like, dude, blow away.

43

Daro Attilane, dressed in grey chinos and a suede bunny jacket, stands in the office overlooking the forecourt watching the black Golf GTI pull up, tinted windows, throaty exhaust, the driver kicking some revs into the switch-off. Has to be the client. On the phone the client sounded like he fancied a statement car, but now needed something less obvious.

'Perhaps a BMW,' he said, the client.

'I've got a full-house Audi A4, new shape,' Daro said. 'A very nice car. Clean. Agile. But I can get you a BMW if you'd prefer. Depends on you. That BM's a statement car. The Audi's more sporty. The car of the serious executive, but also says you've got spark. You know, that you're on your game. Depends on you.'

'Sharp,' the client said, made the appointment.

Now the Golf, stopped in the visitors' bay, stays shut, Daro can see the man's on his cell. He gets out, he's still on his cell, walks away from the car remote-locking it, very cool customer.

Daro picks the Audi's electronic key off his desk, goes outside to meet the man he's begun to think of as a player. Snappy dresser, suit and rollneck, lace-ups. A smiling man with a little kick in his walk, not a limp, more a sort of skip. Like the player's stoked to be alive.

Daro waits at the door while the man finishes his conversation. The man in no hurry, no worries about Daro overhearing his conversation.

The man saying, 'I don't care what the story is, there's an obligation. Legal, moral. It's on paper. You're locked in, my brother.' Ending with a run of Zulu, probably, no clicks in it.

The man listening.

The man back in English saying, 'You're not hearing me, my brother. I am saying there is no other way. I don't want to hear about your troubles. I don't want to hear that. I want to hear you tell me it is finished. Over. You hear what I am saying.'

The man holding the phone away from his ear, rolling his eyes at Daro.

The man back on his cell, saying, 'No, no, no. My brother, you phone me when it is done. Before that I don't want to hear from you. When it is done, then. Before that, we have nothing to talk about.'

The man disconnecting, sliding his cellphone closed. Saying to Daro, 'Sometimes people don't understand. Even when they've signed a piece of paper, they don't understand. It's a contract. It's legal. You honour it, or you pay the consequences. Not so?'

Daro shrugs. 'That's the way I see it.' Steps back into the office, the man following him.

'Not this guy. No, this guy believes the situation can be changed. For this guy everything is negotiable, all the time. If that was the case, where'd we be? If nothing's for sure. If everything's flexible. One thing today, another thing tomorrow. This would be a mess.'

Daro holds out his hand, introduces himself, realises he doesn't know the player's name.

The client doesn't give it, says, 'Very boutique,' – pointing at the two cars Daro's got in the showroom.

'It works for me,' says Daro. 'Personal service.'

'You've got a reputation. Highly recommended.'

'Pleased to hear that.' Daro nodding, saying, 'You called. You're Mr ...?'

'Velaze. Mart Velaze.'

'The man after the executive vehicle?'

'That's me.'

'Excellent,' says Daro. 'You like a coffee? Tea? Coke?'

'Water,' says Mart Velaze. 'Sparkling.'

'No problem.' Daro bends down to a minibar fridge, lifts out a sparkling water, hands it over. 'A glass.'

'Nah, this's fine.' Mart Velaze twisting off the cap, taking a

mouthful. 'So what've you got? Not much I can see.' Mart Velaze
pointing the bottle at the two cars Daro's got on display. 'Just
the Benz here, that car outside, the Audi. What about a BM?'

'I can get you that,' says Daro. 'I can get you any car you
want.'

'That's no good, Daro,' says Mart Velaze. 'What I wanted
was to see it now. Test-drive it.'

Daro holds up the Audi key. 'The car I mentioned on the
phone.'

'What's that?'

'The A4.'

'No, that in your hand?'

Daro gives it to him.

'This's a key?'

'Electronic. You lose that it sets you back two thousand bucks
for a replacement.'

Mart Velaze whistles.

'That's her out there,' says Daro, pointing at the silver car
under the awning. 'Leather interior. Built-in GPS. Good sound
system. As I said, comfortable. But look how she sits. She's got
presence. She's taut. Ready.'

'Game.'

They both laugh.

'It's what you said.' Mart Velaze stepping towards the car,
taking a swig of sparkling water. 'She looks fast.'

'She is. Want to get the feel?'

Mart Velaze running his hand over the bonnet. Daro smiling
to himself, letting the guy get involved.

'Showroom car,' he says. 'Six thousand on the clock.'

Mart Velaze opens the door, settles into the leather, slots
home the key. Daro buckles up in the passenger seat.

They head for the Blue Route highway, Daro singing his sales
pitch down the Tokai Road: spark ignition, direct fuel injection,
turbocharge, power outputs, gearbox specs. Mart Velaze nodding along.

'There's turbocharge on the petrol?'

'Sure.' Daro glances at Mart Velaze, wondering if he's saying this because he knows about engines or if he's winging it. The man's focussed on the road, his eyes hidden in wraparound shades.

They get onto the highway, Mart Velaze floors the pedal, the A4 powering through the gears at two hundred still accelerating up the rise.

'In about a kilometre there's a speed camera,' says Daro.

'Know it,' says Mart Velaze, taking his foot off the juice. 'Nice vooma.'

On the ride back Mart Velaze sings the car, Daro's turn to nod along until there's a break in the praise song, Daro coming in with, 'What line of work're you in?'

Mart Velaze turns in at Daro's showroom, switches off. 'Marketing consultant. Strategic planning. Company's called Adler Solutions. We come in and sort you out. Pump your strengths, beef up your weaknesses. The company's been around for, I don't know, twenty years, twenty-five years. I joined ten years ago just after the guy who started it sold out, went to Australia. Guy called Ray Adler. Sorry story that one.' Mart Velaze unbuckles, gets out of the car.

Daro does likewise. 'Yeah, why's that?'

Mart Velaze brushes it off. 'Another time.' Pats the car on the boot. Says, 'This is mine. Give me a couple of hours, two, three this afternoon I'll be back to sign the papers.'

'I can hold it that long,' says Daro.

'Sharp,' says Mart Velaze, heading towards his GTI. 'Till later.'

Daro watches him pull away, thinks, This wasn't about cars. Not about an A4 at all. This was about something else. Something he's been dreading.

44

Samson and Daphne Appollis sit opposite Fish on a couch. The couch has heavy wooden arms, ball and claw feet. Cushions patterned in brown and orange.

On every surface in the room are family photographs. Self-standing, silver-framed. The three of them: in this room, at a wedding, on the Sea Point promenade. Twosome combinations: Fortune and his dad fishing; Fortune and his ma at a school function; Fortune in his school uniform, badges on his blazer. A lot of pictures of Fortune by himself: studio portraits. One stands on the glass-topped coffee table staring at Fish.

Fish's been through the sympathy spiel, heard about their good son. He's told them he's working for their lawyers. He's told Mrs Appollis he likes her shortbread biscuits. There's a plate of them next to the photograph of Fortune on the coffee table. The room smells of home-baked biscuits.

Mr and Mrs Appollis sit uneasy on the couch. They're perched more than sitting. They're not eating biscuits, they're holding their teacups. Occasionally the teacups tinkle on their saucers.

Fish's got to how glad they must be that Fortune's in a private hospital now.

'Oh yes, Mr Pescado,' says Mrs Appollis, 'thank the Lord.' Her teacup tinkles. 'Has Mr Pescado ever been into a government hospital?'

Fish nods. 'Bit rough.'

'You can die in a government hospital. They forget about you, Mr Pescado. They don't care, not so, Pa?'

'They were good to Forty, Ma,' says her husband.

'My friend's mother died in hospital, Mr Pescado. They didn't feed her. They didn't wash her. It's terrible. She got an infection.

In the days when the whites were the government, the hospitals were clean. Not like now.'

'Ma ...'

'It's true, Pa,' she says to her husband, 'blacks can't run a country. Look at what's going on. All the scandals. The young people can't get jobs. This is not our country anymore.'

She stands up, rushes from the room.

'Ma ...' Samson Appollis looks at Fish. 'Sorry, sorry,' he says, getting to his feet. 'I must ... We are very upset, Mr Fish.' he says.

'That's okay,' says Fish, watching Mr Appollis head after his wife. 'Take your time.' He can hear them in the kitchen, Daphne Appollis sniffling, her husband comforting her. He sits drinking his tea, eating biscuits.

Five minutes they're back, apologising, perched again on the edge of the couch.

'Don't worry,' says Fish, 'I understand.' He lets that settle. Then tries. 'You sure you can afford the private hospital? It's expensive. My firm can help you. Tide you over until the court case.'

'There's going to be a court case, Mr Pescado?' says Daphne Appollis, looking from Fish to her husband. 'Pa, I thought ...'

Samson Appollis puts his arm round his wife. 'Alright, Ma. It's fixed up.' He looks at Fish. 'It's alright, Mr Fish, we don't want a court case.'

'Has to be a court case,' says Fish. 'Your boy was injured. Badly injured.' About to mention their son's still in a coma but doesn't. 'That's why I'm on the case, to find out who did it.'

'Pa?'

'What we want's our son to get better,' says Samson Appollis. 'Mr Fish, that's all we want. No court cases. We want our son ...' He rocks his wife. 'It's okay, Ma.'

Fish shifts forward on his chair. 'I know what you're saying. But you see, the law's been broken. Your son was watching an illegal car race. The cops have to investigate what's happened. They've got to find out who did it. Otherwise somebody else could get hurt. Maybe next time somebody dies.' He looks at them, neither of them looking at him. 'Mr Appollis, Mrs Appollis we need your help. The police will need your help.'

Nothing from the couple, Samson and Daphne Appollis sitting there in their unhappiness.

Fish tries other bait. 'What's fixed up?' he says. 'You said something was fixed up.'

'The hospital,' says Samson Appollis. 'We've got what-you-call-it … a policy.'

'Insurance?'

'Ja, insurance.'

'Like a hospital plan?' says Fish.

Samson Appollis nods. 'That's what they call it, ja. We don't have to pay.'

'That's lucky,' says Fish. 'That's why Fortune was moved?'

'Ja.'

'Pa,' says Daphne Appollis.

'Not now, Ma,' he says.

Samson Appollis keeps his eyes down. Daphne Appollis stares at her teacup.

Silence. Fish picking up on the thump of bass vibrating in the walls. Nice neighbours.

Fish thinking what's the scene here? No ways they had a hospital plan. No ways they could afford a hospital plan.

'Ah, listen,' he says, 'I'm just trying to help, okay?'

Now they both look at him. Quickly. Flashing glances like startled mongooses wanting to make a dash for it. The bad part of this job, thinks Fish, pushing where people don't want to go.

'Your son,' he says, 'did you … know about the car racing?'

'Pa,' says Daphne Appollis.

'Forty didn't drive,' says Samson Appollis.

'Pa.'

'Wait, Ma,' he says. 'Let me tell Mr Fish …'

'He's a good boy, Mr Pescado,' says Daphne Appollis. 'A good son.' She's not far off letting the tears flow. 'Tell him, Pa.'

Fish says nothing.

'Mr Fish, we told him, his Ma and me, that the car racing was wrong. Please, we told him, don't go to the races. The police say it is dangerous.'

'But his friends like it,' says Daphne Appollis. 'They like the fast cars, not so, Pa?'

'Ja, Ma,' says Samson Appollis. 'Forty liked them too. He told me.'

'Do you know these friends?' says Fish. 'Their names? Where they live?'

The couple shake their heads.

'The one boy was Willy. Big boy, very polite, not so, Pa? He came inside the house one time. He and his girlfriend. Also very nice. Quiet, a very soft voice, ja, Pa.'

Samson Appollis glances at Fish. His brows furrowed, his eyes scared.

'Willy was the one with a new car,' Daphne Appollis is saying. 'They went to college with him.'

'You got a phone number for Willy?' says Fish. 'Or the girl?'

Blank looks from the couple.

'Fortune's cellphone then? He must've had a cellphone?'

'It wasn't with his things,' says Samson Appollis. 'We asked the police but they don't know. They never found a cellphone.'

'Either of the friends phoned you, Willy or …'

'No, Mr Fish. No one.'

'Okay. Alright.' Fish standing up. He fishes a card from his shirt pocket, sets it against the photograph of Fortune on the coffee table. 'In case you need me.'

'All fine, Mr Fish. We won't need you will we, Ma?'

'No, Pa,' says Daphne Appollis. To Fish she says, 'Does Mr Pescado have a map to get out of Mitchells Plain?' Fish nods yes, she gives him directions to Baden Powell Drive anyhow.

Fish sits in the Perana outside the Appollis's house in Beechcraft Street. The street quiet this time of the morning. The boom-boom music inaudible. A woman sweeping her stoep watching him, two doors down. End of the road a grease monkey peering into the bonnet of his Nissan. In the rear-view mirror, Fish sees a black Golf GTI with tinted windows parked about a hundred metres back. The reflection's bad but he reckons the driver's behind the wheel. Nothing wrong with that. Except Fish thinks there is. He's wondering, should he circle, should he leave it? Decides to leave it. Takes the reg number anyhow.

The last time they meet together is over a weekend at a beach cottage. The Commander, Rictus Grin, the Fisherman, Blondie. And a black dude who drops in for lunch. There's a pic of them all, well, minus the Commander who's taking the photograph: Rictus, the Fisherman, Blondie and the black dude. Happy pic, they're all grinning. Holding bottles of beer, showing their teeth.

On the Sunday morning the Commander suggests a braai on the beach. The Fisherman's already in the tideline, fishing. Rictus is knocking back a hair of the dog.

'May as well,' says Blondie, scratching mosquito bites on his neck, arms. He and the Commander haul a half-drum to the beach, collect a pile of driftwood.

When their collecting's taken them off a way, the Commander says, 'Some advice, after this job, disappear.'

Blondie stops. 'What?' He laughs. 'What's this? What're you saying?'

'I'm saying disappear. Drop out of sight. Leave. Scoot the country. Change your name. Vanish.'

'Huh! Come'n, man, I can't do that.'

'You can. This's genuine. I'm genuine. Genuine advice: get lost. Like you say, it's what Dr Gold told you: run.'

'I can't do that.'

'You can.'

'Look …'

'No, you look. We've been through the heap. We know things. We can point where the bodies are.' He laughs. 'Some cases, literally. Big things are happening, okay. Changing. Things are not going our way. The blacks are coming in.'

Blondie wipes sweat out of his eyes. 'What're you talking

about? What things? Come'n, talk sense. Plain English, what's going on?'

'What I'm saying,' says the Commander, 'is you've got no connections. No wife. No family. No girlfriend even. If you disappear who's gonna know?'

'I can't disappear.'

'Why not? Who's gonna know? Head office? Couple of colleagues. In our work it's not strange for men to disappear. When last were we all together? Eighteen months ago, something like that? In between we stay out of touch. If one of us died we wouldn't know, probably not for months.'

Blondie keeps focussed on the Commander, watching his mouth, his lips tight. The man's not playing games.

'We could've disappeared, been killed, for all you knew. Hear what I'm saying, you can go. No one's gonna know for a long while. Even your surfer mates aren't gonna worry. People'll say they heard you'd gone to Durbs. Someone will say no maybe it was South West. Rumours. Nobody gives a damn. You can vanish. Poof, gone. Outta sight, outta mind.'

Blondie bends to pick up driftwood. They start walking back towards Rictus, dragging branches. Blondie twitches, scratches mozzie bites with his free hand. 'You scheme, hey?'

'I do. Work something out, okay, work something out. Something so that nobody knows where you are. Nobody can contact you. What I'm telling you's serious.' He jabs a finger against the other man's head, once, twice.

Blondie steps away. 'Chrissakes.'

'That kinda serious. Bullet hole serious.'

They get back to Rictus, the Commander's talking about taking a swim to cool down.

'There're sharks here,' says Rictus. 'Zambezis. Ragged-tooths. Hammerheads.'

'You're the expert?'

'I went to the shark place in Durbs. They got pictures of what's out there. Sometimes close in.'

'You're shit-scared.' The Commander lets go of the wood he's carrying, angles towards Rictus. 'You're shit-scared, aren't you?' Turning to Blondie. 'Come'n, let's give him some therapy.'

Rictus grins, pulls a stiletto.

'What're you gonna do with that?' says the Commander. 'Stick your mates?' He lunges. Rictus feints. 'Come on.' He lunges again. Rictus steps backwards, stumbles on the sand. And the Commander's got him, knocked the knife out of his hand. Blondie's into the mix too, grabs Rictus by the feet. He's kicking, struggling, swearing. Laughing too. All of them laughing as they stagger towards the water. All of them collapsing in the waves, horsing around. Rugby tackling. Playing silly buggers. Stripping off T-shirts. Causes the Fisherman to put down his rod, join the melee. The four of them riding one another until they can't stand up. Part laughing so hard, part winded. They lie in the shallows, the sea lapping warm over them. Lie there not talking, like four beached corpses.

Until the Fisherman sits up. 'Okay, boykies, time for beer and boerewors.'

Blondie's moving off into deeper water for a swim. Still hears the Fisherman say to the Commander, 'Why're we here? What's the story?' Blondie stops, he's in waist-deep water. Lies beneath the surface, still as a crocodile.

The Commander's rolled onto his stomach facing the cottage couple of hundred metres away across the sand and dune grass. 'A big one,' he says, rising to his knees, standing. 'Makes everything else chickenfeed.'

'So what's it?' Rictus getting in on the act. 'Chrissakes. We gotta torture it out of you?'

'Major communist,' says the Commander. 'Major terrorist. Major ANC bigshot.' He stops, glances at the men. 'Any guesses?'

They shake their heads, no.

'Another away game. A London job.' He stares at Rictus. 'And nobody goes off-plan, okay?'

Rictus grins, salutes. 'No, sir.'

'I mean it. No twak 'n nonsense this time. We stick to the plan.'

Rictus scoops up water, douses his face. 'It worked out alright.'

'It mightn't have. Off-plan's when the crap happens.'

Rictus looks from the Fisherman to Blondie. 'Two weeks surveillance. Nice little holiday drinking flat beer, I don't think.' He walks backwards out of the shallows, talking to them. Beckons to Blondie. 'You want to hear this?'

Blondie hauls himself in, shaking water from his hair as he jogs out of the waves.

Still the Commander holds off with the name until the fire's going, they're standing round it in their damp clothes with long-tom Castles in their fists. Rictus's chasing his beer with brandy nips. In a plastic bucket covered with Blondie's shirt to keep off the flies, they've got two coils of sausage, about a metre's length of meat, eight chops, two racks of ribs: their lunch.

The Commander smiles at them, keeping up the tension.

'Chrissakes,' says Rictus.

'The head honcho.' The Commander pokes at the fire with the tongs to spread the coals. 'The veritable head honcho. One Mr Oliver Tambo, ANC president.'

Rictus splutters, goes into a coughing fit.

'Piss off,' says the Fisherman. 'There's no chance.'

Rictus wheezes out, 'You've gotta be joking.' His voice thin, raspy.

'No way,' says the Fisherman. 'No way in hell.'

'Suicide,' says Rictus, slides rings up and down his fingers. 'A kamikaze number.' He takes a slug of brandy from the bottle. 'We wouldn't walk out of that.'

The Commander looks at Blondie. 'Want to add your two cents?'

Blondie shrugs. 'Nothing to add.'

'Bloody surfer's got water for brains,' says Rictus.

'Better than brandy.' Blondie matching Rictus grin for grin.

Rictus checks him out through slit eyes. 'Watch it, Blondie.'

'Alright,' says the Commander. 'Anyone interested in the plot 'n plan?'

'Course not,' says the Fisherman. 'We're here for the sausage.'

The Commander says, very funny, goes into CO mode. How the job's got to be done chop-chop. How they fly to London separately. He's flying in directly. Rictus to Paris, then by train. The Fisherman to Amsterdam for two days, then a ferry. Blondie to Frankfurt for a day, then a flight to Gatwick. How Blondie joins him in a Wimbledon house. How the Fisherman hooks up with Rictus in a Notting Hill pad. Bit rough, but rough's a wise idea. Once there, the programme is a surveillance roster one by one until the timetable's filled in. Then bingo bongo.

Which is about when they hear a car.

The Fisherman first, pulling a .38 from his tackle bag. 'We got visitors.'

Rictus's conjured his stiletto. Says to Blondie. 'Want to get our guns, china? You're the fittest.'

Blondie's listening, reckons the car's a Golf, something small, the engine whiny on the dirt track. He glances at the Commander, the Commander's unfazed. He's expecting this.

Rictus and the Fisherman are jabbering, going, hey, hey, hey, get the guns, split up, let's move, Chrissakes, man, this is a problem.

The Commander holds up his hand. 'Relax. The visitor's expected.'

Rictus says, 'Now you tell us. Now he says, don't worry we're expecting a lunch guest. Hell, man, hell.'

The Fisherman spits in the sand, says, 'Ag, man, what a cock-up.'

'What's your case?' says the Commander. 'You got some sort of problem here?'

The Fisherman spits again, backs away.

'Get rid of the hardware,' says the Commander. 'Relax, okay. Just relax.'

They listen to the car stop, the engine dies. A door opens,

slams shut. Blondie counts off the paces. Takes about thirty paces to go round the cottage, appear in the front near where they braaied the previous evening. He counts: one, two, three …

On twenty-two a black man, early thirties, appears at the corner of the cottage: colourful dude in his swimming shorts, bright Hawaiian shirt, flip-flops. Kicks off the flip-flops, starts barefoot over the vlei grass towards the beach. He lifts a hand in greeting. The Commander acknowledges.

As he reaches them the Commander says, 'Right on time.'

45

'Can I disturb you a moment?' Vicki Kahn looks up from her laptop, there's Clifford Manuel standing in the doorway to her office.

'Sure, no problem.' She pushes back. 'Come in.'

'Quick one,' says Manuel, not moving. 'We're off the Appollis case.'

'What?'

Manuel shrugs. 'They're no longer retaining us.'

'Why?'

'No idea. Does it matter? Clients come and go. Not as if we're losing fees on this one.'

'I thought ...' Vicki frowning at the senior partner, Manuel taking a step in, half-closing the door.

'I got a phone call, Vicki, a couple of minutes ago from them, from Mr Appollis.'

'You did? It's my case.'

'I know, I know. Hear me out. I don't know why he phoned me, he did, okay? I was the first person he talked to in the beginning, maybe that's why.'

'Yeah, sure.'

'Can I finish?'

Vicki waves her hand, go ahead.

'He said, and I quote, "We're okay now, Mr Clifford, we don't need any lawyers."'

'Just like that?'

'Just like that.'

'You didn't argue?'

'I suggested it was unwise.'

'Oh, great. That would really have made him worry he was doing the wrong thing.'

'His decision.'

'Suddenly he's got a rich cousin paying the hospital bills?'

'I don't know, Vicki, it doesn't matter who they've got paying the bills. We're no longer involved.' Clifford Manuel giving her the stare-down, glances at his watch. 'Lunch at parliament. Time I was off.' At the door he pauses, looks back at her. 'Tell that investigator fellow he can bill us for the time he's done.'

And Clifford Manuel's gone, except for his aftershave. Vicki fans the air in front of her nose. The man smells like a woman. Then again, these days with some of the colognes you can't tell the difference. 'Enjoy your lunch,' Vicki says aloud.

She stares at the screensaver rabbit hopping about her screen. First the man wants to be kept in the loop, then he drops it like it wasn't worth toffee in the first place. She sighs, keys through to Fish's name in her cellphone. He answers third ring.

'Where're you?' she says.

'Cemetery,' he says. 'Staring at awesome surf.'

'You're not. Tell me you're not.' She can hear Jim Neversink singing about zooming out of life, drifting off the stage. The music tonking at a pace.

'I'm not.' A pause. 'But I'm thinking about it.'

'Well, be my guest,' she says.

'Can't, I'm on a case.'

'Not anymore.'

'No?'

'No. We've been dumped.'

'That right?' Neversink guitars and crashing surf filling the gap Fish leaves. A long gap.

'Fish?'

'Umm. When was this?'

'Now. Five minutes ago.'

More drum thrum rattle and crashing surf. Gone, gone, gone, zooming out of life. Vicki thinking, the boy's on the hook. 'Fish?' she says.

'Okay, what can we do?'

'Nothing. Just let me have the invoice.'

'Someone's got to be paying.'

'I know.'

'Probably the driver.'

'I know.'

'Probably someone important.'

'I worked that out.'

'So?'

'So what?'

'Give me one more hour.'

'I can't.'

'Pretend we didn't have this phone call.'

'I can't.'

'Try, it's not that hard.'

Vicki Kahn realising she's been disconnected. Vicki Kahn smiling as she gets rid of the rabbit on her screen.

Her cellphone rings: Cake Mullins. She's been waiting for this. Dreading it. Cake Mullins not one to let a coincidence pass.

It was a surprise bumping into him with Clifford Manuel. Last she heard from him had been four months back. She could thumb him off. That'd be wise. She doesn't.

'How's the programme?' he asks, not keeping the laugh out of his question.

'Good,' says Vicki. 'What you want, Cake?' Knowing exactly what he wants.

'Grand seeing you the other evening, princess,' he says.

'Likewise, I'm not sure.'

'No need to be nasty.'

'I'm not, Cake.'

'Listen,' he says. 'I heard about your problem with the collectors. That was rough, that was the sort of hurt you shouldn't have gone through.'

'It's over, Cake. I've finished. Not going there again.'

'Sure, I know. I know. I've been there. But I've gotta ask you. Gotta see if you'll say yes or no.'

'I'll say no.'

'You don't know what I'm gonna ask.'

'You're going to tell me you've got a game tonight.'

'I have, you're right. Small game. One thou gets you in.'

'One!'

'That's all. I told you, a small game, no big deal.'

'I'm not playing, Cake. Forget it.'

'It's a friendly, Vicki,' says Cake Mullins. 'What's the pot going to go to? No more'n a couple of thousand.'

'Not the money I'm scared of. I do this one, if I win I'll be back.'

'Always the lucky girl, you were, with the cards. What's wrong with a small windfall?'

Vicki stares at the horizon thinking, one thousand's nothing. Even if you go down that plus another grand, it's nothing. You're on the programme, you're taking counselling, everyone falls off once or twice.

'No,' she tells Cake Mullins.

'Can't take no,' he says. 'I need a good player. I need you.'

'Thanks but no thanks. I'm out of it. Signed up to GA. You know.'

'You're out of it when I say you're out of it.' Cake Mullins getting hard-arsed.

She's back staring at the horizon, her hand trembling, that itch in her fingertips.

'You owe me, Vicki. I'm calling it in.'

As she knew he would one day.

'Be good to go a few hands with you.'

'Hell, Cake.'

'Hell nothing, princess. You get your butt here. Nine sharp.'

'Then we're square?'

'Absolutely.'

'No more comebacks?'

'Nothing. My word on it.'

Vicki thinking, for what that's worth. Thinking, what'd one

more game matter? Low stakes, nothing dangerous. If things went against her she'd quit. Say goodnight and walk out.

'You know where I am? Same place as last time.'

'I'll find it.'

'You better. Not a minute late, okay.'

Vicki thumbs him off, thinks, this isn't good. This has bad writ large. Fish's not going to like this. Fish mustn't know. Have to head him off with a story, which isn't easy when Fish's got his mind in a groove.

46

Mart Velaze phones Clifford Manuel.

'You've pulled your colleague off the case, Mr Manuel?' Mart Velaze in the sitting room of Samson and Daphne Appollis looking through the net curtains at the street. But the man in the Perana's long gone.

'As you requested,' says Clifford Manuel.

'Then why's he been snooping around, troubling the boy's parents?'

'I've no idea who he is, Mr Velaze,' he hears Clifford Manuel say. The background noise excessive. The man clearly out to lunch, saying to him, 'Now I have to go, I'm with guests.'

'Your colleague, Vicki Kahn, has some guy playing the private investigator. Some guy called Mr Fish Pescado.'

'I know nothing of that.'

'You don't believe me? You want to hear it from your former clients? I'm right here with them.'

'I know nothing of this Mr Fish Pescado, this private investigator.'

'Then you should. He's causing upset to people who're worried about their son. He's causing upset to me. I told you the situation. The pro bono is not needed any more.'

'Understood. Whoever he is, Mr Velaze, if he was assisting my colleague then he's no longer on our time.'

'Good. Then call your colleague and get her to stop this nonsense.'

Hears Clifford Manuel say, 'I already have.'

'Smart man.' Mart Velaze getting rid of Clifford Manuel, turning to the Appollis couple, smiling. Likes the way they're gaping at him, frightened rabbits. He holds up a finger. 'One more call.'

Keys through to Cake Mullins. 'That Vicki Kahn,' he says.

'You've contacted her?' Hears Cake Mullins take a slurp of something. Says, 'Cheers, Cake.'

Cake Mullins coming back, 'Mart, don't get above your station, brother.'

Mart Velaze looks at the Appollis couple, neither of them meeting his gaze. Says, 'Just checking.'

'You don't have to. It's not something I appreciate.'

'So did you?' Hears Cake Mullins suck up fluid again. Imagines it's probably a cappuccino, Cake vacuuming the froth.

'I did, yes. As it happens, O lord and master.'

Mart Velaze about to rise to the sarcasm, pauses, closes his eyes for a moment. Says, 'Cake, Cake, I was obeying orders, alright. Jacob's request.'

'He might have phoned me.'

'I'm sure he will. He's got a lot on his plate.'

'Good, I'm pleased to hear that. Pleased he enjoyed his safari.'

Mart Velaze is about to ring off, says, 'That a cappuccino you're drinking?'

Hears Cake Mullins snort. 'Only a spook'd wanna know that.'

Mart Velaze puts his phone away, sits down opposite the Appollis couple. 'Please,' he says. 'Look at me.' They do. Not rabbits now, more like pigeons perching close together on a gutter, the two of them sitting on the edge of the couch. 'Now, what did Mr Fish want?'

47

Fish sighs, gives Cemetery a last scan: these neat sets stacking up, rolling in free of charge. Dozen dudes out there pulling aerials, cut-backs, slashes, lip-smacks, tearing up the surf like what else was there to do? Answer: nothing. Except. Except find out who's paying Fortune Appollis's medical bills. Except it doesn't matter anymore. Except to Fish it does. Professional pride. More specifically, valuable information. As valuable as foreign currency. Also means he feels legit about neglecting his mother's job.

His phone rings: Vicki. He thumbs her on, is about to get all mellow with her but she's straight in: 'Drop it, Fish. Please, just drop it.'

'I'm sorry.'

'Clifford's been on at me again to get you off. Not a pleasant Mr Clifford Manuel either.'

'What'd Cliffie say?'

'Precisely?'

'Precisely'll do.'

'Get that lowlife to crawl back under his rock. Quote, unquote.'

'Lowlife?'

'His word.'

'Very judgmental.'

'Fish, look, please.' Fish hearing something different in Vicki's voice, worry, anxiety. 'Just walk away. Not even the extra time we agreed on. You'll do that for me?'

'Okay, cool,' says Fish. 'It's not a big deal. Just fascinating everybody's getting so worked up.'

'I know, I know. It raises lots of questions. But I've got a job, a career. So please.'

'Done, Vics, done,' says Fish, frowning, wondering what's behind it, getting to Vicki.

'I'm sorry. I'm sorry. I've got to go.'

Fish thumbs her off, stares at his phone as if there's an answer for Vicki's weird call going to flash on the screen. He fires up the Perana, thinking, what the hell, the surf can wait.

Half an hour later he's standing at the hospital's reception desk with a bunch of flowers, mostly daisies.

'For you,' he says to the woman behind the desk. Heavily made-up young thing with purple lipstick.

She laughs. 'For me?'

'My friend's in ICU,' Fish says. 'In a coma. He can't appreciate them, but you can.'

'Really?'

'Really,' says Fish. 'He'd want me to do it.'

'You could leave them up there. In the ward.'

'They look better here.'

She smiles, white teeth biting brilliant against her lower lip. A blush darkening on her cheeks. Smooth olive cheeks.

Fish hesitates. Says, 'Could you just check they haven't moved him?' Gives Fortune's name, gets the floor and ward numbers in return.

'Enjoy the flowers.'

The receptionist giggles.

Upstairs, Fish doesn't skip a beat, heads straight down the corridor past the nurse's station to the ward. No one inside but Fortune Appollis wired to monitors, tubed to bags. His leg's in a plaster cast, thigh to ankle, his toes blue. His face's not too pretty: bruises, swellings, white plaster strips everywhere. A turban of bandages round his head.

Attached to the foot of the bed's a plastic holder, inside's a file. Fish flips through the file to the admin sheet, lifts this out. The rest goes back in the holder. He folds the page into his jacket pocket.

At the nurse's station, Fish stops to ask what time is visiting hour. He's told only at four. The nurse glancing up from her paperwork, pointing at the notice across the corridor.

'Didn't see it,' says Fish. 'Sorry.' Then: 'How's young Fortune?'

The nurse stops writing. 'Are you from the family?'

'One of his lecturers at the college.'

She taps her pen on the desk. 'He is badly injured.'

'He's going to make it though?'

The nurse puts her hands together. 'We are praying.'

Fish grimaces. 'That'll be a help.'

The nurse goes back to her paperwork, Fish heads down the corridor towards the staircase.

At the ground floor reception desk he pauses, says to the giggler, 'Nice arrangement.' The flowers now in a vase. 'Much better they're here. From what they tell me upstairs my young friend's going to be pushing them up soon.'

The receptionist claps a hand over her mouth, can't help an explosion of laughter.

Fish winks. 'Got to laugh, haven't we?'

In his car he unfolds the admin sheet: the box marked private patient is ticked. The billing address is Beechcraft Street, Mitchell's Plain.

No joy. Nothing he doesn't know already.

Fish folds the page, slips it back into his jacket pocket. He's about to fire the ignition, he notices a black GTI with tinted windows in the row behind him, two cars down.

Nice coincidence.

He gets out, checks the number plates. Same car. Thinks, Daro can help here. Daro's got access to the car licensing system.

Fish has that feeling he's being watched, ignores it. Dude's hardly going to be standing in plain view. On the way back to his car, he scopes the parking lot. Nonchalant, only taking in what he'd be looking at anyhow. Someone watching would be behind the hospital's entrance doors with their reflective glass, you could stand there without being seen. Fish gets into the Perana, heads out with a low reverb in the tail pipes.

48

Cake Mullins decides doesn't matter how much Jacob Mkezi has on his plate, he connected him to Tol Visagie. Straight business deal. Straight business commission. Finder's fee. Whatever you want to call it. They should talk money.

Might be midday but Cake's in his dressing gown. Standing in his dressing gown at an upstairs window, Cake looks over the vineyard that abuts his property. Shiraz grapes. The wine that welcomes you like a woman with her legs wide open. Cake has this image of a naked woman sitting on a beach, leaning against a rock, one leg crooked, the other spread. Her hair's wet, her arms are up to hold you, her boobs raised, nipples puckered, some curve to her belly, shaved crotch, the vertical smile. Cake Mullins gets a half-rise thinking about it.

Shakes his head to clear the image. Time he phoned Midnight Girls again, ordered a Shiraz.

Instead Cake phones Jacob Mkezi. 'How'd it work out?' he wants to know.

Listens to Jacob Mkezi saying, 'Interesting, Cake. Interesting, my friend.'

'It worked out then?' Cake wandering into his bathroom, checking himself out in the full-length mirror.

'What you mean is what's in it for you? Cake Mullins on his game.'

Cake smiling at himself. 'Something like that.'

'No problem,' says Jacob Mkezi. 'How about one per cent?'

Cake keeping up the smile. 'What're we talking, actual figures?'

Again Jacob Mkezi laughing. 'Cake on the bake.'

'Ha, ha.'

'Couple of hundred grand probably.'

'Rands, dollars?'

'Dollars.'

'Two per cent.'

'One point five. That's it.'

Cake Mullins happy enough with the outcome but not finished yet. 'You could've phoned me yourself about getting Vicki Kahn into a card game. You could've asked me.'

'I could've,' says Jacob Mkezi. 'I asked Mart to handle it. He tell you about Lord?'

'What about Lord?' Cake Mullins letting the dressing gown fall open: the way he does it for the Midnight Girls, giving half an ear to the story of Lord's fuck-up. His father's words, Lord's fuck-up.

Lord always was a wanker as far as Cake Mullins is concerned.

Cake admiring himself in the mirror: the chest hair, the good-life stomach, the hairy thighs, the cock and balls.

'Nasty one,' he says to Jacob Mkezi. 'See you tonight.'

49

Fish takes the drive down Main Road to Daro's boutique car lot slowly, checking the rear-view mirror for a black GTI. Wondering why he should even be bothered to find out the owner. You're off the case, dude, he tells himself. Drop it. Go surfing.

But there's the GTI, way back, five cars behind him. Not getting any closer, just hanging there.

Problemo: let him know he's spotted, or cruise on like who gives a toss?

Options: slip left down a side road, stop in the park 'n ride at Heathfield station. Wait till the cracker passes then swing in behind him. See how he fancies it.

But Fish's not in the mood for high jinks. Fish'd rather stop in at Daro's, drink some of his filter coffee while Daro pops the CA number into the system.

Just for the hell of it.

Just to know.

Which is what Fish does. Listens to Jim, takes a sedate speed-limit shuffle through the traffic lights to Daro's executive wheels. Because Fish plans to hit the beach when this's done.

Despite that, he keeps an eye on the black spot in his rear-view. Out of professional interest. Because the guy's good. The guy knows how to do this. What puzzles Fish is why's he bothering?

He phones Vicki.

'Sorry,' she says, 'I'm in a meeting. Hang on.'

He hangs on. Hears her making excuses, a door clicking shut. Then, a bit hissy: 'What's it?'

'What d'you mean what's it?'

'I'm in a meeting, with clients, please.'

'Big deal. I've got a black VW GTI, tinted windows, hanging onto my every move.'

'Following you?'

'Rocked up first at the Appollis's. Then at the hospital. Now he's breathing my exhaust.'

'I told you to let it go. I told you, Fish. The hospital was a bad idea. We were off the case. Specific instructions. Can't you listen to anything I tell you?'

'It was my own scene.'

'Ah, Fish. Come'n.'

'Anyhow, I didn't get anything at the hospital. Not anything we didn't know already.'

'You're sure? Sure it's the same guy?'

'Same registration.'

'He knows you've seen him?'

'I'd say so. He's a pro.'

'Go surfing, Fish. Show him you're off it.'

'That's your advice?'

'No one's paying you. Leave it. That's what I asked hours ago.'

Fish lets this hang a while until Vicki says, 'I've got to get back.'

'Cool,' he says. 'See you later. What, six, six thirty?'

Hears her hesitation. 'Can't,' she says. 'I've got this work thing that's come up.'

'You didn't have this morning.'

'No.'

'So afterwards?'

'It's going to be late. Dinner with clients. I'll be tired, Fish, you're a long drive from the city that time of night.'

'You want a lift, I'll fetch you.' Fish thinking as he says it, back off, you're getting too intense.

'You're sweet,' she says. 'But no. I'll call you tomorrow.'

Before he can say bye, the connection's cut.

He flips the phone onto the passenger seat. You don't want full-on commitment. You want your pad. She's got her apartment. Nice situation, couldn't be better.

So what's the big deal?

Her tone's the big deal. It's a tone he's heard before. When they first got it together and she was gambling. That kind of defensive note in her voice. Like, leave me, okay, there's a part of my life that's mine.

The part she was ashamed of.

Nah, thinks Fish. Can't be. She wouldn't. She's on the programme, she's been for, is going for, counselling. Most Monday nights she does Gamblers Anonymous. Eight, nine months she hasn't placed a bet. Hasn't sat down to a game of poker.

At least that's what she's told him.

Now he's not so sure.

Now he's recalling those early heart-to-hearts, a year back, longer even. The line he took with her: please, please, please, Vicki, get out of the gambling. Tears from her. How it made him hurt. Once, in the early weeks, he got so emotional about her gambling he headed up the west coast for three days to surf. Left her to face the debts. He came back, she was black and blue. Scared. Really scared. She wouldn't tell him who'd done it, but she hit Gamblers Anonymous right afterwards. Got a loan to cover the thirty grand she was down, told Fish, 'That's the end. No more.'

He whacks the steering wheel, redials. Call goes straight to voicemail.

'Bloody women,' Fish yells, ramping onto Daro's forecourt faster than's wise, skidding on the zooty tiles. Glimpses Daro's face at the office window, alarmed.

He dials again. Voicemail. This time he's come off the boil, leaves the message, 'Phone me, okay? Just phone me.' He cuts the connection, stares up at Daro standing at his car door.

'Skilful,' says Daro. 'To the centimetre.'

Fish grimaces. 'Sorry, hey' – switches off the engine.

'Nothing a hard scrub won't clean off.' Daro turns back to his office. 'Coffee?'

'Good idea,' says Fish.

Daro pours two mugs, gives one to Fish, handle outwards.

'I've come for a favour,' Fish says.

'No?' says Daro, drawing it out, sarcastic.

Fish blows at the steam, looks at him over his mug. Daro's not the sarky type.

'You having a bad day?'

'Two people across the floor this morning. One just looking, the other I don't know what his case was. Maybe he'll be back, maybe he won't. Gut feel, he won't. I need to sell another car.'

'One sale last week's not bad.'

'Not good either.'

The two men focus on their coffee. Fish says, 'My job got canned. Lasted all of three hours.' He goes into a recap. When he gets onto Fortune Appollis's change of fortune, Daro stops him.

'The kids drag racing now,' says Daro, 'use Subarus. Jettas. I'm talking the latest models, half a million bucks worth, they smack in oversized pistons, V66 cam shafts, interceptor carburettor kits, wind these things up to three hundred kays on the R303.'

'They do?' says Fish.

'They're out there one behind the other, that's the thrill, maybe a metre, maybe even less between them. You're travelling at that speed the front guy touches the brakes, you're both history. Bang, flip, mangle. I saw one of those ...' Daro drank off a mouthful, swallowed. 'The front car burnt out in a fireball. The car behind flew, I mean, flew, ended up over the island on the other side of the road. Even then it doesn't stop. Heavens, man, on and on. The metal sparking, scraping for a hundred, two hundred metres, I don't know. The driver disappeared. Poof. Vaporised. Not a trace of him left. Nothing. Might have been a ghost driving that car.'

'Hectic,' says Fish.

'I heard it was a seventeen-year-old kid behind the wheel. His daddy was, is, a major businessman couldn't see any reason not to fork out five hundred grand for his little boy. Even though his little boy was too young to have a licence.'

'That right?' says Fish.

'It's happening two, three times a week on the Flats. And these guys come from money. The new elite. Which is why ...'

'My Appollis gets the private upgrade. Why his mommy and daddy drop the case. Yeah, I got that. Only one thing I want to know, for the hell of it, who owns this car?' Fish smoothes out a piece of paper with a CA registration on it. 'Black VW GTI with tinted windows.'

'Shouldn't be a problem,' says Daro. He taps into the system on his laptop, comes up with a try again message. 'Licensing system's down right now,' he tells Fish, 'I can find out tomorrow.'

'No rush,' says Fish. 'I'm going surfing.' He finishes the coffee in a swallow, says, 'You still want me to speak to my friend? About the drugs talk?'

'Why not,' says Daro. 'No harm in it.'

'Great.' Fish jiggles his keys. He's tossing up: does he, does he not tell Daro about Seven's hit list nonsense? Goes with: 'D'you carry a gun?'

Daro gives him a quick headshake, a frown, a jokey: 'What? Where's that come from?'

'Nowhere.' Fish backtracking. 'Just you being on the forum, maybe it's a good idea.'

Daro keeps staring at him, nods. 'I've thought about it. But why d'you say that?'

Fish shrugs. 'No particular reason. Just guns can be useful.'

Outside it's warm in the sun, the two men feeling it on their shoulders, gazing at the mountains cut out against the sky.

'Close up,' Fish says. 'A surf's what you need.'

Daro snorts. 'It's half past three.'

'There you go,' says Fish, 'almost a whole day wasted. We shoulda been at the beach.'

Daro watches Fish drive off.

'Guns can be useful.'

Puzzles why Fish said that now. Decides it's Fish's way of saying be careful on the forum. Thing is that's the least of it.

Daro's got the piece of paper with the registration number Fish gave him in his hand. He doesn't need the system to know who owns the car.

Mart Velaze.

Understandable why Mart Velaze would need a quieter car if what Mart Velaze does is stake out people.

Mart Velaze and his casually dropped reference to Ray Adler. Dries out Daro's mouth.

He goes back online, keys passwords through to the traffic department's lists. Gets an address for Mart Velaze in Milnerton. It's a block of flats on Marine Drive.

Next he Googles Adler Solutions. No surprise there's no website. No surprise it's not in the phone book.

Daro's not sure how to handle this one.

THE ICING UNIT, MAY 1995

The Fisherman's name is Dommiss Verberg. When Dom gets the bullet, he's fishing off the concrete breakwater – the dolosse – outside Port Elizabeth one bright October morning. The sea's flat, slipping, gurgling among the dolos concrete blocks piled to preserve the beach from washaways. Off in the distance the office blocks of the city stacked in the haze. Only souls nearby two men fishing down the break to his right. Dom sits on a dolos with his feet dangling over the edge. The water's a murky soup, there might be cob passing through, even elf, but he's not had a bite. Doesn't matter. Dom is content to sit there, smoking, eating the cold meat sandwiches his wife made. The fishing's an excuse, gets him out of the house on his off days.

He reels in. The hook is bare. Something's been nibbling the mud prawns. Something not inclined to snatch the bait in a passing gulp.

Dom sighs. Fresh fish once a week would be nice. He hasn't caught a fish in two weeks. His wife jokes that he must be having an affair. It's a joke with teeth because once he had a scene with her sister until he got caught waving his bum in the air. Tears, tears, tears. Weeks of it. He had to make up with a seven-day break at Sun City. And give his wife a thousand to play the one-arm bandits. Which pulled her in eight grand on a straight-across four fruit. Ching. Ching. Did she give him five cents? Not a chance.

'You see,' she said. 'God's watching.'

Dom wipes sandwich crumbs off his moustache, packs up, hurls the tin of mud prawns into the soup. Be a couple of days before he can get back, and one thing cob know it's old bait. Might even be the Greek'd sold him stale bait this morning.

Bloody Nico, and his 'Fish don't know the difference, my friend. Fish eat anything dead. Why you think there's only skeletons under the sea?'

Dom carefully hops across the dolosse, then the railway lines back to the car park.

In the car park two fishermen lean against their bakkie, drinking coffee from a flask, two nice-sized cob on the van's tailboard. Dom remembers they were fishing about a hundred metres down.

'I didn't get a bite,' he says to the men.

'You wanna buy one?' asks the man holding the flask. 'Twenny rand.'

Dom considers this. Twenty rand's a high price for a five-kilo fish. Bloody bushies always trying it on. Other hand he could say he caught it. Give his wife a thrill.

'Alright,' he says, pulling a ten-rand note from his pocket. He jiggles his small change. Says, 'Not used to the five rand yet' – picks out one from the coins in his palm. 'Fifteen rand alright?'

The men look at the remaining coins, mostly coppers.

'What about that?'

Cheeky. Dom squints at them. His cop squint from the old days that he'd follow up with a fist to the face, a nose cruncher. The thing with coloureds, always they're cheeky.

The fishermen shift, unhappy. Dom keeps up the hard eyes, swivelling his gaze from one to the other. He were a cop he'd start hassling these two gents. He holds out the money. 'Fair deal.'

The men shrug. The one takes the note and the coin. 'Ja, okay.'

'Any one?'

'Any one.'

Dom hefts the heavier one by the tail. 'Thanks, hey.'

He walks to his car, flops the fish into the boot onto sheets of newspaper he's got there in anticipation, slams shut the lid. Pleased with the deal. Smiles to himself that they could tell he was a cop. Was once a cop. An attitude you can trade on.

He clips the fishing rod into the brackets on his roof rack, aware of the men watching him. Pretending not to watch him.

Stuff them. Fifteen rand was a good price. More'n they'd have got on a street corner.

Inside the car, he smacks out a cigarette, smelling fish on his fingers. Comforting. He lights up, blows smoke against the windscreen. Which is when he sees the bullet taped there on the outside. A small round.

Fuck! He stares at it. Sucks on the cigarette, exhales. Twists in his seat to look over at the men. They're not watching him anymore. He gets out, shouts, 'Hey, you see anyone round my car earlier?'

The one shakes his head. The other says no.

Dom tears the tape off the windscreen, pulls the cartridge free: a .22 with a cross-hatched nose.

Dom's first thought: it's Ray playing silly buggers. He hasn't heard from Ray in four years after the Tambo job was called off, it has to be Ray. The bullet was Ray's thing from the beginning: send a bullet to the victim in advance. Dom's second thought, it's not bloody funny.

He hears doors slam, the fishermen's bakkie harrah-harrah into life. With a skittering of gravel they pull out, leaving Dom alone.

He waits, expecting Ray Adler to appear from behind a dolos. He even calls out, 'Ray, come on, man, stop the nonsense.'

Nothing. Except seagull squawk, distant motorway noise.

Dom is retired. Has been retired for three years. Well, took a package because he could see the way of things and that way didn't look like he would have a job in the new country. Worse. There might be witch hunts. Tricky questions. Better to duck out, keep a low profile. Which Dom did. Cut his cop mates, kept away from old drinking holes. Went fishing. Found work in a paint shop three days a week and Saturday mornings, selling gloss to homeowners. The paint shop in a small centre in an outlying suburb. Not much chance of bumping into his past.

A sweet enough life. Until now.

Dom worries about the bullet for two days. Keeps it with him in his trouser pocket. Doesn't tell his wife. Doesn't tell anyone. Thing is, Dom has no one to tell. The cops he cut were his friends. Beer and braai friends. He dropped them, he dropped his social life. Men who'd known him all his working days. Proper gabbas. Good mates. Some of them tried to keep it up but Dom didn't respond. Truth? Dom was nipping scared.

He's nipping scared now. Rubs the bullet between his fingers trying to figure out what to do.

He's got one, maybe two cops in the service he could phone. At a push. The one being a former brother-in-law. The brother-in-law whose wife he'd screwed. So maybe only one contact who might have a number for Ray Adler. Or Pat Foreman, with his rictus grin. Though he'd heard Foreman was a drunk. Out of it on an hour-to-hour, day-to-day basis. Completely stuffed.

From a public phone near the paint shop where he works, Dom puts through a call to his contact, Flip.

'Yusses, Dom, you got a cheek, hey,' says Flip.

'Please, man, Flip,' says Dom.

Flip goes off on a diatribe about Dom dropping his mates, not caring about years and years of friendship. Not coming to funerals. Just disappearing. 'As if we were nothing.'

'Don't be like that, Flip,' says Dom. 'You know I had reasons.'

'Reasons? We all had bloody reasons. We were all in the kak after the elections. Why were your reasons any worse?'

'Forget it,' says Dom. 'Forget it. I just asked if you had his number.'

'Listen, my friend. You've heard about this TRC thing. Truth and Reconciliation. A commission, hey. That's gonna be major kak. What're you gonna do about that?'

'Nothing.'

'You tell the truth and they believe you, you get amnesty. Some of the manne think that's the way to go.'

'Not for me.'

'You gonna blab, Dom?'

'I said no.'

'The okes that're gonna try for amnesty, they're leaving. Leaving the force. Rats 'n sinking ships. They're gonna drop us. Name names. Nice, hey? You wanna know what it's like round here these days. Bloody kak. Everybody's on their nerves.'

Dom says nothing.

'Yusses, Dom, you've got a cheek.'

'This's urgent, okay.' Dom keeps his voice low, his lips touching the phone's mouthpiece. There's a woman behind him, staring at him.

'Will you be much longer?' she says.

'One minute, lady,' says Dom. To Flip, 'Please, Flip, I wouldn't ask otherwise. It's an emergency.'

'Alright, alright,' says Flip. 'The last number I've got he was in the UK. But he could be in Oz. I heard that he went there. Maybe.' He gives Dom a London number.

'What about Foreman? Pat Foreman?'

'How much more, hey? You want a roll call?'

'Come'n, Flip. Please, man.'

He hears Flip sigh. 'Foreman's an alkie. Forget about him.'

'Strues?'

'Strues bob. Bag wine and meths. Does blue train.'

'Shit.'

'Ja. Very shit.' And Flip laughs. 'Who wants to be a cop, hey? Not you.' Again he laughs.

'Thanks,' says Dom. 'Thanks, Flip.'

'Easy to say.'

'I mean it.'

'So buy me a beer.'

Dom hears this but hangs up. Flip Nel's a good man, but Flip can go on, moan, moan, moan. He glances at the number he's written down, glances at the woman, decides, bugger it, this's an emergency, she can wait.

'Are you finished yet?'

'One more,' says Dom.

'Can you hurry up, please?'

Dom ignores her, presses the numbers. He's got a pocketful of coins. When the phone's answered he feeds the slot, says. 'I'm looking for Ray Adler.'

'Ray Adler?'

'That's right.'

'No one here by that name, mate.'

'Wait,' says Dom, but the line's cut.

'Can you let me phone now?' says the woman.

Dom doesn't go fishing for two weeks. Mopes about the house getting on his wife's nerves.

'For heaven's sake, Dom, what's with you?'

'Nothing, girlie,' he says, sitting in the lounge watching repeats on television ten o'clock in the morning. Having just got out of bed. And Dom usually a seven o'clock up and raring to go sort of man.

'You don't go fishing anymore. Four days you've skipped work. What're you sick?'

'I'm okay, okay?'

'You're not, boykie. You're a bloody pain sitting here all the time.' She picks up his empty coffee mug. 'I'm going to phone the doctor, you're depressed or something.'

'Ag, girlie.'

'No really, Dom. This's worrying, you sitting here day after day. Look at you. All you wear's that old tracksuit like a poor white. Twenty years of marriage you've never done this. You're forty-five, Dom. Not seventy-five.'

She hauls him off to the doctor, the doctor says there's nothing physically wrong but maybe, yes, he's depressed.

'You anxious about something, Dommiss?' the doctor asks.

Dom's wife's in the consulting room and she comes in with how he spends all day in the chair watching television. Doesn't go fishing. Doesn't go to work. Well, called in sick for the last four days. Doesn't dress properly. Doesn't talk to her. Doesn't have any friends.

The doctor prescribes antidepressants, a tonic, tells Dom to go fishing.

'That's what I tell him,' says Dom's wife. 'Only before you didn't have to tell him that. Before you couldn't stop him. Any excuse he's away like a stray. Before I had to beg him, Dom we got family for a braai, can you get back for that please? To start the fire early so we don't have to eat at midnight.'

All the ride home in the car she's at him to go fishing. Beautiful day like it is, no wind for a change, he should go down to Cape Recife. Buy a tin of mud prawns from the Greek. Go cast a line. She'll make him sarmies, a flask of Nescafe. Maybe take a couple of beers. He can sit there, get some fresh air and sun. Even, if he wants to, on the way home stop in at the old bar for a beer with his mates. Because why'd he drop them? Sometimes the wives phone, say they used to enjoy the fish braais on the weekends. They're not the only ones, she misses it too. So what's your problem, Dom? What's going on?

'Alright,' Dom says. 'Alright, okay, alright.' Anything to get her off his back.

They get home, he clips his fishing rod to the roof rack, checks there're enough hooks and sinkers and line and swivels and bait cotton in his tackle bag, and his knife's in the side pocket.

'Good,' says his wife. 'It'll do you good to get out for a bit.'

He changes into jeans and a T-shirt, sticks his .38 into his belt.

His wife kisses him on the way out. 'Enjoy it, Dom. Catch us a fish.'

'Ja, girlie,' he says.

He doesn't go to Cape Recife, he goes to the dolosse. There's a rusty Corolla in the parking area, the only vehicle. Dom slings his tackle bag over his shoulder, heads for the breakwater to find himself a spot. He's not fully into this, the bullet's nagging at him as it has been all this while. His wife doesn't know but he's been sitting with the .38 under the cushion of the lounge chair every day. Waiting for them, him, whoever it is, to break in. Each day that passes he reckons the heat's going off but you can't be sure. They could be playing him. On the plus side there've been no more little presents.

Dom stands on the dolosse, surveys the scene. There a black guy fishing the Bluewater end, otherwise nobody. The guy doesn't even notice him. Dom skips along about fifty metres in the city direction before he baits up.

This time the Greek's sold him fresh mud prawns that're squirming and clicking in the tin. He threads one onto the hook, binds it fast with cotton. Stands, holds the rod in his left hand over his shoulder, balancing, feeling the weight of the sinker. The sea's got some life today, a chop that cracks among the dolosse, spitting up spray. Its colour's blue, that dark blue it goes in the afternoon. Good elf water. Dom casts a long arc. The line plays out, slackens. He reels in one, two turns, tests the line between his thumb and forefinger.

For a while he stands there, the butt of the rod resting on his belt. A Thursday afternoon, peaceful, the city at work. What's to worry about? But still Dom's edgy, not quite the laid-back happy fisherman. There's that bullet in his pocket with the cross-hatched knob, the way they used to cross-hatch the lead before a job.

One o'clock the Friday morning, more than ten hours after Dom-miss Verburg went fishing, he's not home. His wife's going spare, hysterical. She reported him missing, the cops've said they don't do missing until twenty-four hours have passed, minimum. She called them bastards, hung up in tears. Her daughter's with her but that's small consolation when she's convinced her husband's dead. Convinced he's killed himself. Because his gun's missing.

'He always takes the gun, Ma,' says her daughter. 'Pa doesn't go around without it.'

'You don't understand,' says her mother. 'He's depressed. That's what the doctor said. He's supposed to take tablets.'

First light she and her daughter drive to the fishing spots. First down at Cape Recife, the Willows, then Skoenmakerskop, finally the dolosse. His car's not there, there's no one there. The wind's come up. The last place anyone wants to be is on the dolosse in a full-frontal forty-kilometre-an-hour wind.

They go home.

Round ten o'clock, the phone rings: it's the police. They were told of this car on fire in New Brighton township. They sent a van. The car was burnt out, luckily they could still read the registration. They ran a check, seems the car belongs to a Dommiss Verburg. 'You know this man? That your husband, lady?'

No, the cop woman tells them, no sign of Mr Verburg. She'll put out the alert.

Hijacking is the word nobody uses.

Early in the afternoon, the cops come round. They've found her husband at the dolosse. He's passed. Seems he shot himself in the head.

Two months later, the autopsy hearing into the death of Dommiss Verburg by a gunshot wound to the right temple, hands down a verdict of suicide. This consequent upon the party holding a recently fired .38 in his right hand, said gun owned by said party. Couple of days drag by then Dom's friend Flip Nel calls on Dom's wife to pay his respects.

'Sorry for your loss, Mrs V,' he says to her.

'Come in, Flip,' she says. 'It's been a long time, my word.'

She makes two instant coffees, finds a box of Romany Creams in the cupboard. They sit down in the lounge, Flip plopping into Dom's favourite chair.

Flip comes straight out with it because that's Flip's way.

'The autopsy report,' he says, 'it's kak.'

Mrs V frowns. Surprised. 'I didn't see it,' she says. 'Didn't want to. Why d'you say that?'

'Cos I don't think Dom would kill himself.'

'Dom wasn't my Dom, hey, Flip. For a long time Dom wasn't my Dom.'

They crunch into Romany Creams.

'The thing is,' says Flip, 'I haven't the faintest what was

Dom's problem after he left the force but he stopped seeing the okes. Turned his back on all of us. I don't know why. Maybe he was scared.'

'Dom wasn't scared of nobody. You know, Dom.'

'Not in the old days. But with the change, there's a lotta okes poeping themselves. Worried about what's gonna happen. Some of them are hiding like Dom was.'

'Dom wasn't hiding.'

'He stayed away from us.'

'I know, Flip, I used to tell him, phone your friends, go'n have a drink like before. But no, he just goes fishing. The only time he sees other people is at the paint shop.'

'That's what I mean, Dom wasn't like that before.'

'Never.' She gets teary-eyed, sniffs. 'The day he died, we went to the doctor. I said to him, Dom, you've got to see the doctor. He wasn't going out. Was phoning in sick at the shop. For about two weeks every day he just sat there, in that chair' – pointing at Flip – 'watching TV.'

Flip takes a swallow of coffee. 'He phoned me, you know.'

'He phoned you?'

'Ja, about a week before he died. Wanted the number of one of the okes he worked with, Ray Adler. I gave him the number but that's the last I heard.'

'He didn't say anything to me.'

Flip looks at her. 'He sounded worried.'

'He didn't say anything.' She raises her eyes to meet his. 'What're you saying, Flip?'

Flip shakes his head.

She sighs. 'You can tell me, Flip. Nothing can make it worse.'

He says, 'Ray was into some heavy stuff in the old days.'

'Like what?'

'Security branch ops.'

She nods. 'Ja. Ja.' Puts down her mug on a coffee table piled with magazines. 'So what're you telling me, Flip? It wasn't sui-cide? It was murder? Yusses, man, you think I haven't thought about that? Over and over. Someone shot him. Dumped his car in the township.'

'Report says Dom was shot in the right temple,' says Flip.

She looks at him. 'What're you saying?'

'Dom was left-handed.'

The shudders start in her shoulders, her face distorting. 'I don't want to think about it. I don't want to think about it.'

50

The driveway gate is open. Fish never leaves the gate open. It's a hassle getting out to open it when you're busting for a pee after a long night's stake-out, or close it when you're in a hurry to catch the surf but Fish does, without fail, shut it. Now the gate's unlatched.

The reason Fish keeps the gate closed is dogs. Dogs get in, they foul up the place wherever there's any grass. In the front there're these scratchy patches of buffalo grass holding down the sand. Not what you'd call anywhere near a lawn, but it's got that at-the-beach feel which Fish likes.

What he hates is coming out in the morning, finding piles of gut-processed special canine formula, light brown and mucousy, on his grass. You slide a spade underneath those mounds, they stick. Then you've got to hose down the spade. Only way to really pick up this crap is wrap a plastic bag over your hand, do it manually. Then you're dealing with turd feel, which makes Fish gag.

An option is to wait until they dry out. Only problem then is the sausages break into black pellets, scatter every which way. Cleaning up's a major mission because there're always some you miss.

Also, once a dog's found a spot it's back every day. Only option then, Fish's heard, is spraying Jeyes drain cleaner about the place until it smells like a municipal boghouse. Better not to get to that position.

So Fish keeps the gates closed, no matter the hassle factor.

When they're open it means bergies, strollers, Muizenberg flotsam have come visiting. Gets Fish's ire big-time. But what's to be done about it? You can reason till you're bloody blue in the face, the dude comes back, 'Mr Gentleman, don't be so fierce. Yous'll strike a coronary.' Not a heart attack, a coronary for heaven's sake.

But Fish's got this soft spot for bergies and strollers. They want a place to spend the day, they can sit on his back stoep. One or two of them, that's all, that's the rule. Come night there's the shelter at Kalk Bay, he doesn't want them hanging out on his stoep. Another rule. Charity goes so far then it gets messy.

Fish parps the hooter, expecting some itinerant to come down, open the gates properly. No one shambles round.

Hoots again.

Still no one.

He gets out, slots the gates back, drives up to the garage. His inherited Isuzu's in the yard, invisible from the street. Only when he's stopped, he notices the bakkie's standing lopsided, both tyres on the near side flat.

Then the chunks of surfboard scattered about. And glass. The Isuzu's windscreen shattered, the rear window smashed, same with the wing mirrors.

But it's not the glass that gets him, or the slashed tyres, it's the destroyed surfboard. Broken in four. Hurled about the place. His beloved Vudu Hybrid. That board wasn't just a board, it was a way of life. Worse, his other board, the Beach Break with the Vudu shapers, is in for repairs.

Fucking Seven.

The bastard.

The last thing Fish thought he'd do.

He looks over at the boat, the *Maryjane*: it seems okay. No holes. They'd holed that he'd've been pissed off. Fish thinking to sell the boat.

Unlocks the Isuzu, reaches under the seat for the Z88. Doesn't seem the house has been broken into, but you can't tell. The buggers could be inside. He walks slowly to the back door easing up when there's no sign they got in.

Turns then to stare at the devastation, imagining Seven and

his toothless sidekick going at the bakkie with hammers. Stomping on his surfboard till it snapped. Plunging an Okapi knife into the Isuzu's tyres.

What fun!

A rage coming up in Fish that the lowlife scumbag shitheads could do this. Waltz over here like it was part of a fairground, take a whammo at a couple of target stalls. The lowlife scumbag shitheads not giving a fuck for what they were starting.

Fish thinking, you ratcheted this up, you were talking grievous bodily harm. Which he wasn't averse to. A shithead like Seven.

'Hey, boet,' says a voice. There's a large guy peering over the back wall, got a .45 in his hand. A huge thing. All Fish can see of him is his head and shoulders, an arm like a ham ending in the revolver. 'It was two coloureds. Gangster types. Hard thin okes with sucked-in faces. That's all the ID I got. 'Cept they were wearing black tracksuits, takkies. The fancy Nike ones. They saw my Dirty Harry here they were gone.'

The man wobbles, adjusts his balance.

'I heard them when they smashed the glass. They were planning on taking a hammer to your boat.'

'I owe you,' says Fish.

'No sweat.' The man unsteady, gripping the wall with his free hand. Stares at Fish. 'You a cop?'

'No,' says Fish.

'That's a cop gun.'

'Once was,' says Fish. 'An inheritance. From an ex-cop. You a cop?'

'Organised crime.' The man changing the gun into his left hand, extending his right, the wall clasped under his armpits. 'Flip Nel. Moved in a month ago about. Seems like an interesting place.'

They shake.

Fish says, 'It is. Appreciate you trying you to stop them.'

'They ran fast.' Flip Nel laughing. 'Especially when I pulled off one shot. When Harry talks, he talks big.' He waves the

Smith & Wesson. 'You want any help, sorting it? Police ID can be useful.'

Fish shakes his head. 'Nah. The main man's a dealer called Seven in the ghetto.' The two men nodding at one another. 'Dude needs another talking to.'

'You security?'

'Investigations.'

'Tough job.'

'Not that bad. Gives me time to surf.'

Flip Nel nods, frowning. 'You feel another presence would help persuade him, let me know.' He hands Fish a card. 'My cell's best. You ring the other numbers, no one's gonna answer. Cop life, hey?' He's about to step down, he says, 'Ag, ja, one more thing, I'm a fisherman. Any time you're going out, I wouldn't mind. Share the petrol, you know.'

'I don't fish,' says Fish. 'The boat's another inheritance.'

'Seems a waste not to use it.'

'Maybe you can show me?'

Flip Nel grins. 'A pleasure anytime' – disappears behind the wall.

Fish slips the pistol into his belt. First things first. Seven is first.

He walks down the road towards the vlei. Pissed off that on a day like this, full-on sun and surf, there's an arsehole scumbag shithead in it called Seven. He's carrying a piece of his board, the piece with the skeg, he's planning to smash it into Seven's face.

On the bridge he stops, gazes down at the water the colour of weak tea. Crabs in the shallows, lying black against the sand.

He gets into a thing with Seven it's going to ride and ride. Problem is he can't let it go.

Fish walks into the ghetto to Seven's crack house, through the gate up to the front door. The security grille's locked now.

He knocks. Bangs with his fist.

Toothless answers so fast he must've been crouching behind the door waiting. The house breathes out its foulness: dagga and boiling soup bones.

'Get Seven,' says Fish.

Toothless looks seriously whacked. Pupils filling his eyes, his right leg jigging like it wants to dance on its own. A smirk on his face.

'Not here.'

'Get him,' says Fish.

Toothless doesn't move, except his leg. Fish can smell him, he's ripe, the stench sharp as rotting guavas.

'Just get him.'

Toothless makes to shut the door. Fish pushes through the grille, slams it back. Toothless going down in a heap.

Fish shouts: 'Seven. Seven, d'you hear me? Get out here.'

Nothing. Not a floorboard creak, not a mattress sigh.

Fish grips the grille. 'Seven.' Silence. 'Seven, get out here. Seven.' He hurls the piece of surfboard down the passageway, it clatters against the walls, slides into a corner. 'Seven.' Nothing. All he can hear is Toothless's wheeze. Either Seven's wetting himself or he's really not there.

Fish watches Toothless raising himself. 'You guys had a lot of fun? Smashing my stuff. Very funny. So now we're going to see, my friend. See how fucking funny it was. Where's Seven? Where's he gone?'

'Fok off,' says Toothless, standing there just inside the grille.

'You stink,' says Fish, reaches in, bunches his fist into the crackman's jersey. One yank he has Toothless tight against the grille. Toothless wriggles. Fish gives him slack then jerks him back, holds him hard on the rusty bars. 'Listen. You listening?'

Toothless says what could be 'Yaaah'. Could be pain, 'Aaaah'.

'What's your name?'

'Jouma,' says Toothless.

'So, Jouma,' says Fish, 'you tell Seven this's over. Okay. Right now it's over. All that crap he's caused, he's going to pay for. New tyres. New windscreen. New mirrors.'

Jouma's got his jaw free, says 'Fok off' out the side of his mouth.

'Listen,' says Fish. 'Just listen' – jerking the guy back and forth, slamming his head against the grille. Jouma spitting, whining, calling for help. Fish pulls out his gun, pushes the barrel into Jouma's cheek. This quietens him.

'Shut up. Just shut up.'

Jouma whimpers.

Fish's closer to Jouma than he wants to be. Not only the sweat stench, the gangbanger's got rancid breath.

'You tell Seven before all the other stuff, he owes me a surfboard. I don't get that surfboard tomorrow morning then I'm back here. You don't want me to come back here. Seven doesn't want me to come back here. I have to come back here, I don't even want to think about it. About what could happen. That too complicated for you?'

Jouma doing his 'yaaah-yaaah' sound.

Fish pushes him back. 'You could take a bath, do us all a big favour.'

51

By mid-afternoon Jacob Mkezi has his ducks in a row. He likes that expression, ducks in a row. He can see the ducks on a vlei, Cape teals, swimming one behind the other. He's in the blind with a twelve-bore over-and-under shotgun, take them out bam, bam, bam.

His ducks this afternoon are trucks, an Antonov, and a destination. Two calls settled the logistics, a contact in Yemen sorted the deal. All from the comfort of his sitting room. The one looking over the lawn towards Skeleton Gorge. The mountain in shadow, a high white cloud ridging in.

The lawn's substantial, the size of two tennis courts side by side. Neat spongy buffalo-grass lawn. Some hadeda ibises stabbing their long bills into the turf, picking out grubs and worms. Not the sort of birds Jacob Mkezi wants to shoot. He likes hadeda ibises, likes their harsh cry in the morning. The dawn birds he calls them.

He goes outside onto his lawn, the hadedas moving slowly away. Not bothered; alert, but not bothered.

Jacob Mkezi admires them, the gunmetal sheen on their wings, flashing in the sun.

He phones Tol Visagie, says, 'Thursday.' Hears Tol Visagie whistle.

'So soon?'

'I don't mess around.' Jacob Mkezi bends down to feel the grass, the cool softness beneath his palm.

'I know,' says Tol Visagie. 'I know.'

Jacob Mkezi gives him details, contact names, time schedule, where to meet the trucks. Travel distance to the airstrip. 'There's a team to do the transfer: cave to truck, truck to plane. Treat them well. Food, cold drinks, beer when the plane's gone.'

'That's it?' says Tol Visagie.

'What else you want?' says Jacob Mkezi, straightening. 'A military band?'

Tol Visagie laughs. 'I was out there this morning. Just to check.'

'Check on what? There's something I should know?' Jacob Mkezi frowns, slaps his palm against his pants. With the back of his hand flicks grass blades from the material. 'I'm a long way away, Tol. You've got to tell me what's happening.'

'Nothing's happening.'

'But …'

'No buts. Everything's fine.'

'Except.'

A pause. Jacob Mkezi about to say, Talk to me, Tol. Talk to me.

Tol Visagie says, 'That man we met, he's back.'

Jacob Mkezi taking this in. Standing on his lawn, looking up at Skeleton Gorge, taking this in. 'Vusi Bopape?'

'Ja, him.'

'You've seen him?'

'No, I've found out he's back at the lodge till Thursday.'

'When?'

'Thursday.'

Jacob Mkezi thinks when the ducks get into line too easily, there's always a problem.

'Don't go back to the cave. Okay. Not till Thursday. Stay away from it.'

Again the silence. Jacob Mkezi says. 'You'll do that?'

'Ja,' says Tol Visagie, 'ja, of course.' Then: 'Who is he? Who is this Vusi Bopape?'

'Good question,' says Jacob Mkezi.

Next he phones Mart Velaze, says, 'Comrade, fill me in.'

'On what?' says Mart Velaze.

'Everything, comrade. All the shit happening in my life.'

'It's sorted,' says Mart Velaze. Gives him a status rundown

on Lord, the boy in a coma, Daro Attilane. 'That's it. All sorted.'

'What about Vusi Bopape? Who's he?' Jacob Mkezi wants to know.

'I don't know,' says Mart Velaze. 'No one knows. Maybe he's freelance.'

'*Ein solcher Diener bringt Gefahr ins Haus*. Find out, comrade,' says Jacob Mkezi. 'Find out a-s-a-p. A servant of his kind is full of present danger. Faust to Mephistopheles, comrade. Faust to Mephistopheles.'

Jacob Mkezi swears. Loudly. The hadedas take off: kwaak, kwaak.

52

Fish's been into the back yard three times with a torch to stare at the Isuzu. Once at seven, again at eight thirty and now at ten. He shines the beam at the slashed tyres first, then the smashed windscreen and rear window, the bust mirrors. It still seems impossible. Unbelievable. He clicks off the torch, stands there dumbstruck.

A couple of grands' damage. Just replacing the tyres would take care of most of that.

Then the rest.

Like how much is this going to cost to sell?

Like Seven is ever going to cough up. This thing with Seven has legs. One of those nasty tit for tats. Depresses the hell out of Fish.

What'd he think telling the cop over the wall that fishing was an option? No ways he could get the Isuzu on the road any time soon.

Unless he got a loan from Estelle. Yeah, that was likely. Really likely he was going to ask his mother.

Especially with ten voicemails from her, eight SMSes, four emails.

'You said this afternoon, Bartolomeu. It's now seven o'clock your time. You're letting me down badly. Don't do this to me.'

Ten messages of that order. Every time Fish saw his mother's name on the screen he keyed her to voicemail. Tomorrow he'd sort out her problem. Right now he's got other worries.

He goes inside. On the kitchen table's the plastic bag with Colins's life story. He takes out the first page, reads: 'I am Colins, you will know me by this name.' This written in a neat cursive in ballpoint, filling up the whole line. Not a bad start, Fish reckons. Has a ring to it. On the next line the same sentence: 'I am Colins, you will know me by this name.' Below that a repeat, repeats all the way down the page, the same line like Colins is doing detention at school. Filling up all the pages in the bag, the same line.

Jesus, thinks Fish, this's his life story?

I am Colins, you will know me by this name.

Fish blows out a long breath. Takes a pinch of weed from his herb tin, pestles it with his right index finger in the palm of his left hand. Sprinkles the crush on a Rizla paper, picking out the seeds.

What a wipe-out day!

Starts like it's paradise, ends like it's hell. A tanked job. A good deed turned crap. An ace surfboard maliciously chopped. A stuffed-up bakkie. The bergie Colins dead on his conscience. His mother on his case. You get through all that then you get to the Vicki thing. Her tone of voice that he knows means she's lying. She's not with clients. Not at some business dinner. Not at Gamblers Anonymous. Something else is happening. Something she's ashamed of. Has to be a poker game. Has to be she's on the cards again. And when did that start? Last week? Last month? Tonight?

Not a good situation.

Fish licks along the edge of the paper, rolls it into a tube. Taps the spliff on the table.

The worst was sitting on the beach wall watching the afternoon surfers slicing the waves. The swell building again on the high tide.

'You not going in?' one or two asked him as they strapped leashes to ankles. 'Haven't seen it cooking like this in ages.'

'My boards're broken,' Fish replied. 'Both of them.'

'Ah, bru, that sucks,' they sympathised.

Sucks alright. Sucked so badly Fish thought about going another round with Jouma. Knocking the rest of the pegs out of his mouth. But didn't. Just sat on the wall, hugging himself as the sun dipped behind the mountain, spread a cold shadow across the beach.

Sat there waiting for Daro to pitch. Because Daro had spare boards at home, could loan him one until the thing with Seven was sorted. At least that's what Fish was thinking while he waited for Daro.

Around five he gave Daro a call, got his voicemail. Left a message: 'This is what you missed', held his phone towards the crashing surf.

Then walked home. More hangdog than a township mongrel, obsessing about his misfortune. Again counting off the downers on his fingers: totalled four. When he got home, five was the state of his fridge: one piece of cold lasagne, wasn't even meat lasagne, two bottles of milk stout.

He drank the stout, nuked the lasagne. Vicki's idea of supper, a veg lasagne. The only thing with some chew were the mushrooms. After that, he put Shawn Colvin on the sound system while he smoked a joint. An older singer but sexy, very sexy.

Shawn singing about not getting too close, not going too far.

53

Vicki Kahn's hating this. She's driving around Cape Town's vineyard suburbs in search of Cake Mullins' house, cursing the darkness, cursing Cake Mullins. A bad bad feeling in her stomach. Churning in the pit of her stomach.

That bad feeling and the darkness.

The thing about the vineyard suburbs at night is the darkness, the darkness in between the street lights.

You've got high walls, electric fencing, dense shrubbery, trees overarching the street, you've got darkness. At nine o'clock no one's about. Everyone locked down. The CCTV cameras on. Outside sensors throwing beams across the lawns. Occasionally you get a passing security patrol car, big bloody deal.

She doesn't like the vineyard suburbs at night. At night they're scary. And now she's lost in their darkness.

The last Cake Mullins poker game Vicki played was about a year ago, just before she signed on the programme, so she's trawling the streets trying to recall the route.

Her phone goes. Cake Mullins on the display. She thumbs him on. There've been calls from Fish she pressed through to voicemail. His SMS too that she's ignored. Didn't want to ignore but had to.

'Everyone's here, Vicki,' he says. 'Waiting. You're late.'

'What's a couple of minutes?'

'That's the problem.'

'Help me here,' she says. She gives him a street name, he gives her directions. She's a few houses away.

'Get a Garmin,' he says.

Before she can reply he's disconnected. 'Rude bastard,' Vicki mutters, thumbing her phone off.

The thing about Cake Mullins, Vicki Kahn remembers as she

buzzes him from the intercom box at the gate to his house, is she doesn't know how he makes his money. Poker's more a passion. Ask him about his financial interests he trots out a story about investments. Offshore leveraging. Dubai developments. Vicki thinks not. On the net she found a photograph of Cake Mullins and Mark Thatcher. You're photographed with Mark Thatcher this puts a different spin on offshore leveraging.

The wrought-iron gates open, she drives between the white columns. Since her last visit Cake has added two guardian lions to his entrance. Very Cake Mullins.

There're four cars parked in the driveway. She stops her Alfa behind a Hummer, checks her lipstick in the rear-view. Checks in her handbag: the money, a can of mace. The tiny .32: the Guardian.

She takes out the pistol, releases the clip: six rounds, hollow points. Presses the magazine back, racks a load into the chamber. Better than a full house, aces high.

The garage door swings up, Cake Mullins stands, in the light, behind him a Porsche Boxster, a Lexus coupé. Cake not the sort of man to bother with family cars. Not the sort of man to bother with family. Women, yes. Including a one-nighter with Vicki Kahn, which she regretted. Cake being a sweaty man, all that meat.

Big Cake Mullins, in black chinos and a rollneck, snazzy leather loafers, his hair cut short, his moon face more cratered than the moon, says, 'The gorgeous Vicki Kahn.'

Vicki standing there in skinny jeans, a loose jersey wondering if he's expecting a kiss. She holds out her hand.

'Hello, Cake.'

'Ah, don't give me that,' he says, clasping her into a hug. Cake holds her tightly, whispers into her ear, 'I've got a great opportunity for you here tonight. You won't regret it.'

'I feel I might already,' she says.

He tickles her ear with his tongue. 'This's the making of you.' He squeezes. 'Let's go inside.'

'Yes,' she says. 'Let me go.' Coughing to get her breath back.

'There's a Vicki-chick,' says Cake Mullins, holding her at arm's length. 'Sweetness herself. Come and meet the man himself, the other guys.' Cake pressing the remote to bring the door down behind them, shutting out the darkness.

They thread through the cars to a room at the back of the garage. The room Cake's decked out like a gambling saloon. 'Hell,' as he would say, 'it *is* a gambling saloon.' Round card table covered in green baize in the centre under a low light with a wide metal shade. Five chairs circling it. Bar down one wall, posters, movie photographs on the others: saloon scenes from *Unforgiven, Tombstone, Pat Garrett and Billy the Kid, Maverick, Shane.* Some of them signed, Clint Eastwood, Sam Peckinpah, Val Kilmer. What Vicki doubts is the authenticity of the signatures. Far as she knows Cake's never set foot on US soil, despite his Vegas stories.

There're four men in Cake's saloon. Two men at the bar drinking whisky, the whisky bottle on the counter between them. Jacob Mkezi at the table, a bottle of mineral water at his elbow.

'We meet again,' says Jacob Mkezi, standing, his hand outstretched. 'How wonderful.' Mr Ultra Dude wearing the kind of jacket you don't buy in Woolies. Don't buy in the Waterfront boutiques either. The sort of jacket you buy in Germany or France, Italy. Underneath, a cashmere sweater, V-neck. A chain round his neck, not bling silver, this's delicate. But it's still a chain. Vicki's not into chains on men.

They shake.

The whisky drinkers watching them, their eyes on her boobs and crotch like she's part of the game. Men with wet mouths. Cake doesn't introduce them.

'Sit, please,' Jacob Mkezi pointing at a seat to his right. 'I've heard all about your poker skills. It is a favourite pastime for me, nothing serious. Just something I enjoy.'

Vicki thinking, This'll be fun.

'I asked Cake to arrange this. Thank you for coming.'

Vicki saying, 'I'm on the programme, Gamblers Anonymous. I shouldn't be here.'

'I know,' says Jacob Mkezi. 'Which is why I appreciate your coming tonight. I hear you are called the poker queen. The killer lady.'

'Was.'

'Okay,' says Cake Mullins, 'all good, let's do it.' Saying to one of the men at the bar, the coloured guy, 'Whitey, bring the bottle.' To Vicki, 'You want a drink?'

'Vodka,' says Vicki. 'Lime and soda.'

Cake Mullins goes behind the counter. Vicki nods at the whisky drinkers. They nod back, unsmiling.

'So were you the poker queen?' Jacob Mkezi focused on her.

Vicki meeting his gaze. 'Don't believe everything you hear.'

'I don't. Just some things, from some people.' He leans back, appraising her.

Vicki doesn't like it, glances down at her hands. Decides to shift the terrain. 'Last Thursday, you mentioned you knew my aunt.'

'I did. In the 1980s, when she was in Paris. A dynamic woman.' He pauses. 'What they did to her was … criminal.'

Vicki waits for more but he leaves it there. 'They, the security branch?'

'Not only them. Long story.' He leans towards her. 'For another time.'

'She was assassinated by a government hit squad.'

Jacob Mkezi frowns. 'That's what it looked like.'

'What're you saying?'

He lays a hand on her wrist. 'Another time.'

'You're saying it wasn't that?'

'I'm saying, another time.' His face bland, his eyes hard on her. 'I will tell you. I give you my word.'

Vicki draws her wrist from under his hand. 'I'll hold you to that.'

'I expect it.'

Cake Mullins plonks the drink next to her, says to everyone, 'Your buy-in chips're in a drawer in front of you. Green's ten, yellow for twenty, pink for fifties, purple for hundreds. I'm the dealer. As agreed, seven-card stud.'

The two whisky drinkers shrug, don't say anything. Poker-faced poker players.

Jacob Mkezi says, 'If that's the way you do it.'

'House rules,' says Cake, breaking the cellophane on a new pack. He hands them to Vicki. 'You do the honours.'

Jacob Mkezi intercepts. 'I'll shuffle.'

Vicki says, 'Be my guest.' Thinking, going to be interesting. The thrill starting in her, pulsing at her heart. Going to be a session. But that's okay, she's entering the zone.

54

The side window shatters, the man's inside the car with a .45 at Fish's head before Fish can raise his gun.

'Too slow, my friend,' says the man. 'Give me that.' Takes the revolver from Fish. A snub-nose S&W .38 special. 'Nice. We can use this.'

'Who're you?' says Fish.

'Don't worry,' says the man. 'Tonight I am your guardian angel.' He laughs: Ha, ha, hey. The sound pitched upward. 'Now watch.'

Fish is sitting in the Perana, Sunrise Beach, on the wrong side of midnight. Crazy mad southeaster sand-blasting his precious car. He's got a night scope. He's watching a white Subaru on the other side of the parking area stopped, facing the beach.

'Drop the scope,' says the man. 'You don't need that.'

Fish does.

'Both hands on the wheel.'

Fish clutches the steering wheel.

'You watching?' says the man.

Fish doesn't respond.

'I need an answer.'

'I'm watching,' says Fish.

'Now learn, my friend.'

The area's lit by high mast lights, enough illumination but the salt spray hazing the windscreen.

'Wipers,' says the man with the .45.

Fish flicks them back and forth. The windscreen still smeared, streaky.

A Jetta approaches from the traffic circle, goes slowly towards the Subaru. Stops. The men get out. Wait. The driver of the Subaru joins them. There's talk. Gesticulation. The two from the Jetta separating either side of the other man. Muzzle flash. Four shots.

Fish says, 'Jesus Christ!' leans forward to start his car.

'Don't,' says the man in the passenger seat. 'Keep watching, my friend. This is what happens when you play shit with us. You get fucked up. We know you, Mr Fish Pescado. You are the next one. You kill one of ours, we kill one of yours. Last time, the man you shot died, Mr Pescado. Bad luck for your friend over there.'

Fish sitting helpless. The man getting out, Fish planning to grab the Astra in the glovebox.

The man leaning in, opening the glovebox. 'Very obvious, Mr Pescado.' Looks at the gun. 'What old rubbish is this?'

'Leave it,' says Fish.

The man smiles, shakes his head. 'You whiteys. Use any antique.'

'Leave the gun.'

The man pockets the pistol. 'You better call Emergency for your friend, my friend. They can fill out the, what's it? ... The declaration of death.'

The laugh: ha, ha, hey.

Thing is Fish gets maudlin at times. Times like this. Times alone with doob. Time when things aren't working out. Is inclined to replay moments.

This scene's a top-ten replay. It burns him that he can't remember what he said to the dude. That he didn't react. Didn't shoot first. Smash the night scope into the guy's face. Grab his arm when he leant into the car. Anything. Burns him that the guy had it all his own way.

Has had it all his own way since. Not that Fish has let it go, he's biding his time. Patience being the virtue Fish's father told him it was.

Thing is in this mood Fish starts dredging up other questions. Questions like: what if his father hadn't died? Would he have finished his law degree? If he hadn't gone to work for the insurance company, would he have got into investigations? If he hadn't hooked up with Mullet would he have been shot? Would he have had to watch his partner being gunned down?

At the end of this road is Vicki.

And the question: what does he really know about her?

She's a lawyer.

She's compulsive.

She's a gambler. Now in the programme. So technically reformed.

She's got her own flat.

Drives a zooty car.

But she doesn't talk about family. All she's ever said was they're dead. Didn't want to talk about it further. The most he's ever got out of her is that she grew up in Athlone.

Why's that?

Fish realises he's never pushed it. In their time together he's talked about Estelle, his father. Even telling her his father had died didn't bring her folks into their heart-to-heart. So nothing about her mom, dad, brothers, sisters, grannies, grandpas, aunties, uncles. No past. No background. Like she was loose, an unconnected body wandering the city.

Not so much a lost soul, he thinks, rather an alone soul. He can identify. Despite his family history, despite his mother's distant presence, he knows alone. Only-child alone. The reason he took to surfing, because he could do it alone.

So he hasn't gone after the family bit with Vicki. Figuring eventually it'd come out, just needed time. And Fish is nothing if not patient.

So what've they talked about?

About the jobs she's moved his way. About surfing. Her gambling past. Lots about her gambling. He even went to some meetings with her in the early days, just after she stopped. When she was all jittery. There was some weird stuff had happened then that he'd never got a handle on. That she wouldn't talk about.

Like now. Vicki stringing him a line. He knows it in his gut. But what can he do?

After he's smoked the first joint, he goes out to look at the bakkie. Make sure he isn't imagining it. He isn't. It is as wrecked as it was.

He SMSes Vicki: Some serious prob's happened. That'd get a reply from her. When it doesn't, he phones. Get her voicemail.

He listens to Shawn, cheer me up, cheer me up. Thinks, right, you're all that I've got.

Maudlin Fish.

The dope gets him through the hours.

Now he's about to light up again he realises Shawn's not singing. The remote's on the table. Fish gets her back on the system: 'These Four Walls'.

Shawn singing about dying in some godforsaken room. About being the hell in, had it with all the crap life dishes up.

'She walked in here and said come, I'd go,' Fish told Vicki one time about Shawn Colvin.

'Leave me just like that?' Vicki playing along with laughter in her voice. 'For an older woman?'

'Only if it was her.'

'Thanks, babes,' said Vicki. 'Least I know where I stand.'

Fish never really sure if Vicki was joking or not. He dropped the topic.

He stares at the photo of Shawn on the back of the CD box: she's lying propped against a wooden wall, wearing this yellow jacket zipped tight, a yellow dress puffed around her, a glimpse of thigh between the dress and her long black boots reaching up to her knees. Southern fancy. An edging of black lace to her dress. Her eyes're closed. Maybe she's smiling, recalling every little thing she can. A sad smile. Her heart breaking.

You wouldn't want to look in her eyes, Fish thinks. You looked in her eyes you'd see the hurt of a lot more people than Shawn Colvin.

The same happened when you caught Vicki gazing at you. The same sadness in her face. The same feeling that it wasn't just one woman staring at you.

He shakes a Bic, brings the flame to the joint, takes the smoke into his lungs. Keeps it there. Imagining the grey swirl rubbing against his blood vessels, being absorbed.

He exhales, hits it again quickly. Closes his eyes.

Shawn singing about being a tough kid.

Fish feels the world drifting off. Vicki and Shawn merging. Shawn in her flouncy summer dress, brushing her hair, going out to face the wilderness.

Vicki in that white dress she sometimes wears with the thin straps. The honey colour of her skin against the white. The sheen of the light on her shoulders. Enough to make you cry.

Fish smokes the spliff to the end. Long hits, taking the herb in, releasing it through his nostrils. Herbal medicine for those in what Shawn's calling the dead of the deep dark night. Telling him, don't worry me now.

'Me neither,' says Fish aloud.

He crushes the roach in an abalone ashtray, goes outside to shine the torch on his bakkie. The tyres still slashed. The windscreen still smashed.

He kills the torch, sits in the bergies' chair. Gets a whiff of them that's now part of the fabric.

Shawn stops singing. Fish's spinning his cellphone between his fingers. Can't even remember picking it up. He puts another call through to Vicki. By now the dinner's got to be over. His call goes to voicemail.

55

The card players break after the eleventh for a drinks round, Vicki desperate for a vodka. She's gone through her buy-in, the extra she brought, an advance from Cake. At the eighth she gave him the nod to chalk her up. Thought about it briefly: leave now or try a few more hands? Two more she had a chance to recoup then walk out.

Cake smiled, pushed more chips her way. Mouthed at her: there's my girl.

But the cards didn't favour her. Couple more hands like the last four, the tab would be hefty.

At the bar she whispers to Cake, 'This's making me nervous. Why'm I here?'

'Pleasure of your company.'

'Come'n.'

'I told you. Debt repayment.'

'And the new tab?'

'We can talk about it.'

'Jesus, Cake, what're you doing to me?'

'Your decisions, Vicki. Your choices.'

'And his choice?' Vicki flicking her eyes at Jacob Mkezi still sitting at the table, drinking his mineral water. 'What's his choice?'

Cake shrugs. 'He wanted it, this game.'

'Why?'

'I don't ask him why, Vicki. Nobody asks him why.'

'First Clifford Manuel wants me to meet him. Now this ...' Vicki not finishing as Jacob Mkezi comes up behind her, puts a hand on her shoulder.

'Gamblers Anonymous has taken away your luck.'

'I'm sorry?' She turns to face him, the movement dislodging his hand. 'What's that supposed to mean?'

'You're playing too cautiously. You think if you're cautious you won't be gambling. And people who are cautious lose. So, be brave. You see, I appreciate your sacrifice to play this evening.'

'You appreciate my sacrifice ...' Vicki frowning. 'I should go.'

'Wait.' Jacob Mkezi reaching out to touch her arm, a quick gesture. 'Wait. Indulge me. I have my reasons.'

'Which you're not going to tell me?'

'Not yet. Eventually. Please let's play cards. Enjoy the game.'

'She's touchy,' says Cake, bringing up a tray of cigars, Rey del Mundos, from a small humidor.

'I understand that. I would be too under the circumstances.' Jacob Mkezi running a cigar under his nose. 'You smoke, Vicki?'

Vicki shakes her head. Stay or go?

'She used to,' says Cake.

'I'm sure,' says Jacob Mkezi. 'She has the look of a late-night gambler.'

Stay or go? She should go. She stays. Looks at the card table, the cards, the chips, feels the pull. The need to fan open a hand, arrange the play. As the man says, be brave.

The thirteenth hand gets her close to the edge. It goes to Whitey. Jacob Mkezi doesn't lose much, folding early.

'Come on, Vicki Kahn, where's that old rep?' he says, that yellow spark still in his eyes. 'We need the poker queen. The killer lady. To show these types what it's all about.' His leg brushing against hers, his hand reaching across to pat her arm.

Vicki shifts her leg, crosses her arms.

Jacob Mkezi gives a small smile, sits back.

The fourteenth hand wipes out her chips. She's got a wheel but Jacob Mkezi has a top straight ace to ten.

'Advance me,' she says to Cake.

He shrugs. Says, 'Maybe speak to Jacob. He's bankrolling.'

'Ah, no, Cake. What's going on? You've been chalking me up.'

'You asked, I did it. You didn't ask who's bankrolling.'

Vicki speechless. Trapped. Hearing Jacob Mkezi saying, 'You remember the old man who killed himself?'

'What old man?' Vicki focussing, her heart beating hard, her breathing shallow. Not liking this new tone in Jacob Mkezi's voice.

'After your last card game.'

Vicki all too up on the story of her last card game, the major reason she hit Gamblers Anonymous. She heard the old guy hanged himself.

'You wiped him out.'

'It was a card game,' she says. 'He didn't have to play.'

'You didn't have to wipe him out.'

'I offered him—'

'Double or quits. The gambler's Russian roulette.' Jacob Mkezi now detailing the old man's debt, the miserable lives of his family.

Vicki remembering the old man crying after she took the pot. The management shuffling him off. How he looked at her, said 'Please, my sister' before they bounced him into the street. Not a triumphant moment for her. 'He's why I stopped.'

'Too late for him.' Jacob Mkezi drinks water, half-turned towards her. 'But he's not the issue, he was a gambler: you live the life, you take what the life deals you. The issue is you, Vicki Kahn.' Jacob Mkezi toys with his chips. 'You're down about twenty now. If I offered you the same option, double or quits, what would you do? What will you do?'

Vicki knows she should leave. 'I'd say fuck you.' Making to rise.

Jacob Mkezi clamps his hand over hers. 'That's what I hoped you'd say. Sit. Please. Let's finish what we've started like civilised people.'

Vicki pulls her hand free. 'Deal,' she says to Cake Mullins.

'Double or quits?' Jacob Mkezi pushes chips at her.

'Double or quits,' says Vicki.

'Be my guest, for the luck. Take the chips.'

Vicki does. She's on his tab. Only way off that is to be brave. Play the cards.

The opening bets go down, Cake Mullins slices cards off the pack, face-down, two to each player.

The third card he flips: an ace of spades for the nameless guy, a ten of hearts for Whitey, jack of diamonds for Jacob Mkezi frowning over his fingertips, his hands in the prayer position cover his chin and mouth. Cake turns a seven of clubs for Vicki.

Whitey opens: a twenty into the pot.

The other whisky-drinker checks.

So does Vicki.

Jacob Mkezi puts a yellow chip in the pot, says, 'How're you doing? Going to pull this off?'

It's Cake's call. He folds.

Vicki keeps her breathing steady. The thrill in her stomach, sucking the saliva from her mouth.

Second cards go round: king of hearts to Whitey, eight of clubs to Vicki, nine of clubs to Jacob Mkezi.

Whitey bets the pot.

Ditto Jacob Mkezi.

Vicki checks her hand: there's two sevens, a club sequence seven and a six staring at her. She's got to. She swallows. Puts a pink, two yellow chips into the stack. The pulse is working over her heart, almost electric.

Jacob Mkezi looks up, grins at her. 'You catching fire. Chancing your luck? I like it.' Makes his call, adds ninety to the pot.

Cake Mullins deals. Flips a three of diamonds to Whitey, two of hearts to Jacob Mkezi, seven of hearts to Vicki.

Whitey checks. Jacob Mkezi bets the pot. Vicki and Whitey call. The pot's at three hundred and sixty.

'Getting interesting,' says Jacob Mkezi. 'Fancy your luck's changing.'

Vicki reckons she takes this to the end, she can win. Could win. Might win. Except her next card's a four of clubs. She pickes it up. No expression in her face, no tremble in her fingers.

Cake flips for Jacob Mkezi: a nine of hearts. He checks.

Same for Whitey.

Vicki suddenly calm, shakes her head.

'No bet?' says Jacob Mkezi.

Again she shakes her head.

'Ah, what a shame!'

Cake deals the last cards face down. Whitey finishes his whisky, folds.

Says, 'I'm out. All yours, Mr Mkezi.'

'No problem,' says Jacob Mkezi.

Vicki's holding a flush. Bets the pot and a hundred raise.

Jacob Mkezi sits still, Vicki watching him, not a twitch in his face, his hands either side his cards, at rest. Strong hands. Well cared-for hands.

Vicki raises her eyes, sees the unnamed guy and Cake are focused on Jacob Mkezi. Whitey watching her.

'I call,' says Jacob Mkezi, matching Vicki's chips. 'Your moment.'

The men leaning forward, the creak of their chairs loud to Vicki's ears.

'Let's see 'em, Vicki,' says Cake.

The four men staring at her. Vicki forcing herself to breathe. Showing no tell.

She lays out a flush of clubs.

'Not bad,' says Whitey.

The unnamed guy, clinks the ice in his whisky.

Cake Mullins grunts, shifts his eyes to Jacob Mkezi. 'Let's see yours.'

Jacob Mkezi's got a ten of diamonds, nine of diamonds, jack of diamonds, nine of clubs, two of hearts, nine of hearts, two of clubs. 'Full house,' he says.

He smiles at Vicki. 'I'm pleased we could meet like this. You owe me nothing but a favour, we'll leave it there. We should have coffee some time, I need to tell you more about your aunt.' He stands. 'Guys, been a pleasure.'

After the men have gone, Vicki's still sitting there. Cake Mullins brings her a vodka.

'Fuck you, Cake,' she says. 'You've screwed me. 'I had my life together. Until this.'

'No choice, princess. With Jacob Mkezi I've learnt you don't bugger around. He wants something, you do it. He wanted you.'

'For that bull story about the old man?'

'I don't know. It happened, right?'

'Sure it happened. But it's cards, Cake. Poker. Players lose.'

'Like tonight?'

'You set me up. That's different.'

'Only that I got you to the table.'

'He was testing me.'

'That's Jacob Mkezi.'

Vicki takes her drink in two swallows.

'How'm I going to find forty grand, Cake? Tell me that.'

'You don't have to,' says Cake Mullins. 'He told you: no debt, only a favour.'

'Like that's not worse. I'd rather pay the money.'

Johannesburg. Unseasonal rain hosing down. Crap miserable winter weather. Cold as rat piss. Pat Foreman in his bedroom stares out at the dripping back yard stacked with rusting oil drums. The bullet's clutched in his fist. The stiletto's lying on his bed.

When Pat Foreman gets the cross-hatched bullet he's been out of rehab three months. Cold stone sober, not a drink in his room. Coffee and headache tablets the only drugs he's got. He scratches his moustache, he grins his rictus grin but he's not amused. He's scared.

Foreman holds the bullet tightly. Still he's got shaky hands but that's not the drink. Or the lack of it. Shaky is Pat Foreman's condition. May have something to do with the bullet at this juncture. More likely it's early Parkinson's. Foreman's not a supporter of the medical profession so he hasn't been diagnosed. But Foreman's AA sponsor reckons it's Parkinson's. Not that he's said anything to Foreman. Merely told him he should have a check-up. Guy gets to fifty, fifty-three in his case, he should have a check-up. Prostate. Skin cancer. Heart, cholesterol. Especially prostate.

'No ways,' says Foreman to his sponsor. 'Not having some medic-oke sticking his finger up my bum.' Foreman playing with his rings, jittery as all hell.

'Doctors do it all the time,' says his sponsor. 'No big deal.'

But Foreman doesn't listen. Not drinking takes all his concentration. He's got a job with a security firm pushing beat through the night at a tyre storage depot. The most exciting thing happens there is the occasional cat fight when the ferals let the fur fly.

Fine by Foreman. He's had enough excitement for a lifetime. Just getting through the proverbial one day at a time's proving a ball-ache. Then comes the bullet and the blade. He finishes his shift, takes a minibus taxi home, walks into his room to find someone's been there. Someone's got in.

Foreman lives in a Mayfair boarding house. Five other boarders. Two of them work nights like him. Foreman collars the landlord. Landlady. A McDonald's-size woman in a tracksuit.

'Anything stolen?' she asks.

Foreman says no.

'Then what's the big deal?'

'It's my room,' says Foreman. 'I don't want people in my room.'

'So how'd you know? How'd you know someone was in it?'

'They left something,' says Foreman.

'What? A present?'

'That's my business.'

The woman snorts at him. 'Put on your own lock if mine's not good enough,' she says. 'Just don't go calling us all thieves.'

Except Foreman thinks he needs more than a lock. He needs to skip. Do a runner. He stares at the water pooling in the yard and schemes okay, he's walking out on three nights' wages but he's not going to pay fat-arse two weeks' rent. So he's scoring.

Pat Foreman packs his suitcase. Makes a break when he's sure fat-arse is out of the house. A bus to Braamfontein, a ticket for the evening coach to Cape Town.

Foreman spends the day in the coach company's waiting room. He smokes a pack of cigarettes. Drinks five coffees from the dispenser. The one occasion he leaves is to buy a sandwich at a nearby cafe. Only he throws most of it away. He's nervous. He could do with a drink. Plenty of bars within tempting distance, but Foreman resists.

He phones his sponsor. Blurts out the whole story. His sponsor's a former cop too, knows something of Foreman's past.

'What's this bullet about?' he asks.

'Getting even,' says Foreman. 'Revenge. I don't know. Could be anything. Could be anyone.'

'It's spooked you?'

'No joking.' He pauses to blow out smoke. 'I've been there. Done this sort of thing. I know about it.'

'My advice,' says the sponsor. 'Get hold of the TRC guys. Talk to them. Ask for amnesty.'

'You think?'

'I would,' he says. 'Maybe they've got a protection facility.'

Foreman's not sure. The Truth and Reconciliation Commission's only been on the go a couple of months. No telling which way it's going to play out.

'And Foreman?'

'Ja.'

'In Cape Town, go to AA, hey. Get a new sponsor. There's a guy I can recommend. Was also a cop.'

'Thanks,' says Foreman, smiling his rictus smile. 'I'll call you.'

Foreman's edgy all day. Keeps an eye on the comings and goings at the coach station. Doesn't believe that he's been followed but if they've found him out once they can do it again. He's well spooked. Wonders why now. Wonders where Ray Adler is. Wonders about Dommiss Verburg. And where the hell the young blond oke disappeared to. Thinks maybe it's got to do with the TRC, stirring up all kinds of trouble. The very last place he's gonna go knocking is on their door. Amnesty. Witness protection. More likely a ride to a lonely spot for a quick Mozambique-style: two shots to the chest, one to the head.

At six the coach loads up, heads off. The rain's clearing, the streets are shiny. Foreman's pleased to see the lights of Joburg blurring past in the condensation. He's got a seat next to a man marking up a Bible, but the man's no missionary. The man's lucky, Foreman has a short fuse with holy rollers.

Once the coach's on the highway with the traffic thinning, Foreman tilts back the seat for a zizz. He's buggered. A night pulling duty, a day on his nerves, only now he feels he can relax.

He dozes. Half-sees the towns come and go: Carletonville, Potchefstroom, Klerksdorp, Wolmaransstad, Christiana, Warrenton. The neon glare of the main streets, the dark of the wide country in between. At the stops he gets out for a smoke. The man marking the Bible smoking two to his one.

Before Kimberley he has this dream: he's standing in the passageway of a house, facing the front door. There's a man outside the front door, inserting his key into the lock. The man opens the door, stares at Foreman, says, 'Who're you? How'd you get in?'

Foreman says, 'We had an appointment, remember.'

The man says, 'What's your name?'

Foreman tells him.

The man closes the door, turns to Foreman. 'It's late,' he says. 'Can't we handle this tomorrow?'

Foreman doesn't answer, pulls out his pistol, shoots the man three times. Then has him with the stiletto: in, out, in, out, in, out. His arm working like a pump.

Foreman explodes out of this dream gasping. His mouth dry. The sweat damp in his armpits.

The man marking his Bible next to him says, 'Thought you were having a heart attack. You should come to Jesus, my brother.'

'No, china,' says Foreman, 'I need a drink. A dop 'n dam. Straight-up brandy and Coke.'

Foreman finds the trolley-jockey downstairs, orders five Klipdrift miniatures, a beer and a Coke. He guzzles off half the beer before he hits his seat.

'You're making a wrong move, my brother,' says the Bible man. 'I've been there. Jesus is the only answer.'

'Zip it, okay.' Foreman grins his rictus smile at the man. 'Okay?'

The man shrugs. 'Your hell.'

'Damn right,' says Foreman.

'I'll pray for you.'

'Quietly. Don't even move your lips.'

The man turns his cheek. 'You wanna slap the other one, my brother?'

'Very Christian,' says Foreman, breaking the seal on a miniature, pouring the golden liquid into a plastic tumbler. Slopping some, he's trembling so badly. 'But no. You stick with Mr Jesus, I'll stick with Mr Klippies.' He slugs back a mouthful, swallows, grunts.

'Heaven?' says the man.

'Look,' says Foreman. 'Shut up.'

'You're with Satan now, my brother. Sipping with the Devil.'

Foreman mixes Coke into the brandy. Grins at the Jesus-follower. 'Let me tell you,' he says. 'The old goat's good company. Doesn't say a goddamned bloody word. Got this smile on his dial, keeps pointing his finger at you.'

'You don't scare me.' The man licks his pencil, goes back to his underlining.

'No,' says Foreman. 'But these little bottles do, hey.' Jingling the miniatures in his palsy hands.

That shuts up the Bible-marker. Two hours later Foreman's asleep, dreamless now. At some point he feels the Bible man climb over him but Foreman's out for the count. Thinks the Bible man says 'God help you', only he's not sure. He doesn't respond.

He wakes as the coach comes out of the Karoo hills into Laingsburg. Blue sky, brown earth. Endlessly. His mouth is a cesspit, his eyes like pissholes, he feels sticky, he could do with a drink. The holy roller's left his Bible open at Corinthians, a line drawn under the phrase: 'Let no man deceive himself.'

'Stuff that,' says Foreman aloud, squeezing out of the seat, heading downstairs for a couple of brandies as the coach pulls into a pee stop. Foreman loads up. No deception in that. At a nearby takeaway grabs a toasted cheese-and-tomato sandwich. Bites down, getting a mouthful of packet in his hurry.

Foreman jigs about from foot to foot outside the coach, snarfing the sandwich without chewing.

He's freezing. It's a couple of degrees centigrade. Breath-clouding. He's trying to keep his mind off the bullet, the blade, the dream, off a rising fear.

The dream's left detritus. The slide and rip of the stiletto going in. The slickness, quickness. Wetness.

Foreman balls the sandwich packet in his hands, lobs it into a bin. He wants to get going. He wants to bed down. He's got this sudden scare that someone'll be waiting at the bus station. That they'll have figured out his plan. Before he climbs aboard he buys a half-jack of brandy. That and the clutch of miniatures put a smile into the rictus grin.

He sips the brandy straight from the bottle, stares out at the cold veld, at the scatterings of sheep and buck among the scrub. The brandy keeps the fear level down, but not the shake from his hands. Doesn't stop his teeth clattering against the glass when he drinks. Other passengers do eye-rolls, cluck their disapproval, concentrate on the movie: *Forrest Gump*.

Foreman makes a decision. Hops the bus at the Touws River stop. No one's gonna find him in a place like this. Arse-end of the world, small town, set back on a long plain against a koppie. The only excitement's when the Joburg and Cape Town trains come through. Once a day.

'You paid for Cape Town,' says the driver.

'Changed my mind,' says Foreman.

'Can't refund you.'

Foreman grins. 'Just get my case out, hey.'

The driver grumbles. Foreman's bag is well back in the luggage hold, a lot has to come out, all of it has to be repacked. The wind's sharp. The cold a couple of degrees off freezing. The driver's not pleased.

'You shoulda told me in Joburg,' he says.

'I would've if I'd known,' says Foreman.

He takes his suitcase, pulls out the handle. 'Drive safe.'

The driver mumbles in Xhosa. Foreman knows something of the language. Grins, 'And may the ancestors screw your mother too.'

He hunches into his coat, drags his suitcase up the long street into the dorp. An icy wind whips grit against his face. His eyes leak. The world blurs.

Foreman reckons a week, two weeks at the most, he can be on the move again. Hit Cape Town, get a guarding job, resume his anonymous life. Meantime he's holed up in an outside room behind a railway house. Full board – a plate of baked beans for breakfast, Marmite sandwich for lunch, chops and putu pap for supper. A dollop of tomato sauce over the mealie meal. As much tea as he wants.

Day one he doesn't go out much. Sits in the sun in the yard watching the chickens pick through the dust. The bullet's in his pocket, he toys with the switchblade, flicking it open. Long time since he's had one of these blades. Once he collected them. Pat 'Stiletto' Foreman. A man to be relied on. Pat 'no shit' Foreman. How'd they find him? Why'd they track him down?

Doesn't matter, it's history. He's in the wind. Albeit a bloody bitter wind off the high Karoo.

Day two Foreman finds a shebeen in the coloured quarter that suits him. A quiet place during the day. He sits in a corner over long Klippies and Cokes. He twirls his rings. He fingers the blade in his pocket, rubs his thumb over the cross-hatched nose of the bullet. The brandy takes the edge off his fear.

Right off two women offer him sex for twenty rand. Short little women with high cheekbones, dull eyes in the one, naughty eyes in the other. Naughty eyes comes down to fifteen rand.

'You know how much it costs in Joburg?' says Foreman.

The woman shakes her head, keeps pawing at his hand.

'Blow job, fifty upwards. Proper screw, two hundred.'

'Fifteen rand,' says the woman. 'Touws River special discount.' She strokes his hand.

'Don't do that,' says Foreman, snatches his hand away.

'Come'n, lovey,' says the woman. 'My place is nice 'n warm.'

Foreman considers all his years he's never screwed a Bushman perhaps he should do it now. 'Later,' he says. 'Tomorrow.'

The woman swears at him.

He gives her five rand. 'Buy some wine, hey?' After that she smiles but doesn't come on again. He's left to himself. Just the way he likes it.

Suppertime, day three Foreman says to the people in the main house, 'This's the same as yesterday. Same as the day before yesterday.'

He's standing at the kitchen door of the main house, collecting his plate of food.

The man at the kitchen table eating chops and putu pap looks at his food. 'Same as mine,' he says.

'Lamb chops,' says the woman holding out the plate to Foreman. 'Fresh Karoo lamb. You know how much you pay for that in the city?'

'Ja, I don't mean that. What I mean is,' says Foreman, 'ja …' He stops. Grins at the couple. 'No problem,' takes the plate to his room.

Day five Foreman thinks, time to move on. He can take the train to Cape Town. Maybe not all the way to the city. Get out at Paarl, catch a commuter train in. Maybe only as far as Bellville, Maitland, plenty of places there he can get lost. Cheap rentals above the shops. Plenty of jobs too. Delivery, security, maybe even handyman work.

That evening after he's eaten, Foreman's lying in bed, smoking, drinking from a half-jack. Bed's the only place he can be warm. There's a knock on the door. Foreman shouts out 'Ja', thinking it's the man from the main house. The handle turns, the door opens. He's never before seen the man standing there.

The man says, 'Haita, Foreman.'

Foreman's at a disadvantage: he's under the bedclothes, the only weapon he's got is the half-jack.

'Who're you?' he says, propping himself forward. He's right-handed. His position's awkward. He's got no leverage to throw the bottle. The blankets have him pinned down like he's wearing a strait jacket. If he can get out of the bed, the blade's in his coat pocket. His coat's hanging behind the door. The man's in the way. It's a shit scene.

'Gave me a bit of grief,' says the man. 'Tracking you.'

Foreman's thinking fast, fast as the brandy will allow. 'I'll talk,' he says. 'To the TRC. Ask for amnesty.' He bunches up his legs, pushes down the blankets. Fiddles with his rings.

'Don't get up,' says the man.

'I know stuff.'

'Of course.'

'Where bodies are. Who gave us orders.'

The man nods. Comes forward, pushes Foreman's legs down. 'Relax.'

Foreman whacks him on the side of the head with the bottle. A half-swing that's not got much power in it. The man staggers back, clutching his ear. It's the gap Foreman wants. He rips away the blankets, swings his legs out.

The man kicks Foreman hard in the jaw. Hard because he's wearing chunky lace-up Docs that open a gash in Foreman's cheek, puts a tooth through his tongue. Foreman jerks back, groaning.

'Why'd you do that?' says the man, looming over him. 'We were talking.' The man touches his throbbing ear, brings his hand away, there's blood on his fingertips. 'I'm bleeding. Ah no, my friend.'

'If he's not going to fetch his breakfast, I'll eat it,' says the man to his wife.

They're sitting at their kitchen table, the door into the yard open. They can see the outbuilding where their lodger sleeps.

'Wait,' says the woman. 'He'll come.'

Half an hour later the baked beans are congealed.

'I'll eat them,' says the man. 'You can't waste food.' He stretches across the table for the plate.

'No,' says his wife. 'He paid for them.'

She picks up the plate, crosses the yard to the outbuilding, knocks. 'Meneer. Meneer.' The chickens flock at her feet, expecting food.

'Maybe he's gone,' shouts the man.

She turns. 'He's paid.'

'Open the door.'

The woman knocks again. 'Meneer. Meneer.'

'Ag, man, bring the food here.'

'Maybe he's sick.'

'Maybe he's babbelas, hungover. You see how much he drinks.'

She gives her husband the cold plate.

After he's finished the food the man says, 'Leave him, hey. Let him sleep it off.' He shrugs into a coat, goes outside to unchain his bicycle from the fence. 'The man's a dronklap, bloody drunk.'

'Ja, ja,' says the woman, busying herself in the kitchen washing the pots and plates.

Two hours later she's knocking on the door again, holding a mug of tea. 'Mister. Mister.' This time she's insistent, stands there solidly. The chickens pick around her feet. She raps with her knuckles until they hurt. Then tries the handle. The door's unlocked, opens. After the brightness of the yard, she can't see anything in the dark room until her eyes refocus. She says she's got tea for him, takes a step inside. She can see now his body shape beneath the blankets. He's sleeping. Doesn't even stir at her voice.

The woman backs out. Waits another hour. Sitting on a straight-backed chair in the kitchen doorway, the sun warming her, she's willing the door of her outhouse to open: her lodger to stand there, lighting a cigarette. But he doesn't. Minute on minute he doesn't. Until she can't take it, this anticipation. Muttering, mumbling she goes down the stairs, across the yard, knocks twice, before she enters.

He's in the same position. Hasn't moved. She puts a hand on his shoulder. Asks in Afrikaans if he's sick. Can she get him some soup, perhaps. He doesn't answer. She shakes him, rocks his body – 'Meneer, meneer, meneer.' He flops on his back. He's got a cartridge between his teeth like he's biting on it. There's blood on his shirt, not much but enough to make her scream.

56

'Mr Fish,' says the voice on the cellphone.

Fish grunts, still surfacing from deep in a doob sleep. Might've answered his cellphone but that doesn't mean he's instantly bright and sharp.

'Mr Fish.'

'I hear you,' he says.

'He's dead,' says the voice.

Fish gets the dead bit, starts paying attention. 'Who?' Takes the phone from his ear, squints at the screen, not quite able to make out the name. The room's dark, no herald of the dawn edging the curtain. He rises onto an elbow, trying to clear dreams from his head. Dreams of running. Fleeing. Being chased. Standard nightmare number one.

'Fortune.' The name a whisper.

'Shit.' says Fish.

'They killed him,' says the voice. 'I know that is what they did. They killed my boy in the hospital.'

'Ah, hell,' says Fish. 'I'm sorry.' Not the best reply but the best he can do under the circumstances.

'Ma … Mrs Appollis … doesn't know I'm phoning you.'

The taste in Fish's mouth's sour, stale, furry, thick. He sucks saliva from his cheeks, swallows the glob. It doesn't help. His mouth's still a rat's nest.

'What time's it?'

'Seven o'clock. A little bit afterwards.'

Fish pinches the bridge of his nose. Too much grass, not enough chocolate munchies. The whole mess of yesterday smacking home: his board, his bakkie, Vicki.

Vicki.

No voicemails. No SMSes.

'Where're you?' he says.

'At the hospital, Mr Fish, standing outside the entrance. Ma's still with him in the ward. She can't let him go.'

'What time'd you get there?' Fish operating on auto, asking questions, suppressing thoughts of a creeping anxiety about Vicki.

'In the night the sister she phoned to tell us Fortune wasn't good. They thought we should come.'

'What time last night?'

'About one o'clock.'

'And? When you got there, how was he?'

'Still in the coma, Mr Fish, but restless. Groaning, his leg jerking, for hours and hours. It was terrible to look at, our boy making those noises like that. Ma couldn't take it, she was crying all the time.' Fish hears the man sob, clear the grief from his voice. 'The nurses did their best, Mr Fish. They did their best.' Again the sobs.

Fish waits.

The man blows his nose. 'I'm sorry. I'm sorry.'

'What d'you want me to do?' says Fish.

'Find the people who killed him, Mr Fish. Please.'

'It's not that easy,' says Fish. 'There's …'

'We can pay you,' says Samson Appollis. 'We can sell our car to pay you. Please, Mr Fish. People can't just kill other people.'

This's all I need, Fish's thinking. A charity case, on top of the mess with Seven, and Vicki hiding something. All I need.

'Okay, okay,' he says. 'Listen, Mr Appollis, I'll be in touch. You go back to Mrs Appollis. You look after her. You don't have to tell her you've spoken to me. I'll come and see you, we can work something out, alright. I'll call you.'

'I'm sorry, Mr Fish, I'm sorry to trouble you.'

'No,' says Fish. 'Don't say that. I'll call you.'

The first person he calls is Vicki.

Before that takes a piss, pulls on tracksuit bottoms, shrugs into a sloppy jersey. It needs washing, has that sharp hint of salt in its weave. The wool crusty in places. But Fish's not into caring much about ocean smells. He puts the call through.

Vicki answers first ring. 'Before you shout,' she says. 'Don't. Just don't.'

He can hear tears in her voice. Not a Vicki he's often encountered in their time together. In the early days, yes, but not recently. 'Where're you?'

'Outside,' she says, 'just parking.'

Which is where Fish finds her, stepping out of the bright red Alfa.

They clinch.

'This's early,' he says.

'You smell of seaweed,' she says. Notices the slashed tyres on the bakkie. The broken glass. 'What happened?'

'Chaos.'

'Godfathers, Fish.' Vicki pulls out of his arms. 'Who?'

'Inside,' says Fish. 'Out of this chill.'

What Vicki confesses is that she played poker. She's sitting there in her business suit, very desirable in Fish's eyes. Both of them clutching coffee mugs, close up against the gas heater in the kitchen.

'You played cards?' he says.

'I had to. I owed Cake Mullins. I had no choice, Fish. He called it in. But he lied to me. He set me up for Jacob Mkezi.'

Fish rises, stares out the kitchen window. Over by the rubbish bin are the bits of surfboard he piled there. 'Mkezi's serious trouble. Big-time trouble. Organised crime. Government corruption. Wherever there's a bad scene, Mkezi's got a link.'

'I know.'

'So you go from meeting him to playing cards with him in a couple of days. That's not coincidence.'

'I lost to him,' she says. 'Forty grand.'

'Pay the guy,' he says. 'Just pay the guy 'n get out of it.'

'He converted it. To a favour.'

'You know what that means?'

'Of course I do.'

'He calls it in, you don't know what shit's gonna come with it. All you know is it'll be dirty.'

'I know. Alright!'

'So pay him. Give him the money, and you're out of owing him anything. Hear me, Vicki, you don't want to owe someone like that a favour.'

'I can't.'

'What d'you mean can't?'

'I can't pay it. Where'm I going to get forty thousand?'

'I don't know. Extend your bond. Get a loan from the bank. Get a loan from your firm. Anything, Vics, just get out of this.'

'I can't.'

'No such thing. You haven't asked.'

'You know how much the interest is on forty grand?'

'Doesn't matter. Being hooked's worse.' He turns round. 'So what was it all about?'

'Mkezi said he wanted to play me. He'd heard of my reputation.'

'And you went?'

'I had to.'

'Because you owed Cake Mullins. What d'you gamblers do? Play for favours.'

'You wouldn't understand.'

'No. Try me.'

She tells him the story about the old man's suicide. Fish sits down to hear it.

'Where's the connection?'

'It was an implication.'

'To what? Tweak your conscience?'

'Yes.'

'Big bloody deal.'

Fish's up again, walking about the kitchen. He stops in front of her. 'What d'you want?'

'I don't know. I want to go to work, see what I can do about the money.'

He crouches down, his hands on her thighs. 'No more cards. Promise me, no more cards.'

She smiles. The wan slight smile that's not in her eyes, her eyes are sad. 'I promise.'

Fish doesn't believe her. Nods okay, pretending that he does.

She runs fingers through his hair. 'I promise.' Adds with a laugh, 'Cross my heart.'

'It's not funny, Vics. You had me going last night.'

'I can see, by what's left in the ashtray. A little dagga den all of your own.'

'I had a bad day.' He stands, takes the abalone ashtray with its roaches and pips and sticks to the dirtbin. Tells her his war stories. Tells her about Fortune Appollis. Vicki reaching across the table to stroke his hand.

'And now? You're not thinking of anything stupid?'

'Like what?'

'Like pursuing the Appollis thing.'

'No.'

'And Seven. You can't leave it.'

'Too right I can't leave it.'

His cellphone rings: Daro Attilane.

'There's a nice wave,' says Daro. 'Thought you'd be here.'

'Have to give it a miss,' says Fish. 'Couple of things come up.'

Daro laughs. 'Didn't think I'd ever hear you say that.'

'What size?' says Fish.

'Not yesterday's, but good enough.'

Fish's about to bum a board, he remembers the black Golf. 'Hey, Daro, you get a name on that reg plate?'

There's a pause before Daro says, 'Ummm, actually, ja I did. Man called Mart Velaze. Lives in Milnerton.'

'You got a street address?'

'At the office. I'll SMS.'

Fish disconnects, looks at Vicki. Vicki's got her eyes on him. 'What's it?'

'Got a name for the guy who followed me. The zooty car with

tinted windows, the black Golf, I told you about. That tailed me from the Appollis's to the hospital ...' Fish stops, shakes his head. 'Something else left dangling.'

The second call Fish makes is to Clifford Manuel.

He gives him a bullshit story that he can't get hold of Vicki Kahn, her cellphone's off. Tells him Fortune Appollis has died. That Mr Appollis suspects foul play. How about taking it on pro bono with investigation expenses upfront?

Clifford Manuel's going, 'Wait, wait, wait. Who're you again?'

'Fish Pescado,' says Fish. 'Your investigator guy.'

'I'm in the traffic, Mr Pescado. Can you phone me later?'

'No,' says Fish, 'this's urgent, the boy died, we're talking murder now.'

'Manslaughter.'

'Murder, manslaughter, they're words. The kid's dead.'

Fish hears traffic grind, radio news about a child rape.

Clifford Manuel speaks over it. 'I'm sorry to hear about this case, but we do not handle that sort of work, Mr Pescado. Some firms do pro bono, ours does from time to time. As you're well aware, we were taken off this case. We're hardly going to run back to them. If you're in contact with the Appollis family I suggest you refer them to the Legal Resources Centre. They are geared for this sort of matter. But it's very unlikely there's anything to be done. It's very unlikely there has been any malpractice at the hospital. We're talking about one of our best private facilities. He would've been getting expert care.'

'He's dead,' says Fish. 'Doesn't that say something?'

'Mr Pescado, I'm not going to argue about it. Especially not in the traffic. You have my answer.'

With a have-a-good-day, Clifford Manuel's gone before Fish can so much as open his mouth.

'And a nice day to you to,' he says, keying off the phone.

'What'd you do that for?' says Vicki.

'Just to stir it.'

'I asked you please not to. I told you how he bitched on me.'

'Maybe that's why I did it. Right now he's phoning whoever put him onto the case in the first place. Five minutes time your phone'll ring. No problem in getting things jumping.'

'This is my job you're playing with.'

'You're a lawyer, Vics. Lawyers've always got work. You can walk out of one firm straight into the next one.'

They're inside pouring cornflakes into bowls when Vicki's phone goes: Clifford Manuel. She holds the screen up for Fish to see.

'Told you.'

Vicki catches a strand of hair behind her ear, starts into the conversation, says, 'ummm' twice, one 'but Clifford', a 'yes, okay, about an hour' – end of conversation.

She puts the phone down. Stares at the cornflakes. 'Soon as I get in he wants to see me.'

'There you go. What'd say?' Fish laying out the way she should handle it.

'I just don't know if I want more of his hannnah-hannnah-hannnah complaining.' She sighs. 'Oh well, we'll see.' Sprinkles sugar over the cornflakes. 'How'm I going to get you onto muesli? Cornflakes are so 1970s.'

Fish crunches through a mouthful, says, 'There's milk if you want.'

'What? To make a soggy goo? Thanks. Dry is fine.'

'So what else did he say?'

'He told me to tell you to back off.'

'I imagine. Any reason?'

'It's got nothing to do with us.'

Fish spoons fast through his cornflakes. 'How long d'you think before Mart Velaze wants a word?'

After Vicki's left, the third person he calls is Cake Mullins on the number he lifted from Vicki's phone log while she was taking a pee.

His call goes to voicemail.

'Cake,' he says, 'you don't know me, I'm a friend of Vicki Kahn's. A good friend. Don't contact her again.'

His last call before he leaves is to Samson Appollis. He's back at home. Fish says he'll be there in an hour.

THE ICING UNIT, DECEMBER 1999

Xmas, Ray Adler's got the bullet. Like a stone in the shoe. Nagging. Irksome. Otherwise he'd be content. There he is sitting on his balcony with the cat on his lap, his feet on the railing, drinking beer, talking to his daughter. Happy, except for the bullet.

His daughter's in London, he's in Sydney. Couple or eight hours' time she's going to be on a Qantas flight home for Xmas. Ray hasn't seen her in eighteen months. They talk often on the phone but what he wants is to hold her, hug her.

Her name's Alice. She's twenty-five.

She says, 'Dad, what d'you want? What can I bring you?'

'You,' he says.

'Dad,' she says. 'Come on.'

Ray looks at the day fading, strokes the cat's head. From his balcony he has a corner view of a park where this time of the late afternoon a pusher sells dope to school kids. Ray's told the jacks, but nothing's come of it. Sometimes he feels he should go over, kick the dealer in the nuts.

'I dunno,' he says. 'Beer. A four-pack of Black Sheep.'

'That's a beer?'

'Where're you living? You must get out more.'

'Very funny,' she says. 'That's all?'

He can hear her exasperation, he loves it. Reminds him of her childhood years, how she'd tug at his hand when he teased her.

'Alright. A Terry's Orange. That satisfy you?'

'Dad! From the best city in the world, my father wants a four-pack of Black Sheep beer and a Terry's Orange. That's crazy.'

'Mostly he just wants his daughter,' says Ray, taking a swallow of beer from the tin.

'You're getting her.' He hears teaspoon-tinkle, tries to imagine his daughter in the grey London early morning. He doesn't know what her flat looks like. He hasn't been to London in eight years. What for?

'How's the weather?' says Alice.

'It's summer,' says Ray. 'Summer is summer in Sydney. Full cafes, full beaches. People having fun.'

'I can't wait,' she says.

Neither can I, Ray thinks.

'Got to go,' she says. 'Still have to pack.' He hears her blowing kisses. Putsh. Putsh. 'See you tomorrow. Or whatever time it's going to be. Don't be late.'

'Am I ever?' he says.

Ray rings off. Sets his cellphone on the table beside a bowl of pistachios. Cracks a few, pops the green nuts from their shells. Alice. What a sweetheart. Two weeks. Pure bloody heaven. He pulls another beer from the cooler box at his feet, rips the top.

But the thing in Ray Adler's life that he can't figure out is the bullet. Point two two, the nose cross-hatched. A little present he received through the post. Mailed in Sydney a few days ago. He keeps it in his pocket, brings it out now and then, turns it over, puzzled. What's tugging at him is whether he should make a few calls. He's reluctant. You start something, you don't know where it's going to end. After all these years of peace and quiet, best not to look into the abyss. Best to keep quiet, pretend nothing's happened. Difficult though.

Antsy, Ray glances over at the park. The young weasel's on his corner selling dope. Okay, Ray thinks, enough. He nudges the cat off his lap, gets up, slugs back a mouthful of beer. Ray in his T-shirt and boardies, flip-flops, is about to do his bit for the community when there's a knock on his door. Ray thinks probably the old biddy from upstairs come down for the sherry she phoned for. Last three Xmases she's bummed a bottle of sherry off him in return for a trifle, which is fine by Ray. He grabs a bottle from his booze cupboard, heads for the door.

Standing on his welcome mat is a man he doesn't recognise.

Snappy dresser black dude. The man says, 'I like it, legendary Aussie friendliness.'

'Who're you? How'd you get in?' says Ray. There being a buzz-lock on the block's foyer door. And no one buzzed for him.

'You know,' says the man. 'Not too difficult. Mostly everybody's gonna let in the plumber.' He grins at Ray. 'Can I come in?'

'No.'

'Don't be like that, Ray. There's things we got to discuss.' The man slipping past Ray into the flat. 'Not quite the place I pictured you in. Pictured you more upmarket. Not second-hand furniture, Van Gogh prints. But this's discreet, Ray. Low-profile. Modest. Humble even. But comfortable.' The man flops down on the settee. 'Comfortable.'

Ray says, 'Like what?'

'Like what, what?'

The two men eyeballing one another.

'Get out,' says Ray. 'Bugger off.'

'Sure. I'm going to do that,' says the man. 'But first we've got to talk.'

'About what?'

'About things you did once upon a time.'

Ray's daughter Alice flies into Sydney bang on time and he's not waiting to meet her. She leaves a message on his voicemail: 'Dad, where are you? I'm here. You stuck in traffic?'

She pushes through the crowd to a bench, parks herself, zonked out after the long-haul. Five minutes. Ten minutes. Fifteen minutes pass.

Alice dials him again. 'Where're you?' She stands on the bench to get a view over the crowds. No Dad in sight. 'This's costing me a bomb, phoning you.'

Half an hour later still no Dad, still no answer to her messages. Worried more than pissed off, Alice trolleys her suitcase to the taxi rank.

Forty-five minutes later she's buzzing him from the street

door. No response. She can see his balcony if she backs out into the road, see the door's open, see the cat on the balcony wall. Hear the cat meowing. Calls her father's name.

A woman coming down the pavement carrying grocery bags says, 'He's not answering, lovey. Neither his phone or door. Had to buy a bottle of sherry myself.'

'I'm his daughter, Alice,' says Alice.

'Can see that,' says the woman. 'Told me you were coming, he did. Looking forward to it, he is. Shouldn't he have been out to meet you?'

'Yeah,' Alice says.

'Come up,' says the woman. 'You got a key to his flat?'

Alice shakes her head.

'Old man Arnot must've. He's the caretaker.'

Ten minutes later old man Arnot the caretaker lets Alice into the flat. 'I shouldn't be doing this,' he says, 'even for his daughter.' The moment the door opens, the cat's out, rubbing against their legs.

'Wants feeding,' says the woman. 'Unlike Ray not to.'

Alice hefts her suitcase into the flat. She's not feeling good about this. She's feeling like this is all wrong. She walks into the lounge, looks through the open door to the balcony. Can see the cooler box. Some beer cans on the table. That's unusual. Unusual he wouldn't have cleared up.

The kitchen's spick and span. Like her father always left it. The tidiest man she knew. No wet towels on the bathroom floor. No dirty underwear piled in the bedroom.

She checks his bedroom. He's lying on the bed with his eyes open, a bullet hole in the centre of his forehead. At first she doesn't see it. Just sees him lying there, thinks heart attack. She rushes at him, yelling, 'Dad, Dad, Dad.'

The woman and old man Arnot come running.

Then Alice sees the bullet hole, screams.

Spray painted in red across the bedroom wall the words: sweet dreams. Clutched in Ray's hand a .22 long-rifle cartridge with a cross-hatched nose.

57

Daro Attilane's not a man at home in the world when he opens up his executive car boutique.

His day might've kicked off with a surf but shredding a couple of waves hasn't brought happiness and light to his heart.

Most of the time he was in the sea he sat on the backline, letting the swells pass under him. Not really adrenaline-pumping swells, but swells that would've given him a decent enough ride nonetheless. And the morning was pretty awesome. Bit more cloud in the sky than the day before. Still the mountain went heart-stopping tawny with the rising sun. Spectacular.

Most of the time Daro sat on his board thinking about Mart Velaze. About who Mart Velaze was really working for. That crap about Adler Solutions just so much sunshine. Truth: Daro had a good idea who pulled the strings that got Mart Velaze on the move.

The previous afternoon, agitated, Daro'd driven to Milnerton, waited in the parking lot outside the block of flats for almost three hours. A big block called Unitas. Mart Velaze was on the seventh floor. Daro'd worked out which one: the unit on the end with no curtains at the window.

In those hours, six o'clock to almost eight forty, people working nine-to-fives got home. No light went on in Mart Velaze's window in that time. During those hours Mart Velaze should've come home. Even if just to freshen up before he hit the high life.

Also, Daro couldn't see the snappy Mart Velaze with his Golf GTI living in a flat in Unitas. The style didn't fit.

So Unitas was a drop pad, a convenience.

When he drove away Daro Attilane was a worried man. He was Mr Normal when he got home, but Georgina wasn't fooled. Steffie was fine, giving him the-everything's-cool-Dad-

I'm-handling-it story that he wanted to hear. And he believed her. But Georgina … Georgina nailed him with the sceptical eye when he walked in, sat at the table opposite while he pushed his food around the plate, watched him sink two whiskies, one more than normal.

When he poured the second drink she said, 'Daro, you'd better tell me.'

He wanted to. Lord knows he wanted to. But he couldn't. She'd never have believed him. Then it would've sat in her, nagging, poisoning her against him. Until weeks, months down the line she'd walk out.

'It's nothing,' he said.

'Come on, Daro. Don't give me that. You made a sale last week, it's not all doom and gloom.' She was curled on a couch, staring at him with those green attentive eyes. The once-upon-a-time blonde beach girl he couldn't believe had fallen for him. Miss Unattainable. But they'd got it together at a crayfish braai one evening under the Scarborough milkwoods. Hadn't been for those lobsters, hadn't been for her and her contacts, there'd have been no boutique car dealership. He'd still be on the floor somewhere: McCarthy's, Auto King, Thorp. Didn't matter which one, he'd be at a little desk next to the demos: inbox, outbox, blotter, telephone, coffee mug with the company logo. Couple of spec brochures aligned with the corner of the desk.

'No,' he said to her, taking down a large swallow of that second whisky, 'I didn't make the sale.'

'It's the economy,' she said. 'The recession. Got nothing to do with you. You can live it out. We've got the fat.'

What she didn't say was we've got my income. But Daro knew it was there, the hidden sting. Live it out. Problem, Georgina, the likes of Mart Velaze aren't necessarily something you can live out. You have to run from them. You have to disappear or … Or you have to get them to back off. You have to show you have an insurance policy. But he can't tell Georgina that.

So they sat there talking about her management placements,

he and Georgina, till midnight, till he'd sunk two more whiskies. Back of his mind he was working on what to do about Mart Velaze.

He tossed and turned on it through the night, too, but there didn't seem to be a way out. Certainly not an easy way out.

He faked breeziness when the alarm clock buzzed. Told Georgina he was going for a surf, would grab a croissant at Knead, head from there to the office.

'Daro,' she said, not opening her eyes. 'Just relax, please, about the slow sales. Things'll pick up again.' He nodded, gone to her room to plant a kiss on Steffie's head. Told her to be a good girl. She smiled, which was a bonus.

Out on the ocean he thought if the man pulling Mart Velaze's strings made a move, he'd be ready. In all ways. During the day he'd get the envelope from the bank deposit box, prepare a file of photostats. Maybe consider carrying the pistol. Wasn't much good locked up in the safe, always considering his instincts were right. One thing Daro Attilane trusted, it was his instincts.

This is the kind of anxiety that makes Daro not feel at home in the world when he opens up his dealership. The main consideration: get the documents from the bank first or sit through the morning? He decides to wait, drives the Audi from the showroom onto the forecourt.

There'll be a phone call Daro reckons to pick up on the car sale.

He's eating the croissant with a filter coffee when a courier van pulls in. Package for Mr Daro Attilane. Small padded envelope with something could be a matchbox in it. The sender: Adler Solutions.

58

'When your father was alive ...' Estelle is saying from the cellphone in loudspeaker mode lying on the kitchen table. Fish staring at it, drinking a last coffee before heading out. Thinking he hasn't heard Estelle use that in a long while.

'When your father was alive' being one of Estelle's constant refrains at the time Fish chucked up his degree.

'When your father was alive you got higher marks.'

'When your father was alive you were focussed.'

'When your father was alive you wouldn't have dreamed of doing this.'

'When your father was alive you didn't surf every moment of the day.'

'When your father was alive I used to see you as a man of the city. A top lawyer.'

Then she cooled it, let him get on with his life in the insurance agency.

Now it's back: 'When your father was alive, you weren't a bullshitter, Bartolomeu.'

Fish raising his eyebrows both at the 'when your father was alive' bit and the 'bullshitter'. Not like his mother to swear.

'I'm not bullshitting, Mom,' he says. 'I'm telling you I need more time.'

'It's a simple research task, Bartolomeu. I'd expect a report in a day normally. A first-year could do it in a morning.'

'Mom,' says Fish, leaning towards the phone, 'Mom, listen to me.'

'Yes, I'm listening.'

'I need more time.'

'You keep saying that.'

'For a reason.'

'Which is?'

'This Prospect Deep mine is not some Anglo American sell-off. I read the news. I know that much.'

'What difference does that make?'

'Big difference.'

'How, Bartolomeu? How's it different? A gold mine is a gold mine is a gold mine.'

'This one's about who owns it. About who is going to own it.'

'They all are, Bartolomeu. Give me some credit. I've been doing this for ten years now. I've put together people who've brought millions into our country. Without those investments we'd be a poorer nation. I know what I'm doing, Barto. I know how to do it.'

'I'm not saying that, Mom.'

'Then what's the problem?'

'Another twenty-four hours,' says Fish, putting down his coffee mug. 'Just so I can get the names, the connections. I've got to go, Mom.'

'We're on a cellphone, Bartolomeu. We can continue this while you're going wherever you're going. Unless you're going surfing?'

'I'm on a job.'

'I'm pleased to hear it. Pity it's not my job.'

And Estelle's gone. Fish standing, shaking his head, scoops up the phone. Jesus, bloody mothers. Lights out for the Perana.

59

'It's not policy,' says Clifford Manuel to Vicki Kahn. His eyes catch hers, then slide away. 'The partners made a deliberate decision that there'd be no borrowings.'

Vicki in Clifford Manuel's office. The two of them standing either side of Clifford Manuel's desk. Vicki's staring at him but his eyes are skittish, his focus mostly past her head at the certificates he's got framed on the wall.

'I don't know why you want this money and I don't wish to know. Your financial affairs are your own business.' A quick flick of his eyes.

Vicki takes this as an opening, lays it on. 'I'm in trouble, Clifford. I need the loan. I really need it.' Steps closer to his desk, lays it on more than she intended. Feeling why not, to hell with it. 'Serious trouble.'

'What sort ...' Clifford Manuel stops himself, holds up his hands. 'I don't want to know, it's your business.'

'Please,' says Vicki. Thinking, listen to you, girl. Beg it out of him. 'I've got a big problem.'

Clifford Manuel groans. 'The firm's policy is clear. It keeps things professional. You need to speak to your bank manager, Vicki, not me.'

'I have,' says Vicki.

'And?'

'And no dice. The firm's my last option.'

Vicki bows her head. Gazes down at the harbour ten floors below: container ships being loaded, an oil rig in for maintenance. Six ships waiting in the roadstead. The tourist ferry heading for Robben Island. Says, 'I'm desperate.' Keeps her eyes downcast, sensing Clifford Manuel's embarrassment. He knows about her gambling. Knows she's doing something about it. She hears him suck breath.

'You played cards?'

'I was forced into it.'

'No one's forced into it.'

She laughs. A harsh explosion. 'I was Clifford. I had no choice.'

'I thought ...'

'What, Clifford? Thought what? That I'm on the programme, it'll all be alright. I'm on the programme but it's not alright. That's why I'm asking you. I need to get out of this debt.'

Clifford Manuel sits down, stares at the papers on his desk pad. 'I can't,' he says, shaking his head. 'I absolutely can't. The other partners ...'

'Forget the other partners,' says Vicki. 'Six months, that's all I need. End of that you can have it all back, with interest.'

'We don't want interest. We're not moneylenders, Vicki, we're a law firm.'

'I'm asking you, Clifford. You, personally.'

He frowns, glances at her startled.

'Me?'

'You.'

'No, no, no, no.' Shaking his head. 'I don't lend money, Vicki. Not to anyone, family or friends. It ends in tears. It always ends in tears. Absolutely not. No.' He stands. Adjusts his tie: his blue tie with little red anchors on it. Set against a blue-striped shirt with a white collar. 'I'm sorry, Vicki. I wish you well but this problem is of your own making. You will have to sort it out some other way.'

'Do you know what they'll do, Clifford?'

Clifford Manuel won't meet her eyes, waves his hands.

'They'll hurt me. Beat me up.'

'There're laws ...'

'There're no laws for these people,' says Vicki. No intention of going anywhere near Jacob Mkezi's name. Wanting to keep that part secret. Or Clifford would freak. Didn't matter that it wasn't her fault, that Mkezi had set it up. He would throw his toys. She's glued to Clifford Manuel's face. His hands flat on the desk. His reply on cue: 'Then why do you mix with them? Why do you do this to yourself?'

'Because I couldn't do otherwise. I told you. I had to.'

Vicki thinking, if only you knew, then upping the ante by bringing tears to her eyes.

Which gets Clifford Manuel moving round his desk to lay a hand on her arm, gently turning her towards the door. 'I can't deal with this, Vicki. I can't get involved in your personal life. I'm sorry. I'm sorry you're upset but I can't help you.' Opening the door for her, a hand softly pressing on her back.

In her office, Vicki thinks, that was smooth, the way he ushered her out. But then Clifford Manuel is smooth.

Maybe the way to sort this is another game? She recalls the silkiness of the cards against her fingers. The anticipation of the hand as Cake Mullins dealt. The slow build with each round: the cards flipped, the money down. The intensity of the moment. Her focus zoned on the cards, the table, the faces of the players. Her own face relaxed. The cards fanned in her hand. The sudden calm.

One night and it's all back. She wants another game.

No.

Vicki closes her eyes. No.

Her heart rate's up, that anticipation beating in her chest.

No.

To stop the thoughts she opens her laptop, clicks through to her email. Right at the top, one there from Clifford Manuel, couple of minutes old: 'Again, Vicki, I'm sorry I can't help you. It's a matter of principle, and I hope you understand. Another thing, I had a call from that private investigator, Pescado. Please advise him again we have not been retained on the Appollis case.'

Not no. Maybe.

60

Samson Appollis phoned Fish to tell him, 'Don't come to my house. You know the swimming pool by the beach in Mitchells Plain? It's better we meet there in the car park. For Ma's sake.'

Took Fish another phone call to Samson Appollis to find the place. Off Baden Powell, down through the dunes and rooikrans bush to a deserted stretch of beach. Deserted swimming pool. All very quiet: the day bright, strong smell of salt off the sea, kelp gulls lined up on the changing room roof. Isolated place in Fish's reckoning. You don't want to be here alone, you don't want to come here for an hour on your ace, daydreaming. Deserted down here doesn't mean peace and quiet, deserted means something waiting to happen.

Coming in, Fish scopes the car park: a couple of cars in the front, probably belong to fishermen hoping to catch galjoen feeding inshore. Two dudes in a low-slung Honda playing loud rap.

Fish senses they're watching him behind their shades. He draws level, wags a two-finger horn sign, safe-my-mate, as he passes, the boys nodding back at him. Rumbles on to the farthest car park, there's Samson Appollis in his 1980s Mazda 323, parked facing the entrance. Fish thinks, if he sells that he's gonna get two grand for it on a good day. That's what he's offering as payment: two grand. What's two grand? A day's work. Two days if he's feeling charitable.

Fish stops beside the Mazda, nose onto the sea.

'I'm sorry for your loss,' he says, settling into the Mazda's passenger seat. The Appollis car smells of fabric softener. The inside neat: no sand in the foot wells, no discarded takeaway packets. No sweet papers, cooldrink cans, chocolate wrappings. Tidy people.

Fish turns sideways, looks at the ocean, the view clear to Seal Island. The way the car's facing is empty tarmac fringed with scrub dunes, the sightline open to the resort's entry point. Some of the empty cars visible but not the boykies in their Honda.

'What's worrying you?' says Fish.

Samson Appollis has his fingers tightly threaded together. 'I didn't want Ma to know. Not even that I talked to you.'

'Why not?' Fish thinking, yeah, and what's the other reason?

'Ma believes it was the Lord's wishes.'

'You don't?'

'No, Mr Fish.' Samson Appollis releases his fingers, balls his fists.

'So the thing is then, why not? The thing is, what's got you jumpy?'

For a long time Samson Appollis stares at the empty car park. 'We haven't got the policy,' he says.

'You said ...' Fish stops.

Samson Appollis glances at him, shifts in his seat, restless, uneasy. 'That was a lie, Mr Fish. Sorry, man. That was a lie we told you.'

'There's no insurance?'

'No.' Samson Appollis with his eyes on the distance.

Fish lets the silence drag. Then: 'So why'd you say there was?'

'He told us. Because this is what they wanted. First they wanted Ma and me to think they were sorry and that they will pay Forty's hospital, then they throw us away.'

Fish rubbed a hand over his face. 'Hang on, Mr Appollis, slowly, listen, what're you talking about?'

'He told us, don't worry, Mr Appollis, your boy will get better. Don't worry, Mr Appollis, we will move him to a good hospital, somewhere with the best doctors, the best care. He tells us and it happens. Don't worry, Mr Appollis. We will pay. It's like you've got an insurance. That's what he said. Ma and me we are so grateful. We can't pay hospitals, Mr Fish. We are not rich people.'

'Okay, bit by bit. I'm not with you, okay. Tell me, who's he? This man who's told you these things?'

'Mr Mart.'

'That right?' says Fish, 'Mart, hey. Mart Velaze.'

'Ja. You know him, Mr Fish?'

'Sort of.' Fish tapping Samson Appollis on the shoulder to continue. Fish sitting sideways in the seat, with Samson Appollis in profile. 'Let's go back here, Mr Appollis, tell me from the beginning when Mart Velaze first talked to you.'

'In the hospital, Mr Fish.'

'The first hospital.'

'That's right. We's standing there at Forty's bed, Ma and me, and I'm thinking, dear God, my boy's going to die. Ma's crying. We's alone there with him and Forty's bandaged, in a coma. I hear this man say my name, he asks if he can speak to me. He says he knows about the accident, that he can help.'

'This Mart Velaze?'

'A very quiet man. He speaks softly to me like a priest.'

'Uh huh, then?'

'Then he says to me, that he is going to have Forty moved to a private hospital. I say, no, we can't pay a private hospital. Don't worry, Mr Appollis, he says, all the money's going to be paid for you. Like an insurance. I look at him, I ask him why. Straight out, why? He says he can't tell me. "The man I am working for is doing this." Those are his words, Mr Fish. "The man I am working for is doing this." Trust me, Mr Appollis, he says. We will look after your son until he is better. I look at Forty lying there in that hospital bed and I think this is not a good place, he is going to die here. In the private hospital maybe he has a chance to live. Mr Fish, a father must do everything for his boy. So I say to Mr Mart, alright. Alright, if you promise me on God's name. "I promise you, Mr Appollis," he says. That's what he said to me, Mr Fish: "I promise you, Mr Appollis." Now look where his promise is. Broken.'

'Do you have to pay the hospital?'

'No, there's no fees, thank the Lord.'

Fish sighs, says, 'That's all he told you, that he worked for a man who wanted to help you.'

Samson Appollis nods.

'You didn't ask him again afterwards who this man was? Why he was doing this?'

'Of course I did, yes, man, what d'you think? I'm not a sponger. Oooh la la, Mr Mart he gets cross. I can see it in his face. He doesn't want me to keep asking this. Still he's smiling at me but his face is hard. Be grateful, Mr Appollis, he says. Your son's very lucky.' Samson Appollis picks at a thread on the steering wheel cover. 'When you were there with us yesterday, he saw you. Soon's you're gone, he's there. Who was that man? What's he want? What d'you tell him? I told him, Mr Mart, we told you nothing. I tell him you're investigating what happened. He gets cross, says, what about his boss? Did we say anything? Nay, Mr Mart, I say, we told you we got insurance. We's covered for a private hospital. We told you like he told us. No, Mr Appollis, he says, this is a problem. He says the man he works for is a very private gentleman. He likes to help people but he doesn't want anybody to know. No publicity. For Forty's sake we must never say anything. We swear for him on the Bible we will not say anything. Even if Forty dies, we must accept it is God's will.'

Fish's watching Samson Appollis, the man not blinking. His teeth grinding.

'You don't accept it?'

It takes a long time for Samson Appollis to respond. Fish shifts his gaze, watches a swell rise up and break, too quick and small to bring anybody much joy, before he hears the faint word, 'No.'

'What's changed, Mr Appollis? Why're you thinking this now?'

'Mr Mart said we must trust him, and what can we do? We must trust him. Our boy ...' He breaks off, swallows. 'Our boy, we had to save our boy.'

He stops there and Fish lets it hang. Samson Appollis still lost in the thousand-yard stare, the grinding teeth.

'But I never heard of this before. Of a person doing this before, paying for someone that's not family. The first thing I think is Mr Mart knows this person that hit my son. I'm not stupid, Mr Fish. Mr Mart knows. Also I would say this person he knows is rich.'

'Could be a main man, absolutely. Someone connected.'

'Could be, ja. That's what I think. A politician. Or a businessman. Maybe a gangster. One of the Untouchables, the mafia poaching abalone. You see Mr Fish there's rich people here on the Plain buy fast cars for their sons. They don't care about the racing. They sommer just spoil their children for peace and quiet.'

Fish chews on this, thinks, we're getting there, Samson my man, says, 'Why d'you think he was killed?'

Samson Appollis comes back fast. 'They's not worried anymore. Theys don't need him to be alive anymore.'

'You reckon?'

'Of course. They've paid their people. When you've got money, Mr Fish, you can do anything. Cheaper to pay your people than keep a boy alive. You don't know if the boy comes out of the coma maybe he says something.'

Which is Fish's take. 'You really reckon this?'

Samson Appollis turns quickly to Fish. 'I'm scared, Mr Fish, for Ma and me.'

'Mart threatened you?'

'Not in words.'

'The way he says things? His attitude?'

Samson Appollis nods. 'He comes close, Mr Fish, when he's talking. Close right next to you, breathing in your face. Talking quietly. You understand, Mr Appollis. You hear me, Mr Appollis. That's what he says all the time, over and over.'

'If you're scared why're you talking to me? Why'd you phone me?'

'Forty's dead, Mr Fish. Maybe you can do something?'

Fish let that go, admiring the man's nerve. Samson Appollis sobbing quietly. After a while Fish says, 'What you want me to do about it?'

'I want to know, Mr Fish. I want to know who killed my son. Just the name.'

'Just the name? Then what?'

'I dunno. Just the name.'

They sit there, not talking, while Samson Appollis snorts and snuffles into his handkerchief.

Fish says, 'Two things, Mr Appollis. First thing, soon's I start poking around you'll have Mart Velaze breathing in your face, wanting to know what you told me. Menacing you. Second thing: how're you going to pay me? I can't work for nothing.'

Samson Appollis blows his nose. 'I know I must pay, Mr Fish. I know that. I have money. Also I can sell the car.'

'Fine. You sell your car. That'll pay me for a day. This sort of work takes days and days. And there's still Mart Velaze. Best thing is you forget about this, Mr Appollis.'

Samson Appollis droops his head. 'I can't, Mr Fish,' he says, 'I can't.' He fidgets in his jacket pocket, brings out a piece of paper. A name written on it: Willy Cotton. 'This's Forty's friend he went to college with. He's a nice boy. How much if you just talk to him?'

'This's it? All you've got's his name?'

'Please, Mr Fish. How much?'

Fish thinks, do it for free. Help the man out. Says, 'Three hundred rand.'

Samson Appollis digs out a fold of notes, could be a couple of grand, Fish reckons. Skims three hundreds off the top, holds them out.

Fish takes the money, opens the door. 'I'll get back to you.'

'No, no, Mr Fish,' says Samson Appollis. 'Tonight I'll phone you.'

Fish shakes his head. 'Too soon. Tomorrow rather.' He's about to close the car door, he says, 'Did you see Mart Velaze last night?'

Samson Appollis nods. 'He was there at the hospital.'

'You talk to him?'

'A little bit. He says he is very sorry for us. He also says it is God's will that Forty's gone.'

Fish twigs on the money, almost snorts a laugh. 'He gave you the money?'

'To help us out with things. That's what he says, "To help us out with things".'

Samson Appollis starts the Mazda, the engine cranking before it fires.

'Why'd you take the money if you think …'

A sad smile deepens the lines around Samson Appollis's mouth. 'To pay you, Mr Fish,' he says. 'To pay you.'

When he's gone Fish phones Vicki. Leans against his car taking in the ozone, the lingering fumes of Samson Appollis's car sneaking into the mix.

Vicki comes on: 'Before you ask, I didn't get the loan.'

'It was worth a try.'

'I did get an email from him afterwards telling me to tell you we've got nothing to do with the Appollis case.'

'I expected that.' Fish hears the Honda kick into life, the exhaust roar, pivots to face the entrance to the parking lot.

'Where're you? On the beach?'

'Mitchells Plain. Funny little place with a swimming pool.' The Honda's crawling towards him. 'Got some company it seems.'

'You alright?'

'No probs.'

The Honda stops fifty metres off, the dudes inside invisible behind the tinted windscreen. Low doof-doof reverb Fish can feel in his feet.

'Quick favour,' he says to Vicki, 'can you check out on Facebook if a guy Willy Cotton's got a page.'

'Fish, I'm not …'

'Might've put up contact info. Kids're stupid that way. I would–'

'Fish, that's why you've got a laptop. So you can use it.'

'It's at home.'

The Honda rolls forward twenty metres.

'Got to go,' says Fish, disconnects. Stands there wondering if this is a gun situation.

The Honda stops, the driver leans out, says, 'Hoezit, my bru ...'

Fish squints at him: one sharp-faced individual, deep eye sockets, pointy cheekbones and chin. Gives him the howzit nod.

'My bru, ek sê, you come to the market?'

Fish shrugs. 'Maybe.'

They do the eyeball until the driver laughs. 'You's a roker-man, I can see. A smoker, I can tell.'

'You reckon?'

'I can see, my bru, I can see you's chilled.' The driver keeps the car grumbling, slides forward a couple more metres. 'We's selling, my bru. Come check.'

The passenger door opens, short skinny type hops out. 'My bru,' he says, 'come check.' He hitches his jeans, waddles off a few paces to spit. 'Come check.' Waves Fish over.

Fish pockets his phone, walks towards them. On the back seat are two binliner bags. The brothers grin at him. 'Another in the boot,' says the skinny one. 'What you call grade A1, herbs from Durbs, ek sê.' He opens a bag. 'You don't believe me, see for yourself.' Fish leans in, breaks off a head. It's good stuff, rooibaard variety with the sticky red hairs on the head.

'See what I tell you, my bru. Our grass is mos top class.'

'You wanna score, we's got plenty more,' the driver adding his pitch.

'Alright,' says Fish. 'How much?'

'Five hundred a bag, my bru. Special price for you.'

Fish takes three hundred-rand notes from his pocket. 'Here's what I've got.' Holds them up, fanned.

'Agga no, my bru,' says the skinny one, 'three's too little. This's the best. Five hundred's rock-bottom, going for a song, ek sê vir jou. Low as we go.'

'Three,' says Fish, waving the notes.

'Dis daylight robbery,' says the driver. 'You's stealing the bread and butter from our children, out of their mouths.'

'Three,' says Fish.

The skinny one and the driver stare at Fish, stare at the money until the driver pushes a bag off the back seat.

Fish thinking no ways these guys are dealers, they've ripped it off, they want to unload quickly.

'Okay, my bru,' says the skinny one, snatching the money from Fish's hand. 'You's a thief.'

'Hey,' says Fish, 'it's three hundred you're getting for nothing. Makes three of us're thieves.' He watches them until the car's out of sight before he picks up the bag. A bloody good deal. Stash that lot in baggies he could score four thou, even five thou maybe.

He's about to drive off, his phone goes: Vicki.

'So what's so urgent you have to ditch me?'

Fish laughs. 'Sorry, Vics. Had a little situation developing. Some kids, you know ...'

'I don't, but your situation's over I take it?'

'Oh yes.'

'Then listen to what your personal secretary's got for you: Willy Cotton's cellphone number, email address, lots of photies even some with Fortune Appollis. And the courses he's registered for. Want me to get Willy's timetable as well?'

'Would you? Thanks, Vics.'

Silence.

'I'm having a bad day, Fish. Don't push it. You want printouts of this stuff, come and get them.'

She disconnects.

Fish smiles.

Jacob Mkezi tells Mellanie, no, no more profiles. Doesn't matter who it's for. No more profiles.

She's not taking no as the final word.

'Jacob,' she says, 'hear me, this is the *Sunday Times*. This is major exposure. This is not my touting. This is their request.'

'No,' he says.

'Lifestyle,' she says. 'Not some op-ed Q&A, this is Jacob Mkezi at home. Jacob Mkezi on the golf course. Jacob Mkezi judging a beauty contest of bomb victims. Jacob Mkezi visiting a school feeding scheme. His personal charity.'

'What charity?'

'The one we're going to launch.'

He laughs. 'You're full of shit. You know that, full of shit. What're you doing this for, sisi? I don't need this crap.'

He hears Mellanie sigh. 'My job, Mr Mkezi, is to reinvent you. No more the man in the crocodile-skin shoes. Now it's Mr Heart. Mr At Home. Geddit?'

'What for?'

'Ah, Jacob, to save your career, my former commissioner.'

'What do I need that for? I'm at home in the crocodile-skin shoes. No police career needed, everything's good. I don't need a career. I don't need a cop job. What do I need that for? I've got a company. I've got everything. I don't need that hassle and crap, I need to relax. Take time out. Live my life.'

Jacob Mkezi looking down at his crocodile-skin shoes. He's sitting in his lounge, the sliding doors open to the lawn, the hadedas doing their thing on the grass. What does he need to be in an office for?

'Lunch,' he says to Mellanie. 'Let's talk about lunch. Let's talk Steenberg. Bistro Sixteen82 we can sit there look up at the

Elephant's Eye. Eat their duck confit. Drink that Rattlesnake Sauvignon Blanc. Listen to the water features. Day like today, what d'you say?'

'I say,' says Mellanie, 'that's a nice idea but some of us have jobs, Mr Mkezi. Some of us need to pull in the shekels.'

'Give it a break,' he says. 'Meet me there.' Jacob Mkezi thinking, Mellanie for lunch is a good idea. After that he needs self-time. Self-time to track down that little rent boy. Put the feeding scheme into operation. Up the rent buti's calorie intake.

He catches Mellanie saying, 'One thirty. That's the earliest I can do, Jacob.'

'One thirty's good. Give you something to look forward to.'

He hears her laugh. 'Jacob Mkezi, sometimes, I dunno, sometimes you're too much.'

Next he keys through to Tol Visagie. A stressed Tol Visagie.

'You found out who he is?' Tol Visagie wants to know right off. 'That Vusi Bopape?'

'Not yet,' says Jacob Mkezi.

'He's just sitting there, at the lodge. My friend says he spent all morning on the deck, reading, checking the wildlife drinking at the waterhole. That's all. Makes some phone calls. Sits there drinking beer.'

'Sounds like he's having a good time. His wife there?'

'No. She didn't come back with him. He's waiting for something. Waiting for someone.'

'Hang loose, Tol,' says Jacob Mkezi. 'Stay away from the horns. Thursday morning you meet the trucks at the river o-five-hundred. Got it?'

'Ja,' says Tol Visagie, 'I'll be there.'

Jacob Mkezi's onto Mart Velaze next.

Mart Velaze says, 'The boy died. Didn't come out of the coma.'

'I'm sorry to hear that.'

'Happens all the time.'

'Daro Attilane?'

'Being handled.'

'Vusi Bopape?'

'Nothing. Not NIA, definitely. Not military. Not police.'

Jacob Mkezi gets up, closes the sliding doors. 'You're a good man, comrade. Keep trying.'

He thinks about phoning Vicki Kahn. Thinks about it, but doesn't. Better to let a few days pass. Let her contemplate owing him a favour. He likes that, the thought of someone owing him a favour.

62

Daro stares at the unopened package on his desk.

Adler Solutions.

There's a city address, suite twelve, fifteenth floor of an office block on Long, and a telephone contact.

Daro knows if he rings he'll be told wrong number. If he does the legwork he'll find it's the office of a management consultant or a forwarding agent, anything but a company called Adler Solutions.

He pushes aside what's left of the croissant. There's that nauseous feeling in his stomach. Reaches for the package, cuts off the plastic courier bag. Inside's a box wrapped in brown paper. The size box a jeweller'd have for a diamond ring. Taped to the box a card for Adler Solutions. Same address, same telephone number. The sort of card you could have run off at an instant-print booth.

Daro pulls off the card, tears the wrapping. Inside's a black box with a hinged lid, a little brass fastening clasp. Someone's got a sense of style.

He flips up the catch, springs back the lid. Lying on a cotton wool bed's a bullet.

Daro tweezers it out with the thumb and index finger of his right hand, lays it in the palm of his left. So light it's no weight at all.

The bullet is a .22 long-rifle. Not a big bullet, the brass and lead no more than fifteen millimetres. Not an impressive bullet, small, insignificant. But give it a chance it'll do death and damage at three hundred and thirty metres per second.

Daro doesn't know the specifics here.

Doesn't know, for instance, that way back in 1887 in Chicopee Falls, Massachusetts the J. Stevens Arms & Tool Company started churning these out and nowadays it's a popular bullet everywhere: good for plinking, good for hunting pest animals, good for hitmen. Not much noise. With a silencer little more than a pop.

Another advantage, this cartridge works for both rifles and pistols. It's the inauspicious nature of this bullet that deceives. A mere two point six grams of lead but you put that into your target in the right spot, job done 'n dusted.

One case: a photographer covering the township wars back in the early 1990s copped a .22 long-rifle load fired by the peace-keeping force. Copped it in the chest. Small hole, invisible if it hadn't leaked just a tear of blood. Inside the lead tumbled about his ribcage chewing up heart and lungs. End of his story.

What Daro doesn't think about is that the example lying in the palm of his hand is one of millions, the brass tarnished, the cross in the lead snag-edged from the cut. Apart from the cross, a common bullet. Can be bought by the box at any gun shop.

Might be common but it gets Daro's heart racing. His mouth's dry, the sweat's damp in his armpits. He keeps himself seated, the bullet clutched in his fist.

What Daro thinks about is who made the cut? Mart Velaze springs to mind. Except Mart Velaze is a messenger. That being the case, Daro decides, he needs him to deliver a message. Well, a whole dossier.

63

Fish makes a mental list: Seven, Cake Mullins, Willy Cotton. His mother doesn't crack the list. Despite that she's his mother, despite the hours he could bill, he's got a reluctance here. He promises himself, tonight he'll handle her job. First things first.

He tools along Baden Powell beside the sea, half an eye on a neat wave rolling in at Cemetery. Very rideable. Not much excitement in the swell but still would be a better thing to do than any of the calls he has to make.

Fish buys a croissant at Knead, munches down on the pastry for the short walk into the warren.

Seven's not at the house of bad breath. Nor is Jouma the Toothless. Who's there is the chick he found Seven shagging the day before. Her and a coloured girl. They stand in the passageway, tell Fish Seven's upped and offed.

'We don't know where to, dude,' the white one says. 'He's gone. You want to see?'

'He's taken his bag,' chips in the coloured one. 'And his CDs.'

'What about the other guy, without the teeth?' Fish taps his own front teeth.

'Both, gone.'

They stand there staring at him, these two urchins can't be more than sixteen years old wearing baggy tracksuit pants and jerseys, grey school socks, no shoes. Lank hair that could do with washing. The coloured one says, 'Can you give us money for food?'

Fish laughs at her. 'No. You should be in school. Sleeping at home.'

'Please, dude, we're hungry.'

'Go home then,' says Fish.

She gives him the finger.

'Fuck off, cunt,' says the white one, slams closed the door.

Nice, thinks Fish. Gives his cop neighbour Flip Nel a call.

'Runaways're not my scene exactly,' says Flip Nel. 'But I'll check it out for the promise of a fishing trip. You getting your tyres fixed?'

'Sort of caught up in other things,' says Fish.

'Weekend's coming, china. Thank Christ. I'm baiting up.' Flip Nel rings off, Fish hoping the cop's not going to be a pain in the arse about going fishing.

Cake Mullins has much the same attitude as the teenage girls, though he puts it differently at first. At first Cake Mullins says, 'I don't know who you are. Go away.'

They're talking through the buzz box: Fish leaning out the window of his car at the gate of Cake Mullins's Constantia house. Fish recognising the place where Daro Attilane came to sell a Subaru. Nice-looking pad. Double-storey, porticoed entrance, neat lawns, swimming pool, a gardener weeding the grass. Fish thinking, How about that? One of life's little coincidences. Fish taps his fingers on the buzz box. He hates buzz boxes. The crackle's bad, there's a CCTV system projecting him onto a screen somewhere in the house, giving Cake Mullins all the advantages.

He says, 'Can we do this face to face?'

'No,' says Cake Mullins. 'I don't know who you are.'

'I told you, Fish Pescado.'

'That supposed to mean something, Mr Pescado?'

'Yes. Plain curiosity should have you opening the gates for me. Can't be every day you have an investigator investigating.'

'Go away, pal. I'm a busy man.'

Fish tries a different angle, says, 'Vicki Kahn, know her? I left a message about her on your answer phone.'

'Never heard of her.'

'Quick refresh: she was here last night for a game you set up. Ring any bells?'

'Do me a favour, pal, bugger off will you?'

Fish looks up at the camera, giving the raised eyebrows query. Wonders if Cake Mullins has a clear picture. 'Don't be like that. Be nice, Cake. I'll say again: she was here last night for a poker game.'

'Wrong address, pal.'

'I don't think so. You're Cake Mullins, this is your house so far so right. Grand place, by the way. Musta costa plenty. Costa plenty to keep it spick 'n span, I'd say.'

'What you say doesn't matter, pal. Let me run through this one more time: bugger off.'

Fish holds up his hands to the camera. 'Okay, I'm going. You can get back to your scones 'n tea, Cake. But hear me: you do that to her again I'm probably going to bust your balls.'

'Yeah, big man. Whatta hero.'

''Nother thing, your mate Jacob Mkezi—'

'I don't know any Jacob Mkezi.'

'Course you do, Cake. That's why you butted in so fast there.'

'Fuck off,' says Cake Mullins. The crackle dies on the buzz box.

Nice, thinks Fish, twice in half an hour. Enough to make you feel unloved.

Willy Cotton's not the friendliest young man Fish's ever stumbled across either.

Fish's sitting on a bench on the campus gazing up at Table Mountain, rising grey against a winter blue, thinking, he loves this city: the tower blocks, the posh suburbs spread round the lower slopes, like rock lichen at low tide.

Fish thinks it's been a time since he walked St George's Mall, hasn't smelt the early morning fish pong that would drift up from the harbour some days. Hasn't eaten a burger and chips at the Gardens restaurant in a year or more. Hasn't heard the noon-day gun chase up the pigeons in yonks.

Where he's sitting faces towards a lecture theatre where Willy

Cotton is learning the wonders of business information sys-
tems. How Vicki pinned this down Fish doesn't know and Vicki
wouldn't tell him.

When she gave him Willy Cotton's contact details and two
printout photographs of the young man all she said was, 'Don't
think you'll always get this lucky, Mr Pescado. That's where
he is right now, in class.' And pinched his cheek and was gone
back into the building before he could say thanks.

The students come out, Fish stands on the bench to get a
better view. No mistaking Willy Cotton: shaved head like a
gangster's, little moustache and chin beard, body that's gym-
toned. Obligatory jeans, though Willy Cotton's are belted round
his waist. Denim jacket over a 50 Cent T-shirt. Happy chappie
having some laughs with his mates.

Fish phones him. Watches the guy squeeze a cellphone out
of his jeans pocket. Seems to be some sort of smartphone with
a keyboard. Impressive, running a smartphone means Willy Cotton's making money somewhere, somehow.

Only bummer in Willy Cotton's image is that he has this
high-pitched voice doesn't belong to his pumped-up body.

'Got a minute?' Fish says.

'Who're you?' says Willy Cotton in his Cape Flats soprano.

'Friend of Fortune Appollis's family.'

End of conversation. Willy Cotton keys him off on the turn.

Fish stares after the big man, moving away with his friends.
But the jauntiness has gone from Willy Cotton's walk. He's
agitated, not paying attention to them, staring at his phone like
he expects it to ring again.

Fish follows the group off the campus up a couple of streets
to Justice Walk where they've parked their cars. They do parting
hugs and back thumps, Willy Cotton going further along the road
to his drive, a new-model Corolla. Not bad going for a student.

Fish calls to him. Willy Cotton pivots.

'I'm the guy who just phoned you,' says Fish.

Willy Cotton checks him out, faces him with the calm of a

club bouncer. Being given the hard-eye by Willy Cotton's not for sissies. Nice polite boy he might be but he can also throw attitude.

'Stay cool,' says Fish. 'No need to get all aggro.'

'What d'you want?' There's that voice again, high and squeaky.

'Couple of things.' Fish stops about two metres off, at the back of the Corolla. 'Can we talk in your car?'

'Nothing to talk about.'

'Fortune's dad thinks there is.'

'Like what?'

'Like what happened that night.'

Willy Cotton keeps up the stare, says nothing.

'Come'n, Willy, what's going on?'

'I can't say anything.' Willy Cotton opens his car door.

'Fortune's dead, Willy.'

'You lie.'

'Last night. In the larney private hospital, where someone was paying for his treatment, Fortune died. Who was paying, Willy? Not the Appollises because they've got no money, no insurance policy. So who, Willy, who?'

Willy Cotton's looking at the ground now, at his sexy silver-and-blue takkies with white stripes, Pumas. Could be grief he's experiencing.

'Aaaah!' He smacks the roof of the Corolla three times with this fist.

Fish waits, the guy tears up, gets the sniffles. He wipes his eyes, sucks back hard.

'Do this for Fortune, Willy. Just a name. All I want's a name.'

'I don't know any names.'

'No? I think you do.' Fish takes a step closer. 'You were Fortune's big mate. You rolled together, parties, those speed-racing gigs, clubs. Why didn't you go'n see him in hospital, man? You were friends. Why didn't you phone his folks? They'd have liked that.'

'I couldn't. Yusses, man, don't you understand?'

'You couldn't?'

'No.'

Fish leans back against the car. 'What don't I understand, Willy? What'm I missing here?'

'I've got to go.'

'Wait.' Fish grabs a handful of Willy Cotton's denim jacket. Comes up close to him. Willy Cotton raising a fist. Fish says, 'Don't be stupid, okay. You're a big boy but so'm I, muscle's not the end of the story. I know moves you don't.'

Willy Cotton shakes himself free. Fish releases him, staying up close, in his face.

'Think about Fortune, Willy. Fortune got hit by a car. Alright, it was an accident. Let's forget it was an illegal street race. Now Fortune's dead and no one's going to pay. That's not right, is it? Fortune was a good guy. A good friend. You had major times together. Means zilch if you let it go. Let him die when there's this other guy running around like nothing's happened. Like he hit a kitty cat in the street, who cares? How's this play in your head, Willy? At night when you're lying there thinking about your friend. How's it play then?'

Fish gives Willy Cotton time to think on it.

'It's not right, Willy. Fortune's life's worth more than this. Wouldn't you say?'

'His name's Lord.'

'Like the Lord God?'

Willy Cotton nods.

'His surname?'

'That's his handle. That's how he rides. I don't know his surname.'

'Rides?'

'Races.'

'Give me a break. How old's he? Young like you?'

A shrug that Fish takes for yes. 'He's a big deal?'

Willy Cotton coughs a high laugh, points into the sky. 'Up there.'

'Connected, hey? But you wouldn't know who to?'

'Government.'

Fish's turn to laugh. 'All the main manne are connected to government, Willy. You're not telling me anything. I need something specific. What's he? A minister's boykie? Son of a DG? One of the president's kids, grandkids?'

'No idea. Listen, man, I can't help you.'

'Course you can, Willy. You just don't know it.' Fish thinking from the sour breath coming out of Willy Cotton's mouth the boy's seriously nervous. 'So, let me come up with a scenario: after your friend Fortune was hit by Lord's car, everyone made a duck. Lord drove away, someone called the medics.'

'I did. I stayed with him.' Willy Cotton's scratching at his goatee as if he'd like to scratch it off.

'You see, now there's a detail his folks don't know, Willy. They'd like that, knowing their son had his friend with him.' Fish gazes across the vacant ground of long-gone District Six to the harbour. From here the gantries and cranes, the towers of an oil rig seem part of the city centre. Always gives him a thrill to glimpse through the urban riggings the bay beyond, a white scythe of beach. 'Then what?'

'When the medics were there they didn't worry about me.'

'You drifted off?'

'Ja.' Willy Cotton leaves off the scratching.

'Thing is the emergency centre had your phone number. The cops must've called for a statement? You make a statement?'

'No.'

'The cops never called?'

'No.'

'But you got a visit?' Fish pulls his eyes off the view, looks square into Willy Cotton's face. Sees there a young boy terrified. The same look kindergarten-Willy might've had watching a Dobermann bounding, snarling towards him. Huge guy like this with a face full of fear. 'You don't have to say anything, I reckon I could tell you who showed up, even what sort of car he drives.'

'Leave me,' says Willy Cotton, 'leave me out of this. Fortune's folks've got no chance. No chance ever.'

'I hear you,' says Fish, drums his fingers on the car's roof. 'All the same, help me out here. If I want to see this dude Lord racing, how's that happen?'

'There's an SMS comes round. He's racing tonight.'

'That right?' Fish chews on this. 'Tell you what, I'll pick you up, we can go together and watch him race. I'd like that.'

'No ways. No ways.'

'Shouldn't be a problem. Who's going to know? I'll pick you up, Willy, I know where you're living. What time these things happen: ten, eleven, midnight?'

'Eleven,' says Willy Cotton, throwing his bag into his car.

'Don't let me down, Willy. That wouldn't be a good idea.' Fish backs off. 'And, hey, give Fortune's parents a bell, they'd like that.'

64

'Cake, my friend,' says Mart Velaze. 'Not now. I'm in a situation, alright. I'll call you, alright.'

'This could be an issue, I think you should understand that,' says Cake Mullins. 'I am not happy here.'

'I'll get back to you. But now's not a good time, Cake, you with me?' At which Mart Velaze disconnects.

Mart Velaze's situation involves a young woman sprawled naked on his bed. She's German, works in the consulate. They thought a quickie over lunchtime was a good idea.

'I've got this flat,' Mart Velaze said, 'just down Marine Drive, ten minutes out of the city.'

'I can wait ten minutes,' said the mädchen.

Turns out she's waiting a bit longer because now Mart Velaze is on the phone. For the second time. She levers herself onto her knees, reaches up to undo Mart Velaze's belt.

Mart Velaze thought her tits looked lovely when she was lying down, considers they're even better gazing down her cleavage. He reaches for her, tweaks a nipple.

The German consular official unzips him.

Cake Mullins doesn't have a situation, he has a concern. Two concerns: one major, one minor. The first concern, the minor concern, being Fish Pescado winding him up. The second concern, the major one, was delivered by courier. Inside, a photograph of a young boy getting into a Hummer. Jacob Mkezi's Hummer. Also a picture at the hotel: him, Clifford Manuel, Vicki Kahn, Tol Visagie, Jacob Mkezi. This causes Cake Mullins concern.

The first might be a photoshopped picture but Cake Mullins feels it's not. Given the rhino horn venture, you don't want pictures of Jacob Mkezi with rent boys floating around. Cake

Mullins can see how this matter can get out of hand. His own small part in it might become known, well, messy is a word that then occurs to Cake Mullins.

He's standing beside his swimming pool, staring at the Kreepy Krauly chundering on the detritus of leaves, thinking, no, he's not going to wait for Mart Velaze to phone him back. Mart Velaze has a reputation for not phoning back, especially when it's a matter where Mart Velaze can't see the angle.

What worries Cake Mullins here is his own reputation. Cake Mullins in pressed white slacks and boating shoes, a jersey draped over his shoulders, his shirt unbuttoned to show a silver crucifix, does not need complications in his life. He has stripped his life of complications. He is living on investments. Nowadays, Cake Mullins is squeaky clean. Even his poker evenings are small-time. Last evening with Jacob Mkezi and Vicki Kahn being a blip on the radar. The last thing Cake Mullins wants is to have his golf days, his crony lunches, his Wednesday yachting afternoons at the Royal Cape spoilt by any kind of stain. The kind of stain association with Jacob Mkezi can cause, when Jacob Mkezi is pulling a deal involving rhino horns. So Cake Mullins gets right back to Mart Velaze.

Who doesn't answer.

Because the German consular official is doing things with her mouth and hands that concentrates the mind of Mart Velaze. For a moment he closes his eyes, submits to the darkness there. But not for long. He brings his eyes back to those breasts, licks his fingers, tweezers a nipple once more. The phone's in his other hand. He lets it ring to answermail.

The woman stops sucking, says, 'I want you inside me.'

'I was,' says Mart Velaze.

The woman tosses her hair, lies back on the bed, her arms held up to him.

'Come.'

He has never seen a woman with so much hair in her crotch.

He thinks of what the Americans call it. Her snatch. Her bush. He wants to run his fingers through the curlies, feel them.

Mart Velaze steps out of his trousers, unbuttons his shirt, lays it carefully over a chair. He puts his phone on the bedside table.

It gives an SMS alert. Mart Velaze ignores it, smiles down at the young woman.

He combs his fingers through the mat of her pubic hair, raises his hand to judge their length. They're four, five centimetres long. Silky.

'You don't like to shave?' he says.

She shakes her head. 'You know muff dive?'

He nods.

'Please.'

Mart Velaze's cellphone rings again.

'Sorry,' he says, 'next time.' Instead he lays down on the woman, slips inside her. She gasps. Groans with his thrust.

With his right hand Mart Velaze reaches for the phone, sees it's Cake Mullins again.

'I will get back to you, Cake,' he says. 'I told you.'

'No, listen to me,' Cake Mullins says, 'I've got this guy Fish Pescado, an investigator, threatening me about Vicki Kahn. Wanting to talk about Jacob Mkezi. I've got this photograph of a rent boy getting into Jacob's car. You better check with Jacob what's happening there. He listens to you, Mart. He's not gonna listen to me. You tell him I'm out of it. Off the radar.'

The woman beneath Mart Velaze is a groaner.

'This is not my place,' says Mart Velaze. 'I'm a soldier, Cake, like you. Taking orders. You want to tell him something, you tell him yourself.'

She's grinding hard against him. Mart Velaze has to shut his eyes to concentrate.

'I'll ... call ... you ... back,' he says, the words spaced between the thrust of her pelvic bone. He's glad she's bushed, without the cushion he'd be grimacing. He thumbs off Cake Mullins, slides his phone under the pillow. Nothing that can't wait seven minutes.

Across the city in the vineyard suburb, Cake Mullins beside his swimming pool stares at his phone, disconnects. Bloody Mart Velaze. Always fucking around. Banging some bird when there's serious dwang in the land. He sits down to his lunch at the table in the gazebo. Takes a long swallow from a tall rock shandy, gets the taste of the bitters under the soda and lemonade. He chomps on a ciabatta slice spread with pesto. This's what he wants of life: sit here in his garden next to his swimming pool for a quiet lunch. Afterwards, maybe drift into the yacht club for a few toots, a perfect winter's day like this. What he doesn't want is the worry of people like Mart Velaze and Tol Visagie on his mind. Or the hassle of types like Fish Pescado.

Quarter of an hour later his phone goes: Mart Velaze.

65

Daro clutches the bullet in his fist, sits at his desk staring at the cars on his forecourt. He has checked his answerphone, no calls while he was out. How long will Mart Velaze wait before he calls? Will Mart Velaze call?

The pistol is in the desk drawer, within easy reach. He has drawn the necessary documents from the bank security box, made copies of everything: bank statements, letters, tape transcriptions, notes, including the photographs. The originals are back in the bank box; the copies in two envelopes beneath his palm.

Daro has considered the options: best outcome, the matter goes away. Worst case, he's killed. In which case there's a contingency plan; doesn't help him but it puts the whole story out there.

Daro believes out there is not where Mart Velaze and his principal would want this.

He sits through midday, one o'clock, two o'clock. He answers phone calls, does a sales spiel for a couple he knows aren't serious. Passes another half an hour waiting for Mart Velaze to ring.

At three he's had enough. Drives in the Audi, shuts up shop. He needs distraction: phones his daughter.

'How about a surf?'

'Alright,' she says.

'Alright reluctant or alright great idea?'

'Alright great idea.'

'You mean it?'

'Da—add.' The long sigh of resignation.

He laughs. 'Just checking. Be there in ten.'

Next, phones Fish with the same invite.

Fish says, 'I can't. My board's broken. Also Vicki's on my case.'

Daro taps the envelopes, thinks, what a pity. Says, 'What's with the board?'

'You don't want to know.' Listens while Fish gives him a potted version anyhow.

'I've got a spare for you, my old cruiser. Rides in anything, even southeast chop. You could surf the wake of that boat you've got sitting in your back yard.'

'Sharks in the deep water,' says Fish.

'Sharks everywhere,' says Daro.

Fish mumbles some kind of gratitude. Daro brushes it aside. 'Pick it up anytime. It's in the garage, top one on the rack. Pleased to hear Seven's gone.'

After the call Daro still hesitates a minute or two. Stands in the office as if he's waiting. He sighs, walks out. He's locking the door when the landline phone goes. He hesitates, considers it better to take the call.

It's Mart Velaze. He starts in about how he wants to buy the car, couldn't make it out today, how about tomorrow?

'Cut the crap,' says Daro.

Mart Velaze says, 'Daro, Daro, Daro, what's up, my friend?'

'This's up,' says Daro. 'The bullet is childish. You're the messenger boy, and I've also got a message needs to be delivered.'

'I think we're past messages.'

'You mightn't think so when you read this one.'

Silence from Mart Velaze.

'I'm going home now,' says Daro. 'Maybe we can meet later at Surfers' Corner, you can have a little read. This is great stuff. Riveting. Some fascinating photographs too. Not the sort of information you'd want in the public domain, so think about this as a preview. A teaser. I've got more. Hear what I'm saying? Five thirty I'll be waiting.'

Daro cuts the connection before Mart Velaze can respond. Best scenario, it's going to buy time. But time can be useful. He puts the bullet back into its box, takes it with him.

Half an hour later Daro and Steffie on her brand new rounded-pin mini mal sit on the backline such as it is. A tame swell pushing in that's good for a cruise but pretty much nothing else.

'This is like naff,' says Steffie.

'It's a surf,' says Daro. 'Better than homework.'

They catch a ride both of them on the same wave: Daro chasing his daughter, trying to step onto her board. He goes over, comes up laughing. Steffie ends the same way.

They paddle out, swing round to face the beach: the parking lot's still jammed with vehicles, the office shift only now arriving. Daro checks his watch: in an hour he's got his meeting. The shadow's starting across the Corner, dragging a cold with it.

'Last ride,' he says.

Steffie doesn't argue.

On the short drive home she tells him the cops busted two of her classmates in a crack house in the village.

Daro comes in. 'Let me guess, the house of a gangster called Seven?'

'How d'you know?' says Steffie.

Daro smiles. 'I know lots.'

66

Fish spends the afternoon on the balcony of Rafiki's restaurant in town, working his phone, selling dagga. He has the same spiel for everyone, the professors, the lawyers, the advertising execs, the trust account officers: 'I've got some schweet rooibaard, the best. Believe me, you don't want to say no.'

Some of them ask him what's rooibaard? He has a riff ready about hidden KwaZulu valleys where the crop lies rich and green beneath a fierce sun. He tells them it is tendered by women in colourful skirts who draw water from ancient rivers. It is the herb of warriors. He lays it on until his clients are giggling, placing orders beyond the normal.

He's sold off twenty bankies before he's halfway through his list. Twenty bankies will sort his tyre problem, still leave stock in hand. When he gets in among the surfers he can make a killing. For them, manna from heaven.

At twenty, Fish puts down his phone, turns his attention to his Castle milk stout and the fading afternoon. He's watching the mountain lose its light as the sun sets, musing on happenstance: the bakkie's tyres get slashed, he lands a cheap bag of good herb; his board is broken, he's lent another; he obliges a grieving father … The outcome of that isn't written yet. Another way to look at it is he can't leave well enough alone. Story of his life, not backing off where he's got no business. Then again, what the hell. He watches the sunlight lose hold of the mountain's rim, the shadows deepen in Platteklip Gorge.

He thinks about his mother's job. Sighs. Puts through a call to a broker at the insurance company he once worked for. Asks the guy for some background on the Prospect Deep goldmine. The proposed BEE deal. Board of directors. Financial statements. Anything that Google doesn't have.

'Prospect Deep,' says the broker. 'There's a story.'

'What sort of story?' says Fish.

'Let me draw this other stuff. I'll get back to you.'

Fish thinks this is not what he wants to hear.

Then his gaze is drawn to Vicki parking her MiTo across the road. Sometimes, he reckons, the world works.

Like for Vicki now. She slides into a parking space right on drinks hour, right outside Rafiki's. Most nights to get that spot on Kloof Nek you'd need to park at two a.m.

He calls over a waiter, orders another stout, a vodka, lime and soda.

Looks down at Vicki leaning against her car looking up at him. He waves. Gorgeous Vicki. Those white teeth. Lovely.

'Why?' he asked her a couple of weeks after she became the new woman in his life.

She was over for dinner. He'd scored some lobsters from people he knew, steamed them. Made a garlic dip. Added salad, potato wedges he baked in the oven, a great meal. Candles. Cotton serviettes. His Boardmans cutlery. Quiet, romantic evening, right time to ask her why.

'I like a bit of rough,' she said, cracking open a lobster leg, happy too about the mess of the meal. He liked a woman who wasn't fazed about lobsters. Not drinking wine either but beer. Okay, not his stout but Millers, from the bottle.

'Ha, ha,' he'd replied. 'Seriously.'

'Seriously?'

'Uh huh.'

She leant across, took a wedgy from his plate, popped it in her mouth. 'Because I go for macho. You know, the surfing, rootin-tootin type.' She chewed the chip, smiling at him, teasing. Her brown eyes impish. 'I don't know, Fish. You make me laugh. I like your taste in music. Isn't that enough?'

Now Fish rises as she strides towards him.

'Babes, such manners.'

He's never quite sure, is she kidding?

They sit. The waiter brings their drinks, pours the soda into hers.

'All the way,' Vicki says, smiling at the guy.

Fish thinking, a bigger smile than he got.

When the waiter's gone she says, 'How d'you guess? I might've wanted a beer.'

He frowns, shrugs. 'That's what you always drink when we're here.'

'Except at home I drink beer sometimes. Except at Paulaner's I drink weissbier.'

'We're not at home or at Paulaner's.'

'The point is, Fish, I might've wanted something different. You didn't ask.'

Fish stares at her, thinking, what's this? Says, 'What's got your goat?'

Vicki takes a long swallow. 'What's really irritating me, Fish, what's irking me big-time is a call I had from Cake Mullins. A very disturbed Cake Mullins. Disturbed because one Fish Pescado gave him grief. So Cake Mullins phoned one Vicki Kahn and made her pissed off. So pissed off she's fuming right now. Just drop it, Fish, okay, just drop it.'

'Only trying to help.'

'I know. But letting it go would help more.'

'Can you get a loan?'

'I'm working on it.'

Fish runs a forefinger up the side of his glass through the condensation. 'That story about the poker game, the man who lost everything to you, who was he?'

'I told you, an old man.'

'Come'n Vics, that wasn't all of it.'

She stares at her drink, snorts softly. 'Alright, it wasn't all. He was a struggle veteran. MK. Been tortured, done solitary confinement, ended up on the Island for seven years. Was an officer for a while in the new army. But he liked drink and cards. Fourteen years down the line he's facing a discharge or a package. He's dying too, AIDS. He goes for the package, stakes the lot on that poker game. I took it off him.'

'You knew this?'

'Afterwards, I was told.' Vicki's not meeting his eyes, her gaze away towards Lion's Head.

'And Cake Mullins? Where does he come in?'

'I told you, I owed him a favour.'

'All these favours.'

'It's how we do it.'

Fish still looking at her, her eyes not meeting his. 'There're favours and favours. What kind of favour?'

Vicki takes her time. 'A debt. He let me off. Alright? Years ago I went down at a game, I owed him money, he let me off.'

'Why?'

'I don't know why. It happens out there. When the luck's down, players sometimes give you a break. You do it too, for others. It's a kind of honour system, that everything'll even out over time.'

She looks at him, those sad brown eyes.

'You don't know what it's like. Unless you're in there you don't know how tight it gets.'

Fish glances down at the intersection, at young people meeting, their voices rising, their laughter. The winter twilight's losing colour, there're lights coming on in the buildings.

'Why didn't you give the AIDS vet a break?'

'I needed the money. I couldn't. I'd been given one warning. I didn't want another.'

'Hah! This honour system?'

Vicki says nothing, takes a measure of her drink. Her lipstick's smudged on the glass, a pink stain that catches Fish's eye.

'Why'd you hassle Cake?'

'For you. To tell him you had protection.'

'Did I ask for protection?'

'No.'

'Then why …?' She taps a finger against her glass. 'Men! You've got this other world. This weird place you all live in.'

'Talking of which …' Fish pushes back his chair, stands.

'And now?' Vicki looking up at him. 'Where're you off to? I've only just got here.'

'Some things to do.'

'That can't wait?'

'Not really.'

'And Willy Cotton? What happened there?'

'Oh yeah. We're meeting tonight. You want to come?'

'Meeting?'

'One of those drag races. He's going to point out the car that hit Fortune Appollis.'

Vicki takes his hand, pulls him down. 'Sit.'

Fish does.

'Why're you doing this? The old man paid you to talk to Willy Cotton. Nothing more.' She lets go of his hand.

Fish smiles. 'Just because.'

Vicki stares up at the mountain, now dark against the sky. She sighs. 'One night a poker game, the next night car races, how exciting can a life get? Alright, Fish Pescado, you win.'

He's on his feet, all smiles. 'Great. I'll pick you up. Nine thirty, ten.' He's on his way out, he stops. 'Oh, Vics, can you get the bill?'

In the back of his car, Fish makes up five parcels. He's got a roll of plastic baggies for just such emergencies. The other orders can wait.

Top of the list's an advertising exec. Woman about the same age as Vicki. Divorced. Fact is if there wasn't a Vicki, he might've tried something on.

'Jeez, Fish, thanks hey, dude. Thanks for thinking of me.' Leaning over to brush his cheek with a kiss. Yeah, man, a serious contender if there was no Vicki.

He does two more drops in the city bowl, a dentist, an actuary, then tools over De Waal Drive, the city rising bright below, to the academic burbs.

First drop's Professor Summers. The prof in his stained trousers, baggy jersey, standing in the doorway of his Mowbray house. The stench of cat piss and cigarettes all-pervasive. The music of Schumann emanating.

'You like Schumann, Fish?' the prof asked him the first time he delivered. 'Or only Meat Loaf, like your dead friend?'

'Shawn Colvin, Alison Krauss, Laurie Levine, Jesse Sykes,' Fish replied.

The professor sucked on his cigarette, blew the smoke at out the corner of his mouth. 'Interesting. You only listen to women, Fish?'

'A lot of the time,' Fish responded.

Now the professor says, 'This better be good, Pescado.'

'You'll know the difference,' says Fish. 'This is your gold star, the finest in the land.'

The professor shelling out three hundred-rand notes. 'You're a good man, Fish,' he says.

Next academic is the classics academic.

'Fish, what a surprise, how lovely to see you,' she greets him. 'Come in, come in.' But Fish doesn't, keeps the transaction to the doorstep. Always gives her a little extra bang for her buck. She's a country rock fan. Was at Woodstock, though you have to listen closely for the American in her voice nowadays.

'What did you call this?' she asks him. 'Roy something.'

'Rooibaard.'

'Which means?

'Red beard.' Fish explaining about the red hairs.

'How romantic, don't you think?'

'S'pose so,' says Fish, although it's not something he's applied his mind to.

With two grand in his pocket for a day's work, new tyres for the Isuzu are a dead cert. Fish makes his last call at Daro Attilane's to collect his loan board.

Steffie answers his knock, tells him Daro's out but she knows about the board.

Tells him they had a surf that afternoon in low swells. Wasn't much really. Fun being with dad though.

'Got to wait for the next cold front,' says Fish. 'Maybe after the weekend.'

At home Fish puts the board in the kitchen, notices a corner of an envelope sticking out of the foot grip. In the envelope are two photostats: group of guys on a beach; the other in a hospital ward: a man in the bed with a visitor sitting beside him. The faces indistinct but nothing a magnifying glass wouldn't bring into focus.

Fish phones Daro, gets his voicemail. 'Hey,' he says, 'what's with the envelope and the pix? Anyhow, thanks for the board. Give me a call.'

67

Jacob Mkezi has the same sort of envelope in his hands: brown manila except this has got the courier company's tracking note stuck on it.

Jacob Mkezi is in a good mood. He's enough Rattlesnake Sauvignon Blanc in his blood to make the world rosy.

He's got confit duck in his stomach, also lemon meringue profiteroles.

He's got rid of Mellanie all randy from the wine, coming on to him. Wanting to do a blowjob in the car outside the bistro.

On which he'd taken a rain check. Despite the Hummer being the ultimate sin bin.

Then said he'd call her later. When he'd finished the logistics, made sure the ducks stayed in a row.

She said, 'For a man with crocodile shoes you need to lighten up a little.'

Now he's slitting open the envelope, drawing out photographs. Black and white prints of his meeting with Clifford Manuel, Vicki Kahn, Cake Mullins, Tol Visagie. The view from the mezzanine, the moment they've got their glasses raised in a toast. Date and time on the print.

Beneath that's a picture of the rent boy getting into his Hummer. The view from the back of the vehicle, the registration plate clear. Number three: the Hummer in the McDonald's parking lot, five minutes later. Number four: Jacob Mkezi getting out of the Hummer, going into a pharmacy, fifteen minutes later. Number five: he's getting back into the vehicle holding a paper bag. Number six: the Hummer parked on the mountain road with the view over the city bowl. Time difference is twelve minutes. Number seven he's dropping off the boy in the city; number eight he's arriving at home, waiting for his gate to roll back.

Jacob Mkezi rubs a hand over his face, stares into the garden. He knows where this is coming from: his old comrades. The ones he made rich. The ones in power. The ones worried that he might tell his story of what happened in the good old, bad old days.

He keys through to Tol Visagie, says, 'Tomorrow, we keep the contact minimum. Just SMS.'

'Why?' Tol Visagie wants to know.

'It's best,' says Jacob Mkezi. 'This sort of operation we keep the comms down,' trying out a line of spook-speak to give the vet a thrill.

The vet says, 'Comms?'

'You know, communication.'

'Ja, okay,' says Tol Visagie. 'Makes me nervous though.'

'It's okay, my friend, it'll be no problem. Stay away, stay sharp.' Jacob Mkezi thumbs him off, his eyes on the photographs, his thoughts shading to red at the betrayal by his comrades. Their fingers sticky with blood and money. His cellphone rings: Mellanie.

'Fuck, Jacob,' she says. 'What the fuck did you think you were doing? If I've got AIDS, you're … you're … fucked.'

'What're you talking about.'

'The photographs. You've got the fucking photographs?'

'Photoshopped,' he says.

'They better bloody be. I'm coming over.'

'No,' says Jacob Mkezi. 'Tomorrow morning. We can handle this tomorrow morning.' Disconnects. He dials up Vicki Kahn.

'Who's this?' she answers.

Jacob Mkezi clears his throat, says, pardon me, gives his name. 'I enjoyed last night.'

'I didn't,' says Vicki.

'Forget it,' says Jacob Mkezi. 'I'm not holding you to anything.'

'A debt is a debt until payback time.'

Jacob Mkezi laughs. 'I hear you.' Says, 'Then, here's the payback: could I tempt you with a job offer?' Listens to the silence.

Says, 'You still there, Miss Kahn?' Hears her hesitation. Says, 'Don't worry about Clifford, I'll square it with him. Meet me, we can discuss this. I'm offering interesting legal work, a good salary, incentives, easy loan schemes, medical aid, pension.'

Hears, 'This is a surprise. This isn't what I was expecting.'

'Think about it, Miss Kahn. I considered last night your job interview. Maybe we can meet tomorrow? I'll be in touch.'

68

'Say again,' says Mart Velaze to Seven, frowning at him.

Seven shifts his weight from foot to foot, says, 'Like I say, Mr Mart, we's asking you for the horns back.' Seven pointing at the horns on the table. Still in the plastic carrier bag.

Mart Velaze squints at the two men. 'I'm having a problem here, my brothers. You want the horns back?'

'It's better, Mr Mart, we's, me'n Jouma, don't wanna bother you.'

'How?'

'I'm sorry, Mr Mart?'

'How're you bothering me?'

'Asking you to sell them. Giving Mr Mart a big headache.'

'I said I'd do it.'

'Ja, Mr Mart. That's right, that's what you and me'n Jouma agreed' – Seven pointing at Mart Velaze, then at himself and Jouma. Jouma nodding, grinning, his lips pulled tight over his empty gums. 'But we's thinking we shouldn'ta bothered Mr Mart. Like I say, we's asking for the horns back to help Mr Mart.'

Seven not looking at Mart Velaze. His eyes're on the yellow plastic bag with the rhino horns.

Mart Velaze's thinking that Seven's thinking of grabbing them, making a run for it. That's why they're here. Mart Velaze not too bothered by this, even hoping that Seven makes the play. Saying, 'How'm I going to do that?'

'What, Mr Mart?' says Seven. 'What's Mr Mart gonna do?'

'Not do, Seven. It's what I can't do. What I can't do is give you the horns back. You sold them to me. I bought them. You took advance payment.'

'Was only five hunnerd.'

Mart Velaze comes round the table that serves as his desk,

perches on a corner. Seven and Jouma edging back. They're in the warehouse: still the tins of paint stacked against a wall, the broken motorbike, otherwise the place is empty.

'Five hundred is money, Seven.' Mart Velaze pushing the bag with the horns along the table. 'You returning the money?'

'It's gone, Mr Mart. Sundries and petties. We's owe yous.'

'Doesn't work like that.'

Seven doing hangdog, head bowed, his eyes on the rhino horns.

Mart Velaze follows his gaze, smiles. 'What'd I tell you, Seven: be patient.'

'We's been patient, Mr Mart. Patient since last week. But Mr Mart hasn't sold them.'

Mart Velaze looks from Seven to Jouma, back to Seven. 'Rhino horn's not Coca-Cola, buti. You got to find the right buyer. This takes time. Understand me?'

Seven and Jouma nod.

Mart Velaze sits square on the table, swings his legs. Lifts the tone. 'I'm talking to people, you'll get your money, this weekend, maybe early next week. Now. What about the other job? You want the other job? You can have an advance.'

'What other job, Mr Mart?'

'I told you last time it might come up. Twenty thousand. Ten before, ten after. You want it?' Mart Velaze draws his finger across his throat. 'Yes or no? Quick and easy job.' He gets off the table, from one of its drawers takes out a 9-mil H&K pistol. Offers it butt-first to Seven.

'Who's it?' says Seven.

'This matters to you? Twenty grand is twenty grand.' He stretches towards Seven, taps his chest with the pistol grip. 'Easy money.'

From another drawer Mart Velaze pulls out a bag, empties it on the table, five bundles of notes. 'Ten thousand.' Again he holds the gun out to Seven.

'Who's it?'

'Your friend from the forum, Daro Attilane.'

Seven bounces on the balls of his feet, grinning.

'You want to do this favour. Twenty thou.'

'Okay,' says Seven.

As he reaches for the gun Mart Velaze says, 'Let me check the load.' Ejects the clip, holds it up for Seven. 'Fully stocked.' Palms it back into the grip. 'You want to do it?' The gun in his hand, butt towards Seven.

'What'd I say, Mr Mart? We's can do it.'

Seven takes the pistol, weighs it in his hand. 'Nice rod, ek sê.' Racks one into the chamber. Points it at Mart Velaze. 'Ag sorry hey, Mr Mart.' Pulls off two shots.

69

Fish and Vicki in the red Perana trawling slowly from street light
to street light. No one about, the houses curtained.

'There,' says Vicki. 'On the corner.'

Fish pulls to the kerb.

'You're late,' says Willy Cotton, getting into the car. 'You
said ten thirty. I've been standing out here fifteen minutes.'

'It's not raining,' says Fish. 'Could have been worse. I told
you, wait inside, I'll knock.'

'Like that's going to happen. My dad opens the door to some
white surfer dude, he'll freak. Sees a car like this in the street,
he'll freak. Think I'm into organised crime. Thank you.'

'You scared of the streets, Willy? Athlone's okay.'

'Athlone's Athlone. You don't stand in the street at night.'

'What'd I tell you, Fish,' says Vicki.

Fish shrugs. 'Your suburb.'

'Who's she?' says Willy Cotton.

'Be polite,' says Fish. 'This's Vicki, she's a speed maniac.
Drives an Alfa MiTo.'

Vicki turns round in the front seat to smile at Willy Cotton.
She extends a hand. 'Hello, Willy, what's your ride?'

Before he can answer Fish says, 'A very nice Corolla, last
year's model. Seems Willy's doing okay.'

'I'm very pleased to hear it,' says Vicki, shaking Willy Cotton's
hand. 'So where're we going, Willy? To see something exciting?'

'Epping,' says Willy. 'You know where that is?'

Fish laughs. 'Don't be cheeky.'

He's got Jim Neversink on the sound system. Neversink singing of urban grit. Jim Neversink has the vibe for this sort of job.

Willy's running his hand over the black interior, can't help himself ask, 'This's a Perana?'

'It is,' says Fish.

'V8?'

'V6.'

'Nice car.'

'It is,' says Fish.

Fish drives out of Athlone towards the cooling towers, across the highway onto the Pinelands circuit road. They pop over the railway line come down onto Viking Way, nice straight stretch of tarmac with reserves either side. Factories of Gunners Circle to the right, a sleeping suburb to the left.

'This's it,' says Willy Cotton.

'What?' says Fish.

'The drag. This's the drag.'

'They race here? It's a two-way.'

'They're only on that side,' says Willy Cotton.

Fish shakes his head. 'Nice one.'

'You seen any accidents, Willy?' Vicki twists round in her seat.

'A couple.'

'Of racers or people watching?'

'Both.' Willy Cotton fidgets with the goatee on his chin. 'One time this guy's tyre burst, the car flipped. He died, so did a child sitting with her parents.'

'What did you think of that?'

'It was hectic.'

'Like what happened to your mate, Fortune?'

Willy Cotton doesn't respond.

Fish and Vicki let this hang, Fish slowing for a traffic light. Up ahead the road's clear. There's a car parked off on the Gunners Circle side.

'This's the end,' says Willy Cotton, 'the guys in that car call the race.'

'What d'you mean, call the race?'

'You know, who wins. For the punters.'

'You can bet?' says Vicki.

'Of course.'

Fish glances at her. 'No.'

'I didn't say anything.'

'Just don't even think it.'

At the top end of Viking, the crowds are gathering. Fish parks well off in a side street.

'Out,' he says to Willy Cotton, 'let's take a hike.' Willy Cotton's shrugged into his hoodie, his hands buried in the pockets. He walks a pace behind Fish and Vicki.

The corner's a carnival: cars lining the road, headlights on full bore, music pumping from their open doors. Fish's offered a 'sip, my bru' from a flagon of Old Brown sherry doing the rounds. 'Nay,' he says, 'zol's my jol. I'm a smoker.' Which gets the group laughing. Catches the eye of a big dude in a caftan standing like he's Gaddafi, next to a sin bin. The sliding door of the van's open, showing an inside of shaggy carpet, top, bottom, sides. There're chicks lounging inside and out, drinking sparkling from flutes. Except, Fish sees, they're not chicks, they're cross-dresser Flats specials.

'He's a bookie,' says Willy Cotton, 'you don't want to know about him.' Willy Cotton edging Fish and Vicki away from the man, taking them across the intersection into the grumble and scream of engines, the gag of petrol fumes. People bump against them, people shout, signalling for the cars to line up.

'That car,' Willy Cotton yells in Fish's ear, 'the Subaru, the blue one in front with the foil. That's his.'

The car's low-slung on wide rims, rocking as the driver foots the revs. Looks like the one Fish saw at Daro's. Has a half-finished spray job to the bodywork up front.

'Where can I bet?' Vicki shouts at Willy Cotton.

'Hey, my sista, right here come with me,' screeches a voice, a short man with a wispy moustache pulling at Vicki's elbow.

'I want to put it on him,' Vicki says, pointing at the Subaru.

'Fabulous, sista, fab-u-lous,' says the short man, threading Vicki back through the traffic to the carpeted van.

Fish after them nudging Vicki, saying, 'No, no, no, what're you doing? I told you no.'

Willy Cotton's hanging back.

'Gambling,' says Vicki. 'Having a flutter.'

The bookie in the caftan flicks his chin at Fish. 'Ja, mlungu, my whitey,' he says, 'how much for you and the sista?'

'No,' Fish says to Vicki. 'No.'

'Just do it. Stop being so heavy. Get with the scene, Fish. Come on. Do it for both of us.' She holds up her hands. 'I'm not involved. Not breaking my vows. Come on.'

Fish relents, this being no place to argue. Pulls out a bunch of notes. 'Two hundred.'

'Don't be mean,' says Vicki. 'Put it down, Fish. Live dangerously.'

Fish looks at her. The fire in her eyes. Her smile, her white teeth.

'After this, no more,' he says.

'Okay,' she says. 'Agreed.' Takes the money, counts two thousand into the man's palm. 'On the Subaru. What're the odds?'

'Same for you two as for everybody, two to one.' The money disappears inside the van.

'Who's it we're betting on?' asks Fish.

'Lord the Lord.'

'Lord has a surname?'

The man laughs, hands Vicki a chit. 'Lordy lord. The Lord on high.'

'All you gotta do is ask for Lord, baby,' says one of the boygirls, blowing kisses at Fish.

'What's that?' says Fish to the bookie, pointing at the chit.

'Your man wins, you'll want a payout, né? You want a payout, you'd better show me a receipt.'

Fish gives him the thumbs-up, steps away. 'We'll be back.'

'All sorted, my bru?' says the short man with the wispy moustache.

'Uh huh,' says Fish. 'Except who's Lord?'

'No, man, he's just the Lord, my bru. The Lord is the Lord.

Chief of the drivers. Come see, come see. You's gotta watch the race.'

Fish and Vicki follow the short man through the crowd. Willy Cotton's nowhere to be seen. People are pushing and shoving to get to the front but the short man carves a path. The reason, he's waving about an Okapi, pricking people with the blade's point.

Fish says, 'We're never going to see that money again.'

Vicki's grinning at him. 'Course we are. Can't you feel the luck?'

Fish gets close to her ear. 'No. This's gambling. You're not supposed to be doing it.'

'It's research.'

'Giving money to a black guy in caftan in a van like that?'

'Guy in a suit in an office's no better.'

Fish doesn't argue.

They get to the kerb, there're the two cars rocking in the road: Lord in his Subaru, an Audi beside him. Lord gives some juice and screams the engine. The Audi replies. The two dicers going rev for rev, the crowd loving it.

'Here we go, my bru,' yells the short man.

There's a bumper-to-bumper crawl of normal traffic driving past. Freaked-out citizens heading home. Everybody hooting. A man in a white coat steps off the pavement, stands in front of the dragsters. He beckons them forward till they're lined up either side of him, his hands on their bonnets. He looks at Lord, he looks at the Audi driver. He lifts his hands, takes three paces backwards. Looks from driver to driver again. Raises his arms above his head. Holds them there: one, two, three, four – the crowd calling the countdown. On ten he pauses, the crowd chanting go, go, go. Suddenly he drops his arms, bows to the drivers. The two cars fishtail past him on smoking rubber, the burn of hot oil.

Fifty metres out Lord comes in close on the Audi, sheers off the wing mirror, screeches metal against metal. The tail lights of the two cars holding until the Audi puts wheels on the gravel soft shoulder, clouds of dust filtering into the oncoming head-light glare.

Fish can't tell who's ahead. Vicki's jumping up and down next to him.

'Who's in front?' she says to the short man, the short man glued to his cellphone.

The tail lights have blurred to one.

'You scored,' yells the short man. 'You scored, my bru, my sista. Two to one. Praise the Lord.'

The second race is lining up. Fish hears cop sirens. People are running now, scrambling for their cars. The short man's tugging at his jacket.

'Come get your money, quickly, my bru, quickly, my sista.'

Fish grabs Vicki's arm, again they follow the short man through the laughing crowd.

At the van, Mr Caftan's about to close the sliding door, make his getaway. He sees Fish.

'Ah, mlungu. A mlungu never forgets about money.' He throws out a packet. Fish catches it. 'All there, mlungu.' He's grinning a deck of white teeth as he slams closed the door.

'A small commission, my bru,' says the short man. 'A little per cent.'

Fish slides him a blue hundred. 'You's schweet, my bru, you's schweet.' The short man kisses the note, gives Fish a toothless grin. 'Goodnight, my larney, goodnight my cherry. See yous in dreamland.'

Willy Cotton's waiting for them at the car.

'That was fun,' says Vicki as Fish pulls off into the suburb to miss the cops. 'And we scored.'

They're laughing at one another. Fish says, 'One and only time, okay. Never again.'

Vicki leans across kisses his ear.

'Only thing is, Willy,' says Fish, 'I don't believe you that you don't know his surname.'

'I don't.'

'Course you do, Willy. You could've saved us a lot of trouble. Vicki and me could've spent a romantic night. But that's okay. We're good. Now you want to tell me what it is?'

'I don't know it. Strues.'

'Think about it,' says Fish. 'We can drive around a bit until you remember.'

Vicki says, 'Wow. How about three thousand nine hundred. Amazing. That was so good.'

'It was gambling.'

'Last time.'

Fish glances in the rear-view mirror at Willy Cotton. 'How we doing there, Willy. Your memory dredged it up yet?'

Twenty minutes later Willy's still closed up, tight as a zip. Fish's cellphone rings. It's Georgina, Daro's wife.

'Can you come over,' she says. 'It's urgent.'

70

The boys stampede him when he stops the Hummer. Shoving and scrambling over one another to get out of their blankets, to be at the vehicle first. Their faces howling at him. He slides down the window, looks for the boy. Points at him, 'Jy.'

The other boys protest. 'Me, my baas, me, I do's it better.'

Jacob Mkezi keeps his finger pointed at the boy. 'You.'

The boy opens the door, gets in, the others squeezing forward. Jacob Mkezi buzzes down his side window, holds out a hundred rand note. The boys see it, rush round the car.

'Close the door,' says Jacob Mkezi. He lets go of the money, sees it fluttering into the street, the boys diving for it. 'You like a cheeseburger?'

'Ja, my baas, please, my baas,' says the boy.

'Same as last time.'

The boy grinning at him. 'Ja, my baas.'

Again they sit in the McDonald's parking lot in the dark, facing the rising stadium, the boy tearing at the burger, hardly chewing the chunks he bites off.

'Slowly,' says Jacob Mkezi. He touches the boy's cheek. 'It doesn't hurt.'

The boy nods, his cheeks bulging.

'You used the Zam-Buk salve?'

The boy keeps nodding.

'Good,' says Jacob Mkezi, smiling at him, sitting back. He watches the boy eat, bite after bite.

When the boy's swallowed he says, 'Ma-Brenda.'

'Brenda Fassie?'

'Ja, my larney.'

Jacob Mkezi slots in 'Weekend Special', the boy giving a jive of his shoulders even as he jaws into the burger.

'Another one?'

The boy nods his head fast, jams a straw in his mouth to suck up Coke.

'Wait.' Jacob Mkezi gets out, walks around the other cars to the order point. Mostly young couples in the cars this time of the evening. Their idea of a date, have a burger, head up Signal Hill for a screw on the back seat. None of them worried they'll be attacked.

No singles in the cars, no one he can see with a camera. Since he left home he's been careful, eye in the rear-view, took the long way through the suburb until the thought occurred they'd probably have a tracker on him. Be watching him ducking and diving, amused. He stops for too long, they can hone in. But there're ways round that game too, underground parking garages for starters. So Jacob Mkezi wasn't overly concerned. He came out on Rhodes Drive at that point, took it through to Union Avenue, quit arsing about on his way into the city.

If they've worked out where he's stationary, no problem. Pictures at a parking lot aren't what they want. What they want is the full routine. They can wait.

Jacob Mkezi buys the boy another cheeseburger and Coke. Walks slowly back to the car, his gaze on the stadium construction. Amazing the speed of it going up. A project that impresses him: its scale, the logistics. Getting all the ducks in a row. Makes arranging a couple of trucks and a cargo plane seem chickenfeed. Then again, the kickback on his operation more profitable than a civil engineer's take-home pay. Still, have to admire the activity.

He gets back to the car, the boy's slumped in the seat asleep. Brenda Fassie singing softly.

Jacob Mkezi reaches in, puts the burger on the floor, the drink in a holder. He shifts the boy to the back seat, lays him down, covers his body with a blanket.

He sits with the boy's head on his lap, wondering about his comrades. The jealous ones. The ones who don't understand the part he played. The money he took possession of. He strokes the boy's hair, feels grit on the palm of his hand. They got their cut, but a cut wasn't enough. They didn't want the dirt coming out.

He slides his hand under the boy's clothes. Lays his palm on the boy's chest, can feel the pump of his heart. Runs his fingers over ribs, slides them down to the boy's waist, as far as he can reach. He caresses the boy, after long minutes gently withdraws his hand.

He sits with the boy's head on his lap, his hands cradling the small face. Sits there for some moments before he smothers the boy. Suffocates him. The boy is drugged: his legs squirm briefly, his body jerks once. Then lies still.

Jacob Mkezi drives back into the city, in Bree Street leaves the boy's body in a shop doorway, covered by the blanket.

On the way home he has Brenda Fassie up loud.

71

'He went surfing with Steffie. He came back. He changed. He told her he'd be about an hour,' Georgina Attilane tells Fish and Vicki. 'That was at five thirty.'

Georgina's hunched forward on the couch, a whisky in her hands, untouched. Her eyes sunk deep. Her skin zombie white. Over the time he's known her he's never seen Georgina other than made-up glam. She looks a wreck.

'Something's happened. He's been hijacked. He's been attacked. He's lying somewhere injured. I know it. I know it, Fish.'

'Maybe,' says Fish. He gets no further.

'Daro doesn't do this sort of thing. He tells me. Or he phones me. He lets me know.'

Fish's watching her, her hands rigid around the glass, sees her eyes come onto him, pleading. Gone the woman with the world at her beck and call. Fish's never been sure of Georgina, always found her a bit stuck up, like she didn't get the surfing-buddy thing he had with Daro. But this woman's hurting.

'He's been gone seven hours.' She puts the glass on the coffee table. Buries her face in her hands, pushes her hands into her hair, holds them there: gaunt, staring eyes. 'He's dead.'

Fish's thinking, what does he know about Daro? The guy could be screwing his arse off somewhere.

'Let's try his cell again,' says Vicki. Vicki not saying much for the hour they've been there, leaving it to Fish. Now asking Georgina for the number, ready to key the digits into her phone.

Georgina begins, 'Oh-eight-three.' Stops. 'I've done that. Hundreds of times. It's no use.'

'Once more,' says Vicki.

Georgina rattles off the number. Says to Fish, 'Don't you

know someone, someone at the service provider? They can track him through his phone.'

'Not as easy as that,' says Fish. 'Especially not at this time of night.'

They watch Vicki, when the call goes to voicemail she clicks it off. Shrugs.

'I told you. I told you. Don't you think I've been on at it all evening?'

'Is Steffie upstairs?' says Fish.

'I made her go to bed.'

'What'd she say about her dad?'

Georgina stares at him from her skull eyes. 'That he was fine. That he said he'd be an hour.'

'Did he take anything with him?'

'His briefcase.'

'Maybe there's a family emergency? With his folks? His brother? Maybe?'

'His parents are dead, Fish. He's got no brothers or sisters. We're his family, Steffie and me.' She's looking at Fish, staring at him with those dark eyes.

'Alright,' says Fish, standing. 'Let me check out his office, maybe there's something there.'

'I've been through it. There's nothing. No appointment written in his diary. I even checked the rubbish bin. Daro's like a boy scout, everything in its place.'

'Sure.' Fish points at some keys on the table. 'Those get me in?'

'You're wasting time. We should tell the police.'

'You could. They won't do anything, but you could.'

'It's been seven hours.'

'I know,' says Fish, 'seven hours is long.' He glances at Vicki. She reads him. Says, 'I'll wait.'

Fish's already at the front door. Ten minutes later he buzzes himself into Daro Attilane's office. The remote disarms the security system, brings up fluorescent lights.

Georgina's right, Daro would've made a good boy scout. A

man of order and neatness in an office of order and neatness. One desk with two drawers. One grey four-door metal filing cabinet. Neither locked.

In the wastebin he finds a courier's packaging, a card for Adler Solutions. He pockets the card.

Some pens, a notepad in the top desk drawer. Finance forms in the bottom drawer.

The filing cabinet's also sparse: car brochures, car magazines, tarnished trophies for best sales figures from his days as a floor-man, bank statements. In the bottom drawer a bulldog clip of receipts. Top receipt's for a print and photostat shop in the Blue Route Mall. Shows that Daro did a lot of photostatting in the late morning. About fifty pages.

Fish's locking Daro Attilane's office when his cellphone rings: a number he doesn't recognise. The voice he does. Willy Cotton.

Willy Cotton says, 'The man you want is Lord Mkezi.'

Fish gets the keys out of the door, says, 'Hold on, Willy, let me get a pen.' On a bank statement jots down the name, repeating it aloud. 'That's good of you, Willy. I appreciate it, you've come through for your friend. You got an address?'

Willy Cotton tells him Durham Road, Salt River.

'What's that?' says Fish. 'A block of flats?'

'Next to the mortuary,' says Willy Cotton.

'Handy. This Lord related to Jacob Mkezi?'

'His son.'

Fish whistles. 'Explains one or two things.'

Willy Cotton saying, 'I didn't tell you this. I didn't tell you this. Just keep away from me.'

Fish's about to tell him they've never met, but Willy Cotton's hung up. 'There's a good guy,' says Fish to the dead air.

Half an hour later he's showing Georgina the two photostats Daro sent him. Georgina with a tremble in her fingers as she holds the papers.

'You ever seen the original photographs?' he says.

'Daro's got no photographs. Except of us. There are four albums of us.'

'What about pictures of his folks?'

Georgina shakes her head. 'He always said … says … he wished he had photographs of them. I don't know what happened. He lost them, they got thrown away. When I met Daro, he could pack everything he owned in two suitcases.' She gives the photostats to Fish. 'Why'd he give you these?'

'Search me.' Fish taps the group picture on the beach. 'This's so fuzzy it's almost useless. This one, okay, you can make out the face of the dude in the bed but who's the other guy?'

Vicki takes the photostats from Fish, says, 'He's familiar, the man in the bed. I've seen pictures of him.'

'Strikes a bell with me too,' says Fish.

'Not famous, not celeb famous. Maybe a politician, a businessman. I don't know. But I've seen pictures of him.'

'So what's Daro on about giving me this stuff?' says Fish.

'Where's Daro?' says Georgina. Her voice small, breaking.

72

'What did you think you were doing, Jacob? Risking my health! Exposing me to HIV! Are you mad?'

Mellanie in full vent, holding up the photographs one at a time like flash cards.

'Heaven's sakes, rent boys! They're toxic. Diseased. Oh, Christ, what a number.' Throwing the photographs on the coffee table.

She and Jacob Mkezi in his lounge. He's standing at the sliding glass doors watching the early sun brighten his lawn, catch the dew on the cobwebs. Hears, but doesn't listen to her.

'Are you a pervert? A paedophile? A kiddie-fucker. This's sick, Jacob. This is completely depraved. Way, way, way out of line. Way out of my territory. I don't do this, Jacob. I don't talk people out of this sort of crap. Young boys, for Chrissakes. Street kids. Je–sus. How'm I supposed to deal with this? Emotionally. That I'm here with the virus in my blood, killing me. Professionally, how'm I supposed to handle a scene like this? Huh? You tell me? I'll tell you: I don't.'

Mellanie walking across the room, back and forth. Mellanie dressed for war in a black trouser suit with pointy shoes. Mellanie the pissed-off lover. Mellanie the spin doctor with her errant client, clenching her fists, taking another tack.

'God's sake, Jacob. I liked you. I fell for you. Bloody fool, Mellanie. Dumb blonde, Mellanie. Thinking she's got a thing going with Mr Crocodile Shoes, turns out he prefers little boys. He's just keeping her on the ups as his dolly bird. Big ups, Mr Mkezi, thank you very much. Nothing nicer than being his bit on the side. His arm-candy so everybody can see that Jacob Mkezi pulls woman. Jacob Mkezi the kid-banger. Dishing HIV to his dumb blonde.'

She stands still, shoulders slumped.

'Look at me. Look at me, Jacob.' Points at the photographs. 'Tell me these are photoshopped.'

He turns to face her. 'They're photoshopped.'

'They're not. You're lying. This's your car. There's this kid getting into your car. This's you getting out of your car, going into the chemist. Don't lie to me, Jacob.'

'I'm being set up.'

'I can find this boy, Jacob. I can go there right now and find this boy. I can ask him.'

Jacob Mkezi shrugs. 'You can. Maybe you'll find him. Maybe you won't. Those kids move around.' He comes up to Mellanie, puts a hand on her arm. She shakes him off, backs away. Jacob Mkezi smiles. 'Say you find him, say you show him a photograph of me, he's going to tell you, yes, that's the man driving the Hummer. That's the man bought me a McDonald's. That's the man bought me muti. He's going to tell you whatever you want to know. And why? Because he knows you'll give him fifty bucks, a hundred bucks. He'll tell you whatever he thinks you want.'

Jacob Mkezi hikes up his sleeves, gazes at Mellanie. Jacob Mkezi standing there relaxed in stone-washed jeans, leather loafers, the casual businessman. The man with the lowdown. 'They want me out,' he says. 'I know too much.'

Mellanie coming back, 'Who's they? Who's they, Jacob? Name names. Who're they?'

'I'm not going to do that.'

'Then how'm I supposed to believe you?'

'You wouldn't anyhow.'

'Try me.'

'Forget it.'

'The party bosses. The president. Tell me who, Jacob? Who?'

'I said forget it.' Jacob Mkezi relaxing onto a sofa, hands clasped behind his head.

Mellanie staring at him: one arm across her chest, the other resting on it, her hand at her chin, a finger over her mouth. Staring at him. 'You're unreal. What was I thinking taking you on? You're a criminal. A bloody lowlife, Jacob Mkezi. You used me, big-time.'

Jacob Mkezi laughs. 'And you didn't like it? Ah, tell me another one, get real. It's what turns you on, sisi. Knowing you're close to the deals. The bad men. The lowlife. Mellanie getting her thrills. Getting her jollies. Rubbing up against the hep guys with the power. What d'you say, Mellanie? Smell the money, sisi. It's groovy, sisi. It's sharp. Everybody's chilled. Everybody's getting their cut.'

Mellanie, hands raised, shaking her head. Saying, 'No, no, no. Fuck you. Okay, Jacob. Just fuck you. Find yourself another PR. Find yourself some other woman to rub your dick. Your limp prick. Someone else you can give AIDS.' Mellanie slamming out of the room.

Leaving Jacob Mkezi with the smile hard on his face. He hears the front door bang closed. Hears her car fire. He phones Mart Velaze. His call goes to voicemail. 'Comrade,' he says, 'what's happening? What have you got for me on Vusi Bopape?'

73

Fish phones Flip Nel. He needs a cop presence. The two of them side by side would block out the sun, be intimidating. Flip Nel tells him he's doing paperwork on a drive-by.

Fish says, 'Gangsters?'

Hears Flip Nel sigh, 'Yup. Yesterday. Don't you read the papers?'

Fish says now and then. Too depressing otherwise.

'Tell me about it,' says Flip Nel. 'This's also organised crime. One of the Russian mafia. Shot him up, his wife, his daughter. All in ICU. Their muscle and the driver died. Crap job, hey? Some guys shot the hell outta the car at a robot. Happens, doesn't it? From time to time. Chances are we'll never find out who did it.' He hears Flip Nel light a cigarette. 'So, you're gonna tell me we're going fishing?'

'I need a favour,' says Fish.

'Such as a fishing partner?'

'We'll get there.' Fish in his Perana, pulled to the side of the road to make the call.

'Yeah, I heard that said before,' says Flip Nel. 'That boat's been sitting in your yard a while since you got it.'

Fish thinking, Guy, guy you've been checking? Says, 'I've got stuff happening.'

'Haven't we all?' says Flip Nel. 'Haven't we all.'

Fish listening to a deep suck on the cigarette, imagining the pursed lips, Flip Nel probably holding the fag into the cup of his hand.

'What's the favour you want?'

'About half an hour of your time. Probably not organised crime. But it's Jacob Mkezi's boy involved.'

'Hey, ai-yai,' says Flip Nel. 'The man still pulls clout here.

Maybe this isn't something I wanna hear about.'

'It probably isn't,' says Fish. 'The dude was in a hit 'n run. The one he hit died.' Fish letting the information wait there for Flip Nel to soak it up.

'Mkezi's got a boy?'

'He has.'

'Ja, really, I didn't know.'

'It's not much advertised.'

'An accident like what: knocked a kid off a bicycle? Smacked into an old lady crossing the road?'

'Late-night street race. As I said, not organised crime. But close enough. I thought ...'

'What?'

'Not sure. That kind of stuff, street racing's, got people gambling. Gambling means someone somewhere's taking a cut. Somewhere there's an organised crime link.'

'This's why you want me?'

'Ah, not really. Scare tactics, mostly.'

'One condition.'

'Uh huh. And that's?'

'This weekend, we take the boat out.'

Fish pausing. Fish saying, 'Okay,' – drawing out the 'o'.

'Scout's honour.'

'Dib, dib, dib.'

'That's cubs,' says Flip Nel. 'So where, when?'

Fish gives him the address, suggests about twenty minutes. Twenty-three minutes later he and Flip Nel are riding the lift to the sixth floor. Standing side by side, shoulders touching the mirrored walls. A renovated building, still smells of cement and paint. Security on the desk didn't even raise an eye from her Sudoku when they stepped in.

'You know he's here?' says Flip Nel as the lift stops.

'I checked.'

Fish knocks on the door of a corner flat. The door's opened by a short, thin dude in dreads, his pupils pinpricks, he's well goofed. Wafts of sweet herb smell drifting past them.

'Lord Mkezi?' says Fish.

Lord stares at them.

Fish says, 'Invite us in.'

Lord says, 'Who're you?'

Flip Nel pulls out his ID.

'Oh, fuck,' says Lord.

'It's not a big deal,' says Fish. 'Just about someone you killed.' He pushes past Lord. 'Best we do this in private.'

Lord's sitting room has these floor-to-ceiling windows in the corner with a view over the corrugated roofs of Salt River. Mosque minarets, church steeples, in the distance the harbour derricks. Look left there's the city's tall buildings on the foreshore.

'Great view,' says Fish, gazing out.

'That's the morgue down there,' says Flip Nel, pointing. 'You ever seen them drop a body, Lord? It happens.'

Lord says, 'I'm going to call my father.' Fidgeting with his cellphone.

'I'd wait,' says Fish. 'Listen to me first.'

'My father was the commissioner of police.'

'Sure. We know.' Fish moving aside CDs to sit on a couch, the only couch in the room. Flip Nel leaning against the wall. 'Take a seat, Lord.' Pointing at some cushions stacked in a corner. Fish and Flip Nel watching Lord in his half-arse jeans, his blue NYPD T-shirt, that some New York cop must've given his dad. Lord a complete caricature.

'Lord,' says Fish, coming forward to rest his elbows on his knees. 'Here's the story: last Sunday night you flattened a young guy watching you street-race. You didn't stop, you got the hell away. So did mostly everybody else. The young guy called Fortune Appollis died yesterday. Someone, probably your daddy, paid for his treatment in a private hospital but he died anyhow. Fortune's got a mother and father. Nice people. Heartbroken people. Really aching for their dead son. Grieving, grieving, grieving. Mrs Appollis is spaced out. She can't get her head around it, Lord, that her son's dead. Her only son. Snap' – Fish clicks his fingers – 'like that, gone. You wouldn't want to see them, the pain they're suffering. It's terrible. Emotional. So, Lord, now I know you did this, only thing is I haven't got the hard stuff, the evidence. And I reckon it's unlikely I'm going to get it. I saw your car last night with the half-done spray job on the front but right now I reckon it's being made like new. So no joy there. One witness is too scared to give a statement. Can you believe that? So no joy there either. This leaves only one thing, Lord: ubuntu. Okay, how's it go? I'm a person through other people type of nonsense. My feeling here, Lord, is that your ubuntu wants you to do the right thing. You with me so far?'

Lord staring at him, frowning.

'Maybe you're going too fast,' says Flip Nel.

'I don't think so,' says Fish. 'Lord's got a private education. He's a Bishops boy. Not so, Lord?' Fish snapping his fingers again to get Lord's focus.

'See what I mean,' says Flip Nel, 'he's not with us.'

'Sure he is,' says Fish, leans forward, taps Lord on the foot. 'I'll talk slowly, Lord. What I want you to do is go round to see Mr and Mrs Appollis. Here's the address' – taking a folded note from his shirt pocket – 'first thing you do is apologise, then you come to a financial arrangement.'

'A what?' says Lord.

'You agree to pay them some money, Lord. Your daddy's rich, you're rich, a couple of hundred K would help the people in their grief.'

'I can't.'

'Course you can. Believe me, Lord, you'll feel much better afterwards.' Fish stands. Gives a light nudge to Lord's foot. 'Hang loose, bru.'

Lord stuttering, 'I can't. You don't understand … My father …'

'I understand,' says Fish, dropping a business card in Lord's lap. 'Do the right thing. That's where you can get me. A couple of days' time I want to hear how you've done. Please don't disappoint me, Lord. You mustn't do that.'

He and Flip Nel leaving the speedster, their last sight of him staggering up from the cushions, gaping at them like a guppy fish.

In the lift, Flip Nel says, 'What was that about?'

'Appealing to his good nature.'

'He's not gonna do anything.'

'He'll tell his daddy.'

'And his daddy will be onto you big-time.'

'Exactly what I want.'

'And why was I here?'

'To aid communication. Cops scare people.'

Flip Nel shakes his head. 'Keep me out of it when Mkezi calls. The man eats human beings.'

'Of course, no problem.'

'So this weekend then?' Flip Nel grinning at him in the lift mirror. 'Hope the cold front stays off a while longer.'

Fish thinking how much fun it would be with Flip Nel in the *Maryjane* two kays out on a heaving ocean. Surfing the swells would be better.

74

Clifford Manuel walks into Vicki Kahn's office, says, 'So, Jacob Mkezi's after you?'

Vicki deeply into some research: away in another time and place. She looks up from her laptop, catches hair behind her ear. 'I'm sorry?' Trying to focus on the man in the pink-and-white-striped shirt standing in her doorway.

He comes in, sits opposite her. 'Jacob Mkezi's just been on the line.' He smiles. That smarmy smile Vicki's come to know means Clifford's pleased with himself. 'He told me he wants you.'

'He ...' Vicki stops.

Clifford Manuel grinning at her. 'He phoned you, yesterday. He told me.'

'He did?' Vicki feels heat in her cheeks. 'I ...'

'Stop.' Clifford Manuel holds up a hand. 'It's fine. We're not losing you. That's not the way I see it. I see it meaning we'll get more work from him. This is win-win, Vicki.'

Vicki flicks her eyes to the screen, a new page opening. 'He hasn't made an offer to me. He phoned, but nothing's definite.'

Clifford Manuel sits back, hands clasped behind his head. 'He told me the figures. They're impressive. It'll get you out of your ... your trouble.'

'He told you what he'll pay me?'

'In confidence.' Clifford Manuel does the smarm smile again. 'Relax, Vicki. It's useful knowing your value.'

Vicki staring at him. Aghast. Like she's a barter cow, a kind of lobola payment. Like these two men are involved in some deal, some trade, using her as merchandise. 'What's going on?' she says.

'What do you mean what's going on?' Clifford Manuel letting go of the smile, creasing his brow.

'It's my private business.'

'Absolutely,' says Clifford Manuel. 'Absolutely. And I'm not interfering. But with the former commissioner, well, with the former commissioner things are different. He has his own style.'

'I don't know, Clifford,' she says. 'I haven't thought about it. I don't think it's where I want to be.'

Clifford Manuel stands. She has to look up at him: the neat trousers, the waist carrying no excess weight, the shirt not even creased yet. The clean-shaven face, the dark nostrils showing no hairs. His trim eyebrows. The eyes solid as mahogany.

'He'll phone you about a get-together. He told me he would. Hear him out, Vicki. This is an opportunity.'

Clifford Manuel leaving it there, walking out, pausing at the door to look back at her. He nods.

Vicki bows her head, closes her eyes: recalls the hotel drinks session with the vet guy, Tol somebody. Thinks, that's when it started. Clifford trying to get her in with Jacob Mkezi.

75

Tol Visagie cannot stay away. In a sense it's his stash of horn, he found it, he needs to see it one last time. One last time in situ. He wants to be alone in the cave with the stack. So he drives there in the afternoon after he's finished treating some cows for heart water. How the hell is Jacob Mkezi gonna know anyhow?

He crosses the river, boys fishing in the shallows, otherwise no one around. No trucks, bakkies, beaten-up cars for the ten kays on the other side. As he approaches the turn-off, Tol Visagie takes a look in the rear-view mirror, no one even in the distance behind him when he swings right onto the dirt track. He drives two clicks towards the distant koppie, pulls up under a tree. Waits there ten minutes. No one's following him.

He goes on around the koppie, stops where he stopped when he brought Jacob Mkezi and his woman. That was something worth watching in her jeans. Pretty face, though too much make-up perhaps. Nothing that a shower wouldn't wash off. Tol Visagie shivers at the thought of stepping into a shower with Mellanie Munnik, soaping her down.

He takes the Remington, stands looking about, scanning the ridge line with the feeling he's being watched. He knows he's alone. Who would be out here? But the feeling persists. Makes the skin crawl at his neck. He breaks the rifle, checks the loads. There're more in his backpack.

His eyes on the ridge, Tol Visagie walks towards the boulders. At the cutting, pauses, does a one-eighty of the bush, nothing's moving. The vlei water's a mirror. He slips between the boulders into the koppie. In the clearing, the bones lie as he found them. Inside the cave, the horns in their neat pile. Everything the way he found it two, almost three weeks back. No one's been there.

It's quiet, as if this's a sacred site. Which is the feeling he had from the beginning. Always the silence in the cave. 'Ag no, Tol,' he says aloud. 'It's rhino horns. It's a bloody bank.'

But he doesn't linger. Doesn't sit in the calm as he did when he found them. This time he gets out sharply. Strides across the clearing to the cut in the rock wall, heads back to his double-cab without checking for animals, humans, new tracks in the dust. Only in the Nissan, with the engine running, he looks over the bush, up at the skyline. Sees a movement there. Thinks he sees a movement there. Something passing into the shadow of the rocks. He unclips his binoculars, focuses slowly left to right along the koppie face. Nothing. A trick of the light. 'You're spooked,' he says. 'You're seeing things.' But his heart's going, his adrenaline's up.

'Take it easy,' he tells himself all the drive back. But the unease persists.

And there's Vusi Bopape sitting on his stoep when he gets home. Sitting there with a six-pack of Windhoek cans on the table, one in his hand.

Tol Visagie parks his double-cab, thinking, this's a bad scene. Stands on the steps to his stoep, Remington in one hand, backpack in the other, says to Vusi Bopape, 'What d'you want?'

'A chat.' Vusi Bopape holds up the six-pack. 'I brought some beer.'

'What's to talk about?' Tol Visagie unlocks his front door, pushes it open. He's holding the rifle in his right hand. 'We've got no business.'

'No?'

'No.

'I think we do.' Vusi Bopape breaks a can from the package. 'One drink. Five minutes. Please.' He eases up the ring-pull, there's a fizz of foam and gas. 'Come on.' Holds up the can to Tol Visagie. 'Take it.'

'I've got frosties.'

'Sure. We can drink those too, later.'

Tol Visagie shifts the Remington to his left hand, takes the beer. 'There isn't gonna be a later.'

Vusi Bopape shrugs. 'Cheers.' Standing to tap cans. 'Let's go inside.'

'We can talk out here.'

'We can. But inside's better. More private.'

'Talk about what?'

'Mr Jacob Mkezi.'

'What about him?.'

'Rhino horns.'

Vusi Bopape grins at Tol Visagie.

'What? What rhino horns?'

'Come on, my friend. I know everything.' Vusi Bopape pushes open the front door, puts a gun in Tol Visagie back, ushers him inside. 'Let me have the rifle rather' – working the weapon from Tol Visagie's grip.

It's dark and cool in the house, smells faintly of antiseptic. Vusi Bopape sniffs. 'You treat animals here too?'

'There's a room I use.'

'Dedication. I like it.'

The front door opens straight into the lounge, a couple of chairs grouped around a glass-topped coffee table. No pictures on the walls. A TV set in the corner, piles of DVDs beside it on the floor.

'Homely,' says Vusi Bopape, prodding Tol Visagie towards a chair. The vet sits on it straight-backed, clutching his beer. 'Relax,' says Vusi Bopape. 'Enjoy the drink.' He sits opposite, places the Remington on the table.

'What d'you want with me?' Tol Visagie fighting the tremble in his legs.

'Hey, buti, slowly. Piece by piece. Now listen, okay, hear my words.' Vusi Bopape takes a long pull of beer, wipes the back of his hand across his mouth. 'This is it, we know what you do, we know you are a good vet. We know you are a good man for the people. You should stay a vet, Dr Visagie, here where the people need you.'

'So ja. What're you saying?'

'I'm saying, we know you found the cave with the rhino horns.' Vusi Bopape taking another swig, his eyes on Tol Visagie.

Tol Visagie feels damp fear between his buttocks.

'What rhino horns?'

'Stop,' says Vusi Bopape, waves his gun hand, 'no, no, no, no more, please, accept this fact. We have been in the cave, the cave in the koppie near the waterhole. We have seen the horns. Accept this, Dr Visagie.' Vusi Bopape finishes his beer, tears another one from the pack. 'These horns are not your horns, Dr Visagie, they are not forgotten treasure for you to be Indiana Jones.' Vusi Bopape laughs. 'You look like Indiana Jones, my friend Ford Harrison, hey. You remember those films?'

Tol Visagie hearing Vusi Bopape saying something about not coming to a gun fight with a knife.

Then hearing him say, 'You understand they are state property, Dr Visagie. Those horns. State property. South African Defence Force property from the border war. They are not for Mr Jacob Mkezi to sell. They are not his private business.'

'They're in Angola. They're Angolan property.'

'A technicality, Tol. Nothing to concern you.'

Tol Visagie watching Vusi Bopape lift the ring, pull it off the can. 'They are not for you to sell. You understand?'

Tol Visagie staring at this man, Vusi Bopape, sitting in his lounge, drinking beer, holding a gun. Hears himself saying, 'Get out of my house.' Sees Vusi Bopape shake his head. Hears himself say, 'Who are you? A government man?' Sees Vusi Bopape raise the gun. Hears him saying something but there is too much noise in his head, too much rushing blood.

76

Fish, in the Perana, drives at his own pace down the Blue Route, going home. Ignores the guys in Polos zipping past, giving him the challenge glance: wanna see if you can cut it? Has Laurie Levine singing but ignores her too. Is not looking at the mountains, the patchy sky. Is looking inward. Thinking thoughts about the meaning of life.

Like why are rich guys so often such pricks? Take Lord. What a wanker. But then having a daddy like his hardly helps.

Like why do ordinary people have to suffer? They don't do anything. Don't hurt others. Take the Appollis folks. Whammo, all the joy gone out of their lives.

Then the big one: can we know other people? Take Daro.

Causes Fish to sigh.

His cellphone rings: his mother. Fish keys her on, presses loudspeaker.

'What's that noise?' Estelle says. 'You're driving, Bartolomeu, aren't you? You're on a handsfree, I take it.'

'Loudspeaker,' he says.

'You should get a handsfree, they're cheap enough.'

'This works fine.'

A pause. Then:

'Bartolomeu,' she says. 'I don't want to do this but I can't wait for you any longer. I've given you plenty of time. I'm engaging another researcher.'

'Maybe you'd like to see what I've got anyhow?' says Fish.

Silence. Fish grins. Pleased his broker contact came through with the goods. Imagines his mother walking round her office, feeling the leaves of pot plants for dust, straightening piles of papers, a Bluetooth receiver tucked round her ear. Not expecting him to come up with the info. A bit taken aback. At least that's what he hopes.

She responds: 'You've got something for me? I'm impressed. What's it?'

'Some stuff you need to know.'

'Of course I need to know. That's why I asked you to go digging.'

'I'll email it.'

'Thank you, Barto. Thank you.'

'You don't know what it is?'

'I do. It's background. Any background's more than I've got. It'll be excellent. Excellent. Exciting, Barto. Really exciting. I'm meeting them tomorrow. They're very keen. This will be a major investment. This'll make news.'

'Mom,' says Fish. 'What I've heard is not good. You should reconsider.'

A hesitation. 'What could be bad news about it, Barto?'

'The people involved.'

'The people involved? Who?'

'There's a front company doing a BEE deal. Empowerment deals are dicey. You know that. They're high-risk. High failure rates.'

'I know this. Doesn't mean this one's like that.'

'There's not a good track record with these people.'

'Which people?'

'The families involved.'

'And who're they?'

'The president's nephew, for one.'

'But that's brilliant. Absolutely brilliant. A connection like that is brilliant.'

'It's not.'

'It is, Barto. This is just wonderful news.'

'There's another big family in it. Major strugglistas.'

'Excellent.'

'Far from excellent, Mom. You don't want to mix with these people.'

'Of course I do. Of course I do. My clients will be thrilled. Honoured. This is the best news.'

'They'll eat you alive.'

He hears his mother laugh. Knows she's impressed. Flattered that this could involve the high and mighty. Hears her say, 'Don't exaggerate. You can be such a drama queen, Barto. Relax. Go have a surf.'

She's gone.

Fish sighs. The way he did before her call. Maybe he is being over-anxious. What's his mother do anyway? Introduce people. Pour their drinks. Take a commission off the deal. But the big families are bad news. Especially the presidential connection. You got into that mix, you got into serious shit.

But what can he do? He's thousands of kilometres away with another kind of serious shit.

77

In two days Fish has got nowhere. Not a trace of Daro Attilane to be found. So much for his rep for finding people.

Nix about Daro's car.

Nix about his cellphone. It's been switched off since the time he disappeared. Getting the records will take a while.

Nix from Vicki. 'Give me a break. I'm working on it. I've got a job too, you know.'

Fish goes back to working it over and over, coming up stumped. Thinking, I haven't got anything to work with. Each hour thinking Daro's had it.

He's not the only one with this line of thought: Georgina is on tranks. Steffie too.

Fish keeps at what he knows. Dials the numbers he has. The one he's got for Mart Velaze going to voicemail.

Adler Solutions is no solution.

The woman on the desk at the courier company says, 'No, man, we do hundreds of parcels a day. How'm I supposed to remember everyone? Huh? How'm I?'

The photostat shop guy says, 'Ja, there was a man statting a lot of pictures, newspaper clippings, stuff like that. I asked him if he wanted help, he said no worries. But it like took him a long time, for sure.'

Fish's gone over everything in Daro's office. Twice. Gone over everything Daro owns. Gone over Daro's life according to Georgina. Which wasn't much.

Born on the peninsula. Family moved around because his dad was a vacuum cleaner salesman. Went to half a dozen schools. Moved back to Cape Town after matric. Sold motor cars all his life. Lived in communal pads in Gardens, bachelor flats in

Wynberg. A beach bum when he wasn't working. Daro's life until they met under the milkwoods at Scarborough.

Fish going over and over old ground. 'What about his folks?'

'I don't know, for Chrissakes. I don't know. He told me they died upcountry, in Kimberley I think. Somewhere in some old-age home, years and years ago. Daro didn't like talking about them. He'd go all vague when I asked, and say he couldn't really remember stuff from that time. No happy family moments. I guess they'd gone out of his life long before we met. Or he'd pushed them out of his life, more like. I always felt maybe he hadn't had a happy childhood. You know, that he wanted to forget it, about them, his parents. I think they had him late. The only thing he said was that they were old. To him they were always old.' She stares at Fish. 'What more can I tell you? I don't know any more. Why do you keep asking about them?'

Fish doesn't answer this. Says, 'Did he talk to Steffie about them?'

Georgina sighs. 'Not that I ever heard.'

'Steffie ever want to know about them?'

'Of course, she's asked me. I told her I never met them. That they died ages ago. I told her to ask her dad. So it's best you talk to her.' Georgina's riding close to breakdown, drawn, skull-eyed, her skin the colour of old newspaper. 'Why're you asking me these things? Why aren't you out there looking for him?'

Some of the time Fish is out there looking for him. Staking out the car lot, sitting at Knead, flashing a photograph of Daro at surfers everywhere: Crayfish Factory, Outer Kom, Boneyards, Dangers, Cemetery. No one has seen the guy.

He asks Flip Nel to jolly the local detectives. Flip comes back that there's zilch. No sightings of Daro's car, no activity on his phone, no credit card withdrawals.

Fish wants to say tell me something new, but holds his tongue.

Flip Nel says, 'There's yellowtail running. This weekend, hey? Put us back on a equal footing.'

Fish thinks, Hey, bru, I've got this missing friend. Says, 'Always a possibility.'

One thing comes through for Fish. He's had Georgina give him printouts of Daro's bank statements, there's payment for a car a week back: an EFT from the personal account of Jacob Mkezi. Takes him no more than a few calls to get Jacob Mkezi's address. A couple of Googles to find a biog of the one-time police commissioner: widower, one child, a son called Lord.

But he already knew that.

Problem is Jacob Mkezi's not at home when Fish rocks around. The place's closed up like a bottle store on Sunday. CCTV cameras aimed at the gates, outdoor alarm passives on the walls. No matter how many times he ding-dongs the buzz box, there's not even a flutter at the curtains. Doesn't the guy have servants? Buti like Mkezi is going to have them in every cupboard. But no dice. Only other place he can go is say hi to Cake Mullins.

At the intercom outside the imposing gates of the Mullins residence, Fish gets to speak to a domestic. 'Mr Mullins has gone away,' he is told.

'When'd he leave?' says Fish.

'Earlier,' he's told. 'Mr Mullins will return in three months' time.'

Fish frowns at the gate. 'Shoo. A long holiday. Where's he gone?'

'Over the seas. To his other home, sir.'

'That was sudden.'

'Mr Mullins is on the business. Goodbye, sir.'

Which is all Fish gets.

He tries the Appollis household on his cell, Samson answers, his voice a whisper. Fish goes straight to it: 'Your son was hit by a man called Lord Mkezi,' he says. 'Son of the former commissioner of police. He's coming to see you, Lord that is. If he doesn't, I think you should sue. I've got the paperwork, I can take this further.'

He hears Samson Appollis drawing in short gasps. Saying, 'No, Mr Fish, no, we are ordinary people.'

'It's not going to cost you anything,' says Fish. 'I told you, contingency. You don't have to sell your house.' He hears Daphne Appollis calling, 'Pa, what's it, Pa? Who's on the phone?'

Samson shouting back, 'I'm coming, Ma, I'm coming.' Says to Fish, 'We can't do that, Mr Fish. Not to important people.'

Fish closes his eyes, imagines Samson Appollis standing in the tiny lounge cluttered with furniture, a winter sun on the lace curtains, a silence in the house. 'You can. You must,' he says. 'I thought that's want you wanted to do? That's what you told me?'

'Not anymore.'

'Pa,' he hears. 'Pa, who's on the phone?'

'It's Mart Velaze, isn't it?' says Fish. 'What's he said to you?'

'No nothing, Mr Fish, please. Okay. We mustn't speak to you. Goodbye, Mr Fish,' says Samson Appollis. 'Sorry for the trouble.'

The line goes dead, Fish disconnects. Bloody Mart Velaze.

Next he connects to Professor Summers.

'What can I do you for, Mr Fish Pescado?' says the professor. 'This is out of the ordinary.'

'Your expertise,' says Fish.

'Oh, my, my. The private investigator's in need of academic assistance. What is the world coming to? How can I help?'

'You're into politics, aren't you?'

'Political science.'

'You'd recognise some of the old guys from apartheid times? On a photograph.'

'I most certainly would.'

'Can I come over? Are you at home?' says Fish.

'Well, now, let me see. Yes, this looks like my lounge, my furniture. So I'd say as it happens, yes, I'm at home. Only joking, Mr Fish Pescado.'

'I'll be there in ten.'

'Such speed, Mr Pescado. A man of urgency.'

Fifteen minutes later Fish's showing the professor the photo-stats. Standing on the doorstep, not wanting to go any further into the foul den. Not that the professor's asked him in. The professor running a magnifying glass over the faces of the white man and the black man in the hospital ward.

'Yes,' he says. 'I know who that is.' Pointing at the man in the bed. 'He was the minister of finance. Then ambassador to Switzerland. Dr Gold he was known as in the newspapers. Shall I tell you why?'

He does. Fish thinking, So the little guy's clued up.

'What's going on here, Mr Pescado?' says Summers at the end of his mini-lesson. 'Something juicy? Who's the black man?' He takes a closer look. 'Well, well. I recognise him too. A lot younger but you can still tell he's our former commissioner of police. Interesting picture. Very interesting. You wouldn't let me have a copy?'

'Not now,' says Fish. 'It's confidential.'

The professor back at the photostat with his magnifying glass. 'You know the thing about him, Mr Pescado, a lot of powerful people don't trust him. Didn't then, don't nowadays either. But then what I heard from the people in the know is Jacob Mkezi had a lot of dirt on a lot of people. He knew who'd been colluding with the enemy, so to speak.'

Fish's phone rings: Vicki. He takes the photostat from the professor, says to Vicki, 'Hang on.' To Summers, 'Thanks, Prof. Much obliged.'

'Pleased to be of assistance,' says Summers. 'You can repay the favour in grass. And a copy of that.' Fish waves, heads out the gate.

'Babes,' Vicki's saying in his ear, 'I've found out some stuff about Jacob Mkezi.'

'How about my place?' he says.

'I'm on my way.'

'What're you bringing to eat?'

'Godfathers, Fish,' says Vicki, 'don't you think of anything else?'

All the drive home Fish's thinking of something else: he's thinking of Daro. Of who Daro really is. Thinking how can a man vanish? Drive away and disappear. Completely. Gone. No traces. Like aliens have zapped him. Walk out on his family. Fish saying out loud, 'I've got nothing to work on. This's killing me.' Except for the photostats. He gazes up at Muizenberg mountain at the end of the highway, at the fire in the sky, the dying day. Thing is, he likes Daro. Daro is okay. That's the problem. Because he's got a sense that Daro was into heavy shit.

78

Through the morning Jacob Mkezi watched porn on his laptop: men in togas lounging with boys. Young boys with shiny skins and stiff little pricks over puckered balls, reminded him of chicken flesh on a drumstick.

Sat at his desk in his study in the quiet house, not completely distracted, troubled. Troubled by the rent boy photographs, troubled by silence.

The silence of Mart Velaze, most of all.

He'd left two voicemails. One at 7.30: 'Comrade, what's happening? Call me.' The second at 9.50: 'I am worried about you, comrade. You need to talk to me.' An hour later he put a missed call on Mart Velaze's log.

This was strange, this was not Mart. Mart was his man.

Then there was Tol Visagie. At 5.30 he'd been woken by an SMS: 'The trucks are here.' Half an hour later he'd phoned the vet, his call going to voicemail.

He'd phoned his point man, been told they'd met the contact, were proceeding.

At 10.30 there'd been another message from Visagie: 'Loading the aircraft.' He'd phoned back immediately: voicemail. 'Tol, phone me,' he'd said.

No response.

Again he'd got his point man's confirmation. Then had messaged Tol Visagie, 'It's okay to talk.'

After that took to watching the porn, watching his phone out the corner of his eye.

Emails pinged on his phone, totted up in his inbox. He scanned them: the daily traffic at his company: invoices, statements, newsletters, notices of sales, investment opportunities. Nothing that wasn't being dealt with by his staff. He wondered to whom else the photographs had gone? He needed Mellanie doing R&R: research and restitution. Damage control.

Each email he hoped was hers. None of them were.

He wondered about phoning her, but didn't.

Instead went through to the kitchen, made coffee. Drank it standing at the sink, looking into the back yard. The empty washing lines, the wheelie bins for recycling. Mellanie's insistence that the recycling would make a photo-story: police commissioner goes green. The enviro-friendly commissioner. And then when he was suspended: Time to recycle the commissioner. And then when he offered to resign: Former top cop dumped.

He'd told his household staff to go. No dusting, no vacuum-cleaning, no washing windows, cleaning silver, polishing brass handles. No raking leaves, no shining the cars. Take the day off. They'd looked at him as if someone had sent them the pictures too.

When the house was his, he'd spoken with Cake Mullins, an agitated Cake Mullins.

He'd suggested lunch.

'I'm outta here,' Cake Mullins had said. 'Off to the Caymans. I'm packing as we speak.'

'What's happened?' Jacob Mkezi had asked.

To which Cake Mullins had come back brittle, 'What d'you mean, what's happened?'

'This's sudden.'

'It's been on the cards.'

Jacob Mkezi about to tell him the rhino horns were in the air had bitten down on his words, had said instead, 'Pleasant flight.'

'Yeah, all twenty hours of it. Connecting in Miami, yeah it'll be pleasant.'

Causing Jacob Mkezi to wonder if Cake Mullins hadn't got the photographs as well, was getting away ahead of any fallout. Had been about to ask him straight but Cake Mullins had rung off.

Then comes another SMS from Tol Visagie: 'Mission accomplished.'

Mission accomplished. Jacob Mkezi laughs out loud at Tol

getting with the Bush-speak. Puts through a call. Voicemail. Redials. Same thing. Goes again. Voicemail. Swears, 'Wena! Visagie, stop being an arsehole. I didn't mean don't speak to me at all.' Keys the number once more. No dice.

He does what he did earlier: phones his point man. Is told, 'All good, chief. All sharp.'

Eases the troubled mind of Jacob Mkezi. Five, six hours the plane's in Sana'a, he'll be a rich man, a richer man. Stuff the old comrades. Fuck them all and their ancestors' cattle.

Jacob Mkezi sits down to his porn. He's getting back into it, the toga men playing chase with the boys in a garden, when the gate buzzer rings. He clicks through to his security links, brings up on the screen this picture of a white guy in a car at his driveway gate: a mlungu with surfer's hair, deep-set eyes, squinting up at the camera, his finger working the bell button ding-dong, ding-dong, ding-dong like he's not seen this technology before. Like he's a kid with a new toy. Jacob Mkezi wants to yell at him to voetsak, fuck off, wants to fire off a couple of shots, put a spike in the man's pulse rate.

He doesn't. He sits it out till the man stops his foolishness. Watches him reverse into the street, drive away. Muscle, Jacob Mkezi reckons. Someone's muscle. Something in his attitude, the way he leaned out his window, stared into the camera, kept his finger on the buzzer. A mlungu with attitude. Could even be the photographer.

Time to go, he decides. Hang loose in a couple of places he knows, Mzoli's place in Gugulethu not a bad idea. Until he's got the confirm from Sana'a.

Jacob Mkezi shrugs into a leather jacket, picks up his sunglasses, decides against taking the Hummer. Times like these he needs to fly under the radar. Times like these he uses his other car, a white Honda Civic. He walks through to the garage, remote-triggers the door which slides up on silent runners. There, turning into his driveway, is Mellanie.

79

The man lies on a bed. He is cold. He is unkempt. He has been sleeping in his clothes, he has not changed since he was brought here. He has not washed. He teeth feel furry, his scalp itches. He lies curled up, hugging himself for warmth, facing the wall.

When he gets too cold he does squats, awkwardly because of the leg irons. He can manage forty before his thigh muscles scream with agony. Or he does push-ups. His arms are stronger than his thighs, he can rise and sink seventy times before the pain gets him. Then he collapses on the concrete floor, his breathing loud, urgent. Once he could've done double that.

The room's small, windowless, two air vents high up. There's a single light in the centre, a bulkhead screwed to the ceiling. It's never switched off. The man doesn't know if it's day or night.

He can hear no sounds of activity. Only the distant, dull throb of a generator. He doesn't know how long he's been there.

His meals are slid in through a hatch at the base of the door. The door is metal, a safe-room door, solid on its hinges.

When his first meal arrived, he shouted: 'What d'you want? Why'm I here? Talk to me. For God's sake, talk to me.' But no one answered. The hatch slid closed. His food was in a varkpan, the sort of pressed metal tray he remembered from his army days. Two slices of toast, a dollop of pap, stiff, long-solidified. A tin mug of tea, sweet milky tea. The same food at each meal. Sometimes a sauce with onion bits on the porridge, sometimes peanut butter with the toast.

Always the same routine. The hatch would slide back, a voice say, 'Give me your tray.' When he refused, he got no food. He learnt quickly, it was better to eat their offering than starve.

The man is lying on the bed when he hears door bolts being drawn back. He sits up. The door swings open.

Mart Velaze says, 'Phew, Daro, buti, you stink.' Mart Velaze fanning the air with his hand.

'You would too,' says Daro Attilane. 'Have you had your fun now? You going to let me go?'

Mart Velaze laughs. Turns to the man beside him. 'He's tough, né, for a car salesman.'

The man smiles, says, 'Maybe we should hose him? Clean him up first?'

Mart Velaze says to Daro, 'You want that?'

'Does it matter what I want?' says Daro.

'Nah,' says Mart Velaze. 'You're right. Let's do it.' He disappears, the other man standing there, gazing at the prisoner.

'Who're you?' says Daro.

'Vusi Bopape,' says the man. 'Mart 'n I are colleagues.'

'Men in black suits.'

'No, we don't wear suits. But, yes, in that zone.'

Mart Velaze comes back holding a garden hosepipe, a trickle of water at the nozzle. He throws Daro Attilane a bar of soap. Says, 'I'm going to turn this on. For a cleaner wash you better strip.'

'While you watch?'

'We're not perverts,' says Mart Velaze.

'We're all men,' says Vusi Bopape.

Mart Velaze opens the nozzle, directs the jet at Daro Attilane still sitting on the bed. Daro stunned by the cold drenching, taking the force full in the face.

'We haven't got all day,' shouts Mart Velaze. 'Wash.'

Daro raises his hand to block the spurt, stands to undress. Keeps on staring at them. The two men grinning at him, Mart Velaze playing the water, face, stomach, crotch, until Daro's naked, only his jeans leg dragging at his ankle.

He washes, the two men watching him, their faces closed. Mart Velaze twists the nozzle, shuts off the water.

'I haven't finished,' says Daro. There's soap lather in his hair, streaks of it on his body.

'Got to conserve water, Daro,' says Mart Velaze, throwing clean clothes on to the wet bed. 'Get dressed, we need to talk.'

'What about the irons?'

'The key's in the pocket. Unlock them yourself.'

They wait while he dries himself with the blanket, dresses, not taking their eyes off him.

'The lock and the key,' says Mart Velaze, 'throw them on the bed.'

He does.

They take him barefoot across a courtyard to a small building that's part office, part storeroom for shovels and picks. There's a table in the room, four plastic chairs around it. A briefcase on the table. In a corner, a heap of clothing, two pairs of black takkies on the pile.

Daro points at them. 'Those available?'

Mart Velaze shrugs. 'The owners don't need them anymore. You want them, help yourself.'

The two men sit, wait for Daro to join them. Daro Attilane saying, 'You're Mkezi's men? You've read what I had in the file. Seen the photographs. He's finished.'

'That's right,' says Vusi Bopape. 'He's finished.'

'Yesterday's man,' says Mart Velaze. 'All the same, Daro, we want you to kill him. Shoot him.'

Daro glancing up from tying his laces.

'No big deal for you, Daro. Maybe you're out of practice, but no big deal.' The two men smile at him. 'What d'you say?'

Daro Attilane goes back to his laces. When he's done, sits opposite Mart Velaze and Vusi Bopape, his eyes on the briefcase. 'That was then,' he says.

'Then,' says Vusi Bopape. 'Then, now, it's all the same.'

'No,' says Daro. 'I finished with that stuff.'

'Let me tell you something,' says Mart Velaze, 'let me tell you that Mr Mkezi is out of control. This week he organised to steal state assets. Rhino horns, worth millions. This's no problem for Mr Mkezi. Last week he puts a hit on his friend because the man's turned state witness. And look.' Mart Velaze takes some printouts from the briefcase on the table. 'That's Mkezi's Hummer. Mkezi screws rent boys, Daro. Street kids. This's not very nice.'

'Your problem,' says Daro. 'I gave you the file.'

'You gave something to other people too.'

'I did.'

'That was not clever.'

'It was insurance.'

Mart Velaze shakes his head, looks at Vusi Bopape. Vusi Bopape says, 'Now they know too much. You must shoot them too.'

Daro Attilane laughs. 'What? Are you mad?'

'No.'

'Doesn't work like that. What've they done?'

'Not done. It's what we said, they know.'

'They don't know about the money. The money that went from Dr Gold to Jacob Mkezi. The state money.'

'You're not going to say anything, Daro. You'll keep quiet.'

'You think so?'

'We do,' says Vusi Bopape.

Mart Velaze saying, 'There's Steffie and Georgina. There'll always be Steffie and Georgina, Daro. Our mutual insurance' – Mart Velaze giving a grin to the word.

The men pausing there.

'Vicki Kahn's the problem,' says Mart Velaze.

'What's she got to do with it?'

'You gave her the information, the documents.'

'You're wrong.'

Mart Velaze smiles. 'Alright, you gave them to your surfing buddy, the hotshot PI, Fish Pescado. That's why he keeps phoning me, leaving messages in my voicemail. I can work these things out, Daro. So if Pescado has seen the pictures then so has his girlfriend Vicki Kahn. And what I think is that you realised or found out her aunt was the Amina Kahn you guys killed. The one in Paris, the stabbing. How'm I doing?'

Daro Attilane looking down at his feet in the black takkies. 'You're wrong.'

'We don't think so. Which is why we think Vicki Kahn's a problem. Because Vicki Kahn's a lawyer, and lawyers ask questions. And the people who deploy me, Vusi and me, don't want her asking questions.'

'Why not? It was a hit, a Special Branch job. One of many.'

'Yes and no, Daro. You see, what you don't know and what I've found out is that you guys did the job for us.'

'Us?'

'The struggle. MK. The ANC.'

'We got her for you? Rubbish.'

'Strange, né? Problem was Amina Kahn was interfering. Getting in the way for both sides.'

'You expect me to believe this nonsense?'

'Doesn't matter, Daro. We're cleaning up.'

'We're cleaners, my friend,' says Vusi Bopape. 'Fixers, cleaners making our new country neat and tidy. Getting rid of all the bad karma. We want a history that tells a nice story, us the good guys and you the bad guys. Jacob Mkezi was both a good guy and a bad guy, but this complication doesn't work for us anymore. We only want good guys.'

'Daro.' Mart Velaze puts the printouts back into the briefcase. 'Daro, it is a simple matter. You don't do this we will kill Georgina and Steffie, Vicki Kahn and your mate Fish Pescado. Then we will kill you. We gave you the bullet, né?'

'And I should believe you? That you'd kill all those people?'

'Doesn't matter. Mkezi and your friends are history, one way or another. Georgina and Steffie, that's up to you.'

'Your call. Get your own back on Jacob Mkezi for your chommies. You know what, he arranged for you to be taken out, every one of you in that unit: Ray Adler, Verburg, Foreman, you. So get even. Save your family. What'd you think?'

Mart Velaze pushes back on his chair, 'Come, let's show

you something. Some housekeeping we've already been doing.'

Daro Attilane follows him into another outbuilding, Vusi Bopape bringing up the rear. A room of chest freezers, must be eight or nine, Daro reckons. Mart Velaze opens one. 'Abalone, taken from poachers.' Another: 'Lobsters, taken from poachers.' The third has two naked corpses. 'You knew these gentlemen.'

Both have been shot in the forehead.

Daro Attilane leans over, sees the frosted bodies of Seven and Jouma. 'That's no loss.'

'Exactly,' says Mart Velaze. He tells how Seven tried to shoot him, how the gun was loaded with blanks. He tells the story of the museum rhino horns. 'What we've decided' – he points at Vusi Bopape – 'is to take them back. The museum can glue on the horns, no one will know the difference. It's the right thing to do, né? Cleaning up, it's the right thing to do.'

Mart Velaze closes the freezer.

'These are his shoes?' says Daro, looking down at his feet. 'Seven's shoes.'

'Seven's. The other guy's, I don't know which,' says Mart Velaze.

'Christ!' says Daro. 'This's all I need.'

'They're shoes,' says Mart Velaze. 'Shoes are shoes.'

'Dead man's shoes,' says Vusi Bopapi, laughing.

The three men leave the room, return to sit around the table. 'So?' says Mart Velaze.

'So why aren't you doing this?' Daro Attilane comes back.

Mart Velaze nods, puts his hands flat on the table, stares at them. Raises his eyes to Daro Attilane. 'Some work we do ourselves, some work we contract out. This one is yours.'

80

'What's this?' says Fish to Vicki, looking at the plastic shopping bag she's hefted onto his kitchen table. 'I thought you were bringing food?'

'I did,' she says. 'Smoked snoek. Basmati rice. Four tomatoes. Two onions. Packet of raisins. Bottle of Mrs Ball's chutney, extra hot. You've got some sweet wine, I'm hoping?'

'Somewhere,' says Fish. 'You want me to make smoervis?'

'That's the general idea,' says Vicki. 'Reason I bought all those ingredients. You cook, I tell you what I've found. You tell me what you've learnt. Means you've got to multi-task, but you can manage that? A big boy like you?'

Fish pulls out a bottle of sweet jerepigo from a cupboard. Says, 'Very funny.'

Vicki slaps down a notepad on the table. 'In the bag there's also a Pinotage. I'll have some of that.'

Fish pours two glasses, smacks his lips at the first taste.

'You could say cheers.' Vicki holding up her glass.

'Just checking it wasn't corked,' says Fish.

'To the man in the crocodile shoes,' says Vicki. 'May the wrath be upon him.'

'I'll go with that.'

'The very same charming man who offered me a job.'

Fish frowns at her. 'You didn't say.'

'I was thinking about it.'

'And now?'

'I'm not.' She points at the rice. 'But let's have some action, babes, some of us're starving.'

'Simple as that, you're not thinking about it? About taking his job offer?'

'Simple as that. First my smarmy boss came over all cootchycoo, then there's this.' She points at the photostats.

'Okay, you go first, I'm listening.' Fish gets the rice steaming. Weeps over the onions as he dices them.

Vicki says, 'This goes back to Dr Gold in the 1970s, when he was minister of finance.' Tells how the government salted gold bullion away, millions and millions of taxpayers' money, mostly in London. A long story of who and what and when and how.

'I know that,' says Fish.

Vicki stops. 'How? How d'you know?'

'A birdie told me.'

'Come on, Fish.'

'This professor I know. He's into politics, lectures it. I showed him the photostat of the man in hospital, he told me what you've just said. I'm ahead of the curve. Also he recognised Jacob Mkezi.'

'So he told you how Dr Gold moved the gold from London to Zurich for a small percentage per ounce sold?' Vicki asking Fish this in her quiet way. Her lovely voice filling his head as he fries the onions.

'He did.'

Vicki saying, 'But here's the thing, I've been going through the Truth and Recon papers. You don't find the minister's name anywhere there, but you do find Jacob Mkezi.'

'Oh yeah?' says Fish. He's set aside a cupful of raisins in water to soften. He's chopping up the tomatoes.

'I think Jacob Mkezi worked for both sides.' Vicki takes a swig of her wine, shuffles papers. Says, 'Three times Jacob's name comes up. The first time it's mentioned is after an attack in Swaziland. At the hearing this woman says she prepared a meal for Comrade Jacob Mkezi.'

'What woman?'

'A woman who was there. The Security Branch shot her, but she survived. She told the hearing they were waiting for Comrade Jacob Mkezi. They'd cooked food but Comrade Jacob didn't come.'

Fish nods, adds more butter to the onions, says, 'Hang on,

you're saying that back then there was a link between young Jacob and this Dr Gold?'

'What I'm saying, Fish ... All I know is Jacob was MK from sometime early in the 1980s. How he got from there to sitting on Dr Gold's hospital bed in Switzerland, I don't know. You read Jacob Mkezi's biog details you're reading about a revolutionary. A man the security police want dead.'

Fish unwraps the snoek, starts easing the flesh from the bones with a knife.

'There's another hit attempt on Jacob Mkezi a year later, back home in South Africa.'

'Uh huh.'

'Uh huh. Look,' Vicki glancing hard at Fish, 'suspension of disbelief, okay.'

'Get on with it.' Fish waving the knife in the air, bits of snoek flying.

'There's a mysterious car wreck with three comrades on a mountain pass. The car leaves the road, catches fire, they all die.'

'Stuff like that happened.'

'Sure, but they were supposed to be driving Jacob Mkezi to a political meeting but Jacob Mkezi never pitched at the rendez-vous. Hear what I'm saying?'

'Sort of. You're saying because he misses two attacks that can't be coincidence. That someone tipped him off.'

'Right.'

'Bit of an assumption.'

'But a possibility.'

'I've heard stranger stories.'

'Exactly. But I've got another story, about Paris.'

Fish tastes the rice. It's done. 'Paris?'

Vicki waves a small diary at him. The cover's a blue plastic worn at the edges. She thumbs through it to a yellow Post-it sticker. 'Here, 15 September 1987 at eleven thirty Swiss ambassador written in ballpoint. That was a Tuesday.'

'So?'

'So my aunt Amina was a big-time strugglista. In the movement's finance section. She ran their money. She would've seen payments coming in, payments going out.'

'Your aunt?'

'My aunt.'

'Okay.'

'She was killed. Stabbed in the metro, five days later.'

Fish upends the rice onto the onions and tomatoes, adds the snoek bits, raisins, a cup of white wine. Mixes it all with a spatula.

'So she met Dr Gold. So what? Maybe the assassination's a coincidence.'

'I don't think so. We got the diary anonymously, separately. It wasn't with her other effects. They were all in a cardboard box: clothing, some books, ornaments, a few records, photographs, letters she'd received from family and friends. Nothing out of the ordinary. The diary pitched up with our post, except it hadn't been posted. It was a hand drop.'

'You're saying someone who should've got rid of the diary, someone who should've destroyed it, didn't?'

'Exactly.'

'We didn't get any of her other diaries, just that one for 1987. I've been through it day by day. The only person she met who was not part of the struggle was Dr Gold.'

'Still doesn't mean anything.'

'Something happened at their meeting.'

'You're assuming.'

'Then why is her file secret? We tried to get her death investigated by the TRC. They got nowhere. The investigators got death threats. I got a death threat.'

'What sort of death threat? A letter? A phone call?'

'A phone call. African voice. Told me I didn't want to go the same way as my aunt. That was it. That and the investigators telling me there was a file on my aunt but it was secret.'

Vicki sweeps up her papers. 'There's a story, a family story that my aunt knew something. Something she didn't like.'

'Such as?'

'That the struggle heroes were doing a deal with Dr Gold. Probably involving the bullion. I don't know. I've only met Jacob Mkezi twice, both times he said he's got something to tell me about my aunt. Why would he do that? Why say that?' She forks a mouthful of smoervis from the simmering pan. 'This's ready. I need to eat.'

Fish dishes. Twists open the cap on the chutney. 'You want some?'

'Of course.' Vicki's into her second mouthful. 'Delish, Fish.' Grins at the rhyme, the pun. 'I suppose I'll just have to wait till I have the sit-down with Mr Mkezi.'

They eat. Fish clears space for the photostats. 'Which brings us to these. And the thing here I don't want to admit.'

'Which is?'

'That Daro was a Special Branch cop. Part of an icing unit.'

'Tell me.'

Fish takes wine, another mouthful of food. Slides the photostat of the group of men on the beach in front of her. The background's whited out but the vegetation's thick to the side of them. Four men. Three with uncombed hair, probably unshaved, wearing shorts or swimming costumes and T-shirts. The one with a mop of hair's got on surfers' baggies, has a cigarette in his mouth. One's better-dressed, stylish. Looks like he's stepped out of a smart-casual lunch party. All of them with sunglasses.

Fish hands her a magnifying glass. Says, 'The snappy dresser, the black guy, you look closely at his face you'd say it was Jacob Mkezi. Problem is without the original there's no telling for sure. But you compare the two copies and that's who it looks like.'

'Accepted,' says Vicki, bent over the image.

'Now, one thing I've heard Special Branch used to have these beach parties. Like they were an institution. Maybe that's what's happening here. And those guys are an icing unit. Questions: what is Jacob Mkezi doing at a Special Branch beach party? Who took this picture of Jacob Mkezi and Dr Gold? Why is

Jacob Mkezi visiting Dr Gold in hospital? And why did Daro make sure I got them?'

'Good questions.'

'And what connects those two men to Daro is the blond guy with the cigarette in the beach pic.'

Vicki looks closely. Glances at Fish then down again at the picture. 'I don't want to think that.'

'Me neither,' says Fish. 'Because I've got this feeling it's probably these guys who killed your aunt. Daro being one of them.'

81

They come down the street in a black Golf GTI, tinted windows, a faint rumble to the exhaust, keeping below the speed limit. Three men in the car. The driver wears a leather jacket, the passenger beside him a black suit, a white shirt with an open collar, a red AIDS ribbon pinned on the jacket lapel. The man on the back seat's got both his hands buried in the pockets of his coat.

'Hey, man,' he says, 'this is a cold place.'

What's left of the day's clouding over, will be dark in half an hour. A wind's cutting through the trees, shaking off dry leaves.

The men drive past domestics, gardeners, housekeepers hurrying along the street, making for bus stops.

Mart Velaze's at the wheel. Vusi Bopape's in the back seat with a handy Cougar in his pocket. He's told Daro Attilane in the passenger seat, any nonsense he'll shoot him. Daro's hands are cuffed behind his back. He's sitting awkwardly, leaning forward against the seatbelt.

'You want to live in Bishopscourt?' Vusi Bopape asks Mart Velaze. 'All these high walls. Electric fences. CCTV security.'

'Not my scene,' says Mart Velaze.

'There's brothers I know this's what they want,' says Vusi Bopape. 'This place, Constantia, all the larney suburbs in Joburg, Pretoria, Durban. Live like whiteys.'

'That's okay,' says Mart Velaze. 'They've got the bucks.'

'Not okay when you have other brothers who fancy your car.'

'They can do that in the townships. You drive a M5 down a township street, ten jackers roll you for the ride.'

'No respect,' says Vusi Bopape. Laughs as he says it. 'Hey, my brother, we have become our fathers. Always complaining.'

Mart Velaze drives past Jacob Mkezi's driveway, stops on the side of the road.

Vusi Bopape looks at the house, the mansion, rising behind the high wall. 'Nice place. You sure no one's home?'

'Hundred per cent. Got a call from Mzoli. He's there, at the restaurant, nursing scotches.'

They hustle Daro up the steps to the front door. Mart Velaze flips the car keys to Vusi Bopape. 'I'll call you,' he says. Smiles at Daro. 'If Daro doesn't perform.'

'Up to you, Daro,' says Vusi Bopape. 'I'm gonna see how Georgina and Steffie are doing.'

They watch Vusi Bopape drive off.

'He better not,' says Daro.

'Or?' Mart Velaze opens the front door, keys in the disarm code, realising Jacob Mkezi left without setting the alarm. He prods Daro into the sitting room, undoes the handcuffs. 'Up to you now, Daro, my brother. Don't try any heavies with me, you'll wake up dead. Just be nice and civilised. You be good, your little women stay alive. Remember that. You act macho, they're in the morgue tomorrow, simple as that.'

Vusi Bopape drives down the street, pulls to the side. From the boot takes a laptop. He checks his pistol, the fifteen-clip Beretta Cougar. A preference. Six times he's used it for jobs, no misfires. Not that he's gone through a full load. Squeezed off a single, a double sometimes. Once three in an extreme situation when the hit wouldn't die.

On the range he's put maybe fifteen thousand rounds through it. Good accuracy, soft recoil. But especially it's compact, doesn't bulk your jacket, has no snaggy edges to catch on the holster. It's a quick gun, quick into your hand, quick to fire. Most of all a fifteen-clip 9-mil is reassuring.

Back in the car he powers up the laptop, checks out the tracker's position. Not in the city anymore. Now down the peninsula on the coast, Muizenberg.

Visiting the boyfriend, says Vusi Bopape aloud. Okay, no problem.

He checks the clip. Fully loaded. Slips the Cougar into the little holster he wears on his belt. Rock 'n roll. Vusi Bopape fires the car, gets out of Bishopscourt, heading up Edinburgh Drive to the Blue Route motorway. Down Wynberg Hill puts the speed at ninety-five, the Muizenberg mountains ahead, rolls of cloud coming up behind them. Probably going to be a wild night. Probably, make that a certainty. Vusi Bopape grinning to himself.

He keys through a call on the handsfree. It rings and rings. Always the long wait, like the phone's locked in a safe. Vusi Bopape counts fifteen rings, on the sixteenth it's answered. 'Chief,' says the Voice, 'talk to me. What's happening? Tell me things.' Going into Xhosa: 'Good things. Ticks in all the boxes?' Back to English: 'Start with the vet.'

'Dead,' says Vusi Bopape.

'Ja, well, this was unfortunate. He did good work with animals.'

'You said …'

'I said your call on that account. Chief, move on. Where are you?'

'On the way to the woman, Vicki Kahn.'

'You know where she is?'

'Of course.'

'Good. Good.' Vusi Bopape's never met the woman on the phone. The Voice. He's only spoken to her twice before. The first time he was told by his boss to expect her phone call. To follow her orders. Don't ask questions. He did as told. The reward was in cash, lots of it. He's got only a hazy idea of what she looks like: imagines a well-dressed woman behind the quiet voice. A sophisticated woman. Someone at home in foreign cities. There is something in her voice, an accent on some words, that's strange.

The Voice says, 'And Velaze?'

'Afterwards.'

'Velaze is with Mkezi?'

'He's handling that part.'

'Then he goes.'

'I understand.'

'This is critical. No mistakes. Velaze has other agendas. Other loyalties. It is time we got rid of him.'

'I understand.'

'Chief,' says the Voice in Xhosa now, 'you have done very well. We have the rhino horns. Nothing has gone wrong. We appreciate you, Bra Vusi. There are ways we can show you this. Afterwards. You understand when this is finished. There will be people who will be pleased. Appreciative. You understand?'

'I understand.'

'Chief,' says the Voice, 'go with the ancestors.'

Vusi Bopape disconnects, thinks the Cougar's more reliable than the ancestors.

He comes off the motorway, takes Main Road to the level crossing, parks in a side street. Vusi Bopape's preference on a job like this is to walk off. That way nobody gets a car make and colour, a number plate. All they can say is I saw a black man walking away. Black man in a black leather jacket. Every black man's got a black leather jacket. Cops'll just roll their eyes.

It's almost dark, the wind hassling him. He crosses the vlei bridge, finds the house no trouble at all. There's the red Alfa MiTo parked in the driveway. No lights on in the windows, but there's a glow in the frosted panes of the front door.

Vusi Bopape touches the gun in its holster, rolls his shoulders, starts up the path to the door. How this plays out is best played out inside, is Vusi Bopape's plan of action.

'Mart Velaze,' says Mellanie, wheeling a suitcase into the lounge. 'Well, well. Who's he, Mart?'

The two men turning, surprised. 'Hey, Mellanie.' Mart Velaze frowning. 'What're you doing here?'

'Packing my things,' she says. 'We're finished. Finished professionally, finished as his trophy cover-up. Jacob Mkezi is history.' She glances at the handcuffs in Mart Velaze's hand. 'Who's he?'

'Old friend of the commissioner's.'

Mellanie studying Daro Attilane, taking in the ill-fitting clothes.

'He's not here, the former commissioner' – Mellanie putting some grit into the title.

'Yeah, I know. You seen him today?'

'He was leaving. I told him not to hang around.'

'Okay, we'll wait,' says Mart Velaze.

'I'm outta here,' Mellanie moving around them towards the entrance hall. 'Mkezi's had it,' she says. 'The comrades'll nail him, big-time. They already are with those rent boy pics. Make yourselves at home, gents, you could have a long wait. Adios.'

'Where's your car?' says Mart Velaze. 'Wasn't outside.'

'In the garage,' says Mellanie. 'To make my life easier.' Right then noticing the gun in Mart Velaze's hand, her face alarmed. 'What's with the gun, Mart? Point that thing away.'

Fish and Vicki eat in silence, Fish staring at the picture of the group of men on the beach. A group of men on a beach. Could just be fishing buddies. But he thinks not. He thinks it's sinister.

'You really think that?' says Vicki. She finishes her meal, pushes the plate aside. 'That Daro was part of a hit squad?'

'I think it. I don't know it. Big difference. But, yes, I think it.'

'This isn't a nice story.'

'No.' He lifts the lid on the smoervis. 'Some more?'

Vicki shakes her head. 'I'm good.'

Fish helps himself. 'You just don't know. About people. You just don't know.' He starts in on his second helping. 'If you'd told me Daro'd been Security Branch, I'd have said impossible. Never. Never ever. The guy's not like that. He's a family man. He's not a killer.'

There's a knock on the front door.

'Probably Holy Joes,' says Fish. 'Early evening, they're active, gathering stray souls. Leave it. They'll go away.'

Vicki doesn't move. Says, 'Everyone's got a past, Fish.'

He glances at her. 'What're you saying?'

'Just that.'

Now the knocking's louder, insistent.

'Shit,' says Fish.

'I'll go,' says Vicki. 'Finish your dinner.' She slips off the stool, pads out of the kitchen in his woollen socks. 'You can fill my wine.'

Fish thinking, everyone's got a past. Thinking this while Shawn Colvin's singing on the sound system. Hears Vicki call out, 'Okay, I'm coming, hang on.' Hears the bolts drawn back, the door open. Hears a deep low voice, too deep to make out the words. Hears the front door close. Vicki saying, 'How can I help you, Mr …?'

The man growls his response, Fish's thinking, What the …? Pauses. He's about to pour Vicki's wine, he hears her scream.

Hears the shot.

Daro Attilane's thinking déjà vu. Seeing the gun come up in Mart Velaze's hand, the chest shot straight through the woman's heart. Then the man is close-in, working a stiletto.

Takes a long moment for Daro to react. Then he's shouting, 'No, no, no,' pulling Mart Velaze off the woman. Mart Velaze pushing him away, bending down to wipe the blade on the woman's dress, folding the blade into the mother-of-pearl hilt.

'Been here before, hey, Daro?' he says, looking down at the dead woman. He shakes his head. 'What's to be done?' Then says, 'Come, my brother, one more thing. Then we can watch TV.'

He prods Daro out of the lounge down a passage into the kitchen. Opens a cupboard, takes out a spray can from among the cleaning fluids, holds it out.

'That's handy,' says Daro. Realising, 'You put that there. You've planned this.'

'Of course.'

'Jesus.'

'Jesus's not going to help. You know what to do.'

'You're full of crap.'

'Do it. Same as before, RAU TEM, capital letters.'

Daro has the taste of metal on his tongue. A harshness that

was there from the moment Mart Velaze killed the woman.

'Full circle,' says Mart Velaze. 'Give us all a sense of closure.'

'You didn't have to kill her.'

'I did. She saw us. Bad timing on her part. Now spray, buti, let's see the artwork. Over the fridge and the cupboard.'

Daro sprays the letters: R on the fridge door the remaining spread across the cupboards.

'Not bad,' says Mart Velaze. 'Neater than last time, from the pictures I've seen.' He wrenches the can out of Daro Attilane's hand. 'Why'd you guys do that? Tell me, why?' Looking at Daro, expecting an answer. 'What was it supposed to mean? Something. It must've meant something. You don't just spray letters for nothing.'

'I don't know.'

'I heard it's German for dreams: *Träume*.'

'It's nonsense. Meant to confuse.'

'I don't think so. What dreams, Daro?'

'Dissolving dreams,' says Daro. 'The wreckage of lives.'

Mart Velaze drops the tin into a plastic bag. 'Poetic. Very poetic. You're talking shit, Daro. Talk sense.'

'How'm I supposed to know? I was fucking young. A foot soldier.'

'Foot soldier. That's nice. For a hitman that's nice. Gives you hero status: the last man standing. Except you're the disappeared assassin.' Mart Velaze, standing back, indicating the door. 'Let's go, down the passage. At the end's the TV room. We can watch sport or something.' Daro doing as he's told. 'You did good, Daro. Doing that. Wiping out your history, coming up as somebody new. Clever. Your mates should've done the same. What a bunch of sorry dogs. Alkies, wasters, rubbish. But that's over. Truth and reconciliation. Up to you now: sort out the commissioner, and your slate's clean.'

'I should believe you?'

'You should.'

'I don't.'

Mart Velaze laughs, pokes Daro in the back with the barrel of the gun. 'Really, brother, you've got a mouth. Wait and see, okay. Wait and see.'

In the television room, two leather couches face a large flatscreen on the wall. Shelves of DVDs to the right. Mart Velaze punches up the sports channel, the sound coming at them through a home theatre system. 'Sit, my brother, relax' – pushing Daro towards a couch. 'You want sport or some movie? A drink, maybe? Shot of single malt? The former commissioner's got this collection, scotch you've never heard of.' He opens a cabinet. 'How about that?' Probably twenty bottles on display. 'What'll it be?'

'Nothing,' says Daro.

'Your loss.' Mart Velaze pours himself two fingers of Johnnie Walker Blue. 'The nectar of the revolution. Cheers.' He sits on the other couch. There's cricket on the screen: a man in green running up to bowl. 'You watch this sort of thing?' says Mart Velaze. 'I don't. Sport's rubbish.' He gets up, finds a movie on the DVD rack. 'How about a bit of Jennifer? Jennifer and George.' Slots in *Out of Sight*. 'You like George Clooney?'

Daro says, 'I want to phone my wife.'

Mart Velaze shakes his head. 'Watch the movie, Daro. Your wife's fine. What happens to her's up to you. You do your job she's not even gonna know Vusi had her in his sights.' He sips his drink. 'Couple of hours you go back to your life.'

'Except three people're dead.'

'This's true. Not Georgina, though. Not Steffie.'

'My friends: Fish and Vicki.'

'A pity,' says Mart Velaze. 'But I don't see a way round it. You should've thought of that one, Daro. Kept them out, hanging loose.'

Daro Attilane rubs his face. Only thing is to wait. Sometime there'll be a moment he can use.

He gazes at the screen: the character Clooney's playing, Jack Foley, robbing a bank.

'He's a dude,' says Mart Velaze. 'So unfazed. Check this,

where he tells the guy the teller's cute. Hey, you credit that?'

Then Jack Foley's outside in his car, except it won't start. Next there's a cop at his side window with a gun, telling him, Get outta the car.

Mart Velaze laughs. 'See how he takes it. Like it's destiny. Fate. That is so sharp.'

Daro's thinking at some point Velaze has to give him a gun. A loaded gun. Might be only one round in it but one round's enough to zap Mart through the frontal lobe. How he deals with Mkezi's the unknown factor. Like surfing, you take the wave that comes. Daro watches the movie, feels adrenaline making him squirmy. It's all he can do to keep sitting still.

On the flatscreen there's Karen Sisco in her car outside Glades Correctional mouthing 'what the fuck' at the jailbreak. The guys popping out of the ground like rabbits. Here she's racking the shotgun, that long slit up her dress peeling away to show her thigh.

'Wena! Sexy mama,' says Mart Velaze.

Cut to Karen and Jack in the boot talking movies: *Bonnie and Clyde*, *Three Days of the Condor*.

Mart Velaze saying, 'How amazing is that?' He draws on his scotch. 'You a Clooney man, Daro? You seen *Michael Clayton*? Probably the best movie he's done. That scene on the hill with the horses. Haunting. Beautiful. Then his car blows up. Hey, how was that?'

Now Clooney's in the bath with Jennifer Lopez leaning over him, when they hear a car pulling in. Mart Velaze looks out the window, the headlights of the Civic on the garage door opening. 'Here's our boy, Daro. Showdown time.'

They hear Jacob Mkezi coming through the house calling, 'Mellanie. Mellanie. You changed your mind?'

Fish thinks, the Z88's in the bakkie, there's a Ruger in the bedroom. Both of them too far away. Footsteps coming fast down the passageway. He sees Vicki's handbag, knows she carries, pulls out her .32. Not the best gun for a situation like this but what're the options? The barrel hardly extends over his fingers.

He calls Vicki's name. The footsteps stop.

Fish edges back, crouches behind the table.

'Vicki.' Gives it two beats. 'Vicki.' Thinking, she's dead. Thinking, fuck it. This's not Seven's gangbanger style. This's professional. He says, 'I was you I'd run, man. Run fast.'

Fish listens. All he can hear is Shawn Colvin singing how she's gonna die in these four walls.

'Now's a good time, go.'

Hears the floorboards creak. Thing about an old house the floorboards always have their say. Knows the shooter is closing. Time to shut up. Play this on its nerves.

He watches the kitchen door slowly open, till it knocks against a cupboard, half-ajar. Gives the shooter the advantage, he can use it as a shield. Nice solid door like that the .32's going to get stuck in the wood.

What's he got, the hitman? 9-mil? .38? Bloody big noise it made, has to be one or the other. Cocky bastard not even bothering with a silencer. What's that tell you? He doesn't care. His intention is in, out, away before anybody's thought perhaps those were gunshots they heard.

Another shifting of the floorboards. Fish thinks, put one into the door see what happens. One wasted leaves five. It's a good bullet the .32 carries but it'll need two for the job. Maybe three if there's ducking and diving.

He pulls off the shot, middle panels of the door, the lead burying itself.

The shooter's hand comes round, takes three measured positions. Left into the sink, the ricochet zinging round the room. Centre across the kitchen table smack into the wall. Right into the sound system, end of Shawn Colvin.

'I'm still here,' says Fish. 'What's your next play, bru?'

Doesn't let him think about that. Fish's out of the blocks like a sprinter, bam into the door. Hears the grunt as the shooter takes the knock hard against his shoulder, staggers back. Fish ducks, goes low round the door, fires up at forty-five degrees, reckoning that's where the guy will be. Hears the hollowpoint juice in. A round comes down, punches into the door above his head.

Fish lets go a wild third, the lead bouncing off the passage walls. Looks up at the man above him. This man with a hole in his chest, this man with his face pinched in pain. The man's swaying but still standing, bringing up his gun hand.

Fish goes for a stomach shot, best available target. The shooter bends on impact, staggers back against a wall, slides down till he's sitting, staring at Fish. The gun's still in his hand, he's still trying to raise it. Fish steps forward, kicks it away. Four more paces he's down the passage, there's Vicki lying in the lounge, blood splatter on the walls, blood pooling under her.

Daro Attilane hears Jacob Mkezi say, 'Fuck,' at the sight of Mellanie's body in his lounge. Repeat it, 'Fuck.' Imagines the former commissioner seeing the chest shot, the stab wounds, bending down to feel for a pulse in her neck. Then the man shouting, 'Comrade, what's the story here?' Knowing the person watching a DVD in the TV room has to be his man.

Daro sees Mart Velaze turn down the sound, grinning at him. 'Let's talk to the former commissioner.' On screen Karen Sisco's in hospital, mouthing to the FBI dude and her daddy. Mart Velaze waves Daro out of the TV room towards the lounge.

There's Jacob Mkezi crouched beside the body of Mellanie Munnik. He stands, looks from Daro Attilane to Mart Velaze. Says, 'What's he doing here?'

'There's a reason.'

'Explain, comrade, explain. There're things I don't understand.'

Mart Velaze smiles. 'There's a reason.'

'You've said that. Why're you here? Why's he here?' – pointing at Daro Attilane. 'Explain, now.'

'Okay,' says Mart Velaze.

Daro watches Mart Velaze reach under his jacket come up

with the 9-mil he used on Mellanie in his right hand, thinks, this's it. This's where he gives me the weapon, tells me blow away the ex-commissioner. Thinking, I'll take the gun, blow away Mart Velaze, see how things work out with Jacob Mkezi in the aftermath.

Sees Mart Velaze draw out a revolver with his left hand.

Jacob Mkezi frowning at the sight of the second gun, his eyes on Mart Velaze, watching this two-draw, waiting for an explanation.

'Thing is, Mr Mkezi,' says Mart Velaze. 'I've got orders.'

'Orders?'

'Being a servant of the state.'

'Mephistopheles to Faust. Had I not become the devil's— '

Daro sees Mart Velaze raise the snubnose in his left hand, pop a load into Jacob Mkezi's chest, another into his face. The one-time commissioner standing there like he's become a statue, then dropping backwards. Swivels his eyes to see Mart Velaze raise the pistol in his right hand, aiming it at him, lining up the sights. The weapon he used on Mellanie. Daro aware of the play in that moment. Even sees the skin tighten on Mart Velaze's trigger finger.

82

No sunrise flush yet on the mountain. Wraiths of mist upon the water in the grey dawn light. Coming out of the bay these tidy sets, not pushing much punch: half a metre, metre tops. A slight offshore holding them up. Still worth doing the dawn patrol.

Midweek, so it's Fish and maybe a dozen others strung from Surfers' Corner to the vlei outlet. Fish's in the corner. The rocks hard to his left. The break's going nicely right, for the moment he has the spot.

He's taken two rides, no fancy footwork, just standing there: the board slicing along the wave, the thrum in his feet, the cold against his face. Ridden them until they were white water. Then kicked out, headed again for the backline.

His first surf since ...

He's on Daro's board. The one Daro lent him. It's not the best but it's a board.

Fish still trying to figure out Daro. Reckons there's the Daro he knew, and whoever he was before. There's the manner of his death in a gunfight with Jacob Mkezi. There's the picture of the group of men on the beach, Daro and Jacob Mkezi among them. This's Daro's guessed-at life.

There's Mart Velaze.

Mart Velaze phoning him: 'I heard about your invader, my friend.'

Fish saying, 'You did? How's that?'

'I hear things. I'm sorry about Vicki Kahn getting hurt.'

'Of course you are.'

'She's a spritzy woman. I like hot dames.'

'How d'you know her?'

'I don't. By reputation only.'

Fish letting in a long pause before saying, 'Why're you phoning, Velaze?'

'To tell you something. To give you a message for her.'

'A message? Like what?'

'Tell Vicki she has people worry about her. About who she is. What she knows about her aunt's death. We live in a dangerous country. A bad time. She doesn't want to ask questions about her aunt's death.'

'What's that supposed to mean?'

'Tell her, my friend. Ms Vicki will know what I mean. Nice talking, Mr Fish Pescado.'

Fish saying, 'Wait.'

'You've got something to say?'

'Daro Attilane?'

'Daro Attilane: a sad story.'

'I've got this photostat, Velaze, with Jacob Mkezi, Daro Attilane, some other men.'

'Frame it.'

'Who're they, the others?'

'Dead men, Mr Pescado, dead men. All of them.'

Fish waiting for more, the silence lengthening until Fish breaks it. 'What's going on, Velaze?'

Mart Velaze coming back, 'Nothing any more. We're done.'

'You're still out there.'

Hearing Mart Velaze snort a laugh. 'I'm still out here. Yebo yes, I'm still out here. But I'm no hazard. No jeopardy to you or your loved-one. Not at the moment. Enjoy the rest of your life, Mr Pescado. Surfing, smoking doob, investigating. Making out with Vicki. Maybe finish that law degree like your mother wants.'

Fish frowning at this, wondering, how the hell does he know what Estelle wants? Saying, 'Meet me.'

'Not going to happen, my friend. You should be pleased about that. You wouldn't want to meet me.'

'Then one question: why? The gold? The money?'

'There you are. The dreams in our hearts, né, Mr Pescado. The dreams in our hearts. Some or other German thing like that Mkezi always used to quote. Dreams, *Träume*. RAU TEM. You've got the answer to your question.'

Fish saying again, 'Meet me. Tell me about the Appollis boy.'

Mart Velaze saying, 'Goodbye, Mr Pescado. My best to your lady friend. Tell her to take care.'

End of conversation. The trace Fish got a mate to put on the cellphone ended at a stolen SIM card.

My best to your lady friend. Vicki right there and then in ICU but stable, out of danger. If being in hospital is out of danger.

Thing was, not two hours after the call from Mart Velaze, Samson Appollis was on the line.

'Mr Fish, we's got the money. Thank yous, thank yous, thank yous.' Fish hears him calling out. 'Ma, Ma, I've got Mr Fish on the telephone.'

Daphne Appollis saying, 'You's very kind, Mr Pescado. May the Lord bless you.'

'Samson,' Fish said. 'Samson, what's going on?'

'We got money, Mr Fish. I'm phoning to tell you, we's got money. Out of the blue Lord the Father's heaven. Fifteen thousand rands in cash. And flowers, such a beautiful vase of flowers. From Mr Velaze, Mr Fish. He brought them to us, here in our house. He said they was from his rich friend to comfort us in our grief.'

'Fifteen thousand rand? That's it?'

'That's a lot of money, Mr Fish.'

Fish thinking, it's bloody peanuts. Lord Mkezi getting away with murder.

'It's something,' said Fish. 'I thought …' then stopping himself.

Daphne Appollis in the background saying, 'Pa, Pa, that's enough now. Stop bothering Mr Pescado.'

'I've gotta go, Mr Fish,' said Samson Appollis. 'Ma calling me, you know. But we's just wanna say thank yous, Mr Fish, wes know this's because of you.'

Fish hanging up, thinking he should go back to Lord, teach him something about making amends.

Fifteen thousand rand! Fifteen thousand rand is an insult. The sort of figure Mart Velaze would hit on. Too little to be useful, but for Ma and Pa Appollis something to be grateful for.

Fish shook his head. Bloody Mart Velaze.

Now Fish sits on the grey sea thinking of Vicki. Of kneeling beside her on the floor, holding her hand, the dark stain of blood leaking out of her. Talking at her: 'Stay with me. Vics, Vics, Vics keep with me. Tell me your name. Tell me where you are.' Holding up his hand. 'Count my fingers.' Vicki in and out of it. Fish thinking he'd lost her each time her eyes closed. Remembering his neighbour Flip Nel with a gun in his hand, saying the man was dead. Not to worry, she'd be alright, his girlfriend. The weirdness of the scene. Paramedics. Cops. Men in suits. Getting into the ambulance. Sitting in the hospital for hours till they'd operated.

Till they told him, 'Go home, Mr Pescado.'

To his empty house, the bloodstains on the floor. A call from his mother.

Estelle triumphant.

'I've done it, Barto. Took a couple of meetings but I've done it.'

Fish at the kitchen window staring at the boat. Was standing there for long minutes, not thinking, not feeling. Numb. Not with it. Not wanting to face cleaning up. 'Done what?'

'The mining deal. The Chinese investment. Prospect Deep. They're coming out. Mr Yan and Mr Lijun. This is amazing. I'm coming with them.'

'Mom,' said Fish, the phone clamped to his left ear, holding up his right hand. 'Mom, Vicki was shot.'

Silence.

'Vicki? Your Indian girlie?'

'Vicki, Mom. Here in my house.' He lowered his arm.

'Killed.'

'She's on life support.'

'Oh, Barto. Bartolomeu, how dreadful. Why? How? You're not hurt?'

'Long story. No, I'm not hurt.'

'You can tell me.'

'Not now.'

'I'm coming out. Next week. Oh, Barto, I am so sorry.'

'Coming out?' Fish frowned. 'Why're you coming out?'

'With Mr Yan and Mr Lijun to see the mine. I told you.'

'Mom,' said Fish. 'Didn't I …'

'I know. I know what you said about the empowerment people. Warning me off them. But they're nice blacks, Bartolomeu. It's the Indians you've got to watch out for. They're the crooked ones.'

Fish closed his eyes. Wanted to sigh.

'Get new locks, Bartolomeu. And a security gate. I hope she makes it, your friend.'

She was gone. Fish thumbed off the connection, stepped over the bloodstain, heading for the bedroom.

Since then there's been Daro's funeral, the grief of Georgina and Steffie. Georgina's questions: 'Who was he, Fish? Who was the man I married?'

There'd been a day in the *Maryjane* fishing with Flip Nel. The cop minding his own business. Fishing, catching Hottentots, a couple of snoek.

Until he'd said, just dropped it in while he was baiting up: 'You ever heard of Dommiss Verburg?'

Fish'd turned towards him, said, 'No.' Thought: Where's this going?

Flip Nel had cast his line with a casual throw, let the reel spool out to a fair depth. 'Man I used to know in Port Elizabeth. Nice guy at a braai, always telling bad jokes. Awful jokes. He was security police. They did scary ops, those okes. The sort of doings you didn't talk about. Anyhow, he's supposed to have shot himself in the head. Thing is he had this bullet in his pocket: .22 cross-hatched. Thing is that's what they found on Daro Attilane, clutched in his hand. A bullet like that: .22 cross-hatched.'

Fish had looked over the sea towards Cape Point, the bright and dancing sea, had said, 'What're you saying?'

'I don't know. I'm an ordinary cop. Was an ordinary cop those days, too. Murder and robbery. That's what I've always been. All I'm saying is there's the bullet.'

They'd gone backwards and forwards on that bullet until Fish'd said, 'I've got a picture of some men. A photostat, actually. It's poor quality but maybe you can check if your friend's on it.'

And Flip Nel had. And had pointed out Dommiss Verburg.

None of this Fish told Georgina. What was the point? She was still on the question of why Daro'd shot Jacob Mkezi. What was he doing there? Why'd he gone missing for all those days?

Asking the questions over and over, till Fish fixed her a joint. That pushed the pain back. He left her two bankies, told her to go easy on the stuff.

Now he's sitting on Daro Attilane's board about to catch a wave in. Breakfast at Knead, double helping of French toast, slide it down with a cappuccino. Joke with the waitress to get flashed her pixie smile. Then Vicki. Sit beside her bed while she lies there looking at him with those still and mysterious eyes. Neither of them talking, holding hands. Grateful.

Fish thinking, forget all the questions, the connections. The warnings of Mart Velaze. Let it go. She's alive.

Recalling that Flip Nel had said to him about the picture with Dommiss Verburg, 'Doesn't prove anything. Doesn't say anything.'

'Except they're all together.'

'So what?'

'They're an icing unit,' Fish had said, putting the page into a file.

'We don't know for sure.'

'Admittedly,' Fish says out loud, paddling onto the swell, getting up as the wave takes him. The kick of that surge going through his veins. 'We don't know for sure.'

AUTHOR'S NOTE

The killings conducted by the Icing Unit are loosely, very loosely, based on real events.

The murders of Dr Robert Smit and his wife Jean-Cora occurred on 22 November 1977 in their rented house in Springs, outside Johannesburg. Both were shot. Jean-Cora was also stabbed fourteen times with a stiletto. Smit was due to stand for the ruling National Party in a coming by-election. Speculation has it that he had information about bullion held in foreign banks and planned to go public with this information which would have been damaging to some senior members of his party. Because of this it is believed the government contracted the hit. The letters RAU TEM were sprayed on the couple's kitchen wall. No one knows what or if these letters have any meaning.

The murderer(s) were not caught. The Truth and Reconciliation Commission into apartheid crimes investigated the incident during the mid-1990s and concluded that it was politically motivated. During that investigation the Smit's daughter received death threats and was offered money to keep quiet.

In 2006 three security branch men were fingered as responsible for the hit. One, Phil Freeman, committed suicide in Cape Town in 1990. A second, Dries Verwey, was found dead in Port Elizabeth. He had been shot in the left side of his head. Although it looked like a suicide he was right-handed and investigators believed that he'd been killed. The third man, known only by the initials RA, lives in Australia. No application has been made to extradite him.

The killing of the three men on a farm alludes to the murders perpetrated by a death squad under the command of Eugene de Kock – nicknamed Prime Evil – that operated on Vlakplaas, a farm near Pretoria during the 1980s. In 1996 De Kock was sentenced to two hundred and twelve years in prison for crimes against humanity. The eighty-nine charges included six counts of murder, as well as conspiracy to murder, attempted murder, assault, kidnapping, illegal possession of firearms, and fraud. De Kock is serving his sentence in the C Max section of the Pretoria Central Prison.

A unit known as the Civil Cooperation Bureau, a government-sponsored hit squad, conducted killing missions in the countries around South Africa, including Swaziland, during the latter years of National Party rule. In his testimony to the Truth and Reconciliation Commission, General Magnus Malan stated: "During my term of office as Head of the South African Defence Force and as Minister of Defence instructions to members of the South African Defence Force were clear: destroy the terrorists, their bases and their capabilities. This was also government policy. As a professional soldier, I issued orders and later as Minister of Defence I authorised orders which led to the death of innocent civilians in cross-fire."

The incident on the mountain pass in the Eastern Cape where the Icing Unit intercepts a car refers to the assassination of the Cradock Four: Matthew Goniwe, Fort Calata, Sparrow Mkonto and Sicelo Mhlauli. On the night of 27 June 1985, security forces set up a roadblock to intercept their car. They were murdered and their burnt bodies found later near Port Elizabeth.

The assassination of the character Amina Kahn was based on the murder in Paris of Dulcie September in 1987. She had established a strong anti-apartheid lobby that argued for sanctions and disinvestment and had become a threat to the apartheid state. In March of that year she was shot five times from behind with a silenced rifle as she opened the ANC offices. In 2011 the state denied September's family access to documents related to her.

The character of Dr Gold was somewhat based on State President Nico Diederichs in that during his tenure as finance minister he moved South Africa's gold holdings from London to Zurich. Allegedly he was paid a small commission on any gold sales. Speculation had it that the bullion was regarded as an emergency war fund should the Nationalist government be forced into exile. Because of his involvement Diederichs was referred to as Dr Gold.

There is a brief reference to the Numbers gangs through the character, Seven. The Numbers gangs (the 26s, 27s, and 28s) have been a feature of South African prisons for more than a hundred years and owe their origins to Jan Note who had been unfairly incarcerated for stealing a horse. The injustice of his jail term led him to found the Regiment of the Hills – a formally structured gang for men who had fallen foul of the law. By the 1920s their influence extended throughout the prison system.

A Human Rights Watch book on conditions in South African prisons states: 'Each of the gangs has an elaborate quasi-military command structure, involving up to thirty different ranks; each rank has specific hierarchical duties, and internal discipline is strictly maintained. Promotion, particularly to the higher ranks, may be obtained by committing acts of violence on persons outside the gang. The gangs themselves are distinguished according to their aims and activities: the 28s are regarded as the senior gang, and are distinguished primarily by their organised system of "vyfies" [literally little wives] or coerced homosexual partners; the 26s are associated with cunning, obtaining money and often goods by means of fraud and theft; the 27s protect and enforce the codes of the 28s and 26s and are symbolized by blood.' - Africa Watch Prison Project, *Prison Conditions in South Africa*, Human Rights Watch, New York, 1994.

Two informative books on the Numbers gangs are:
The Small Matter of a Horse by Charles van Onselen (Ravan Press, Johannesburg, 1984)
The Number by Jonny Steinberg (Jonathan Ball Publishers, Cape Town, 2006)

See also an interview on YouTube by the British journalist Ross Kemp with John Mongrel, the highest ranking member of the 28s: http://www.youtube.com/watch?v=q27xtHbgXcU

During the war that was fought along the border between Angola and Namibia during the late 1970s and through the 1980s, the rhino and elephant populations in the region were decimated. UNITA troops which were supported by South African forces, 'traded rhino horn and ivory for weapons with South African Defence Force senior personnel, thereby contributing to the almost complete annihilation of rhino in southern Angola,' according to authors Richard Emslie and Martin Brooks. In an IUCN survey they write: 'It also appears that authorities in the former apartheid regime in South Africa turned a blind eye to ivory and horn smuggling from the rest of Africa through South Africa, as the smugglers provided valuable military intelligence.' Emslie, Richard and Brooks, Martin (editors), *African Rhino: Status Survey and Conservation Action Plan*, IUCN Publications, Cambridge, 1999

As far as I can tell the last Miss Landmine beauty pageant was held in Angola in 2008. http://miss-landmine.org/

Some Jim Neversink songs:
Zooming out of Life: http://www.myspace.com/music/player?sid=65692724&ac=now
Western World: https://soundcloud.com/jim-neversink/01-western-world
Always Dreaming of You: https://soundcloud.com/jim-neversink/12-always-dreaming-of-you